SENSIBILITY AND ECONOMICS
IN THE NOVEL, 1740–1800

Sensibility and Economics in the Novel, 1740–1800

The Price of a Tear

Gillian Skinner

First published in Great Britain 1999 by
MACMILLAN PRESS LTD
Houndmills, Basingstoke, Hampshire RG21 6XS and London
Companies and representatives throughout the world

A catalogue record for this book is available from the British Library.

ISBN 0–333–64477–8

First published in the United States of America 1999 by
ST. MARTIN'S PRESS, INC.,
Scholarly and Reference Division,
175 Fifth Avenue, New York, N.Y. 10010

ISBN 0–312–21147–3

Library of Congress Cataloging-in-Publication Data
Skinner, Gillian.
Sensibility and economics in the novel, 1740–1800 : the price of a
tear / Gillian Skinner.
  p.   cm.
Includes bibliographical references (p.   ) and index.
ISBN 0–312–21147–3 (cloth)
1. English fiction—18th century—History and criticism.
2. Sentimentalism in literature.   3. Economics in literature.
4. Emotions in literature.   I. Title.
PR858.S45S57 1998
823'.609353—dc21   97–31889
                                                          CIP

This book is printed on paper suitable for recycling and made from fully managed and
sustained forest sources.

10   9   8   7   6   5   4   3   2   1
08   07   06   05   04   03   02   01   00   99

Printed and bound in Great Britain by
Antony Rowe Ltd, Chippenham, Wiltshire

For Emmeline and Marianne

Contents

Acknowledgements   viii

1 Introduction   1

2 Economic Sense and Sensibility in *David Simple*,
   Tom Jones and *The Countess of Dellwyn*   15

3 Sexual Innocence and Economic Experience:
   the Problems of *Amelia* and *Ophelia*   37

4 'Godlike benefactors': Patriarchal Patterns in
   Lady Julia Mandeville, *The Vicar of Wakefield* and
   Humphry Clinker   59

5 'Above œconomy': *The History of Lady Barton*,
   The Man of Feeling and *A Sentimental Journey*   91

6 'The first soft system': Commerce, Sensibility and
   Femininity in *Barham Downs* and *Anna: or Memoirs of
   a Welch Heiress*   117

7 'The mild lustre of modest independence':
   Economies of Obligation in Novels of the 1790s   154

Conclusion   187

Notes   191

Bibliography   216

Index   224

Acknowledgements

I should like to thank Vivien Jones for her continuing and invaluable support, both practical and moral, over the years since she ceased officially supervising me. I should also like to thank Charmian Hearne at Macmillan for her patience and forbearance. Last but not least, I want to thank my husband, Joe Cassidy, for all his help in the completion of this book, as in every other aspect of my life.

Some of the material in Chapters 1 and 2 first appeared as an article in *Literature and History*. The greater part of Chapter 5 first appeared as an article in *Eighteenth-Century Life* and is reprinted with permission.

1

Introduction

She stretched out her hand to Harley; he pressed it between
both of his, and bathed it with his tears. – 'Nay, that is Billy's
ring,' said she, 'you cannot have it, indeed; but here is
another, look here, which I plaited to-day of some gold-thread
from this bit of stuff; will you keep it for my sake? I am a
strange girl; – but my heart is harmless: my poor heart! it will
burst some day; feel how it beats.' – She press'd his hand to
her bosom, then holding her head in the attitude of listening –
'Hark! one, two, three! be quiet, thou little trembler; my Billy's
is cold! – but I had forgotten the ring.' – She put it on his
finger. – 'Farewel! I must leave you now.' – She would have
withdrawn her hand; Harley held it to his lips. – 'I dare not
stay longer; my head throbs sadly: farewel!' – She walked
with a hurried step to a little apartment at some distance.
Harley stood fixed in astonishment and pity! his friend gave
money to the keeper. – Harley looked on his ring. – He put a
couple of guineas into the man's hand: 'Be kind to that unfortunate' – He burst into tears, and left them.[1]

Eighteenth-century sensibility is linked inescapably to the economic. The classic sentimental tableau, such as this set piece in
Bedlam from Henry Mackenzie's *The Man of Feeling* (1771), in which
the spectator weeps at another's distress, is based not simply on
feeling, but on feeling and *money*: money which the spectator generally has, and which the object of his or her gaze does not. The
centrality of feeling in fiction labelled 'sentimental' has long been a
commonplace of criticism, but the link with the economic has been
largely neglected. Yet sensibility manifests itself again and again
economically and in situations of financial delicacy and exigency.
Mary Collyer, popular sentimental novelist of the 1740s, wrote
(with a telling lack of either finesse or irony) of 'drying up the tears
of the distressed with money'.[2] Richardson's Sir Charles Grandison
quite consciously uses the response to financial generosity as a

1

barometer of moral worth. The possibility of reformation in his ward's wayward mother is confirmed by her new husband's speechlessness and tears on being presented with a large banknote: 'He hurried out, and when he was in the hall, wiped his eyes, and sobbed like a child.'[3]

Work involving the simultaneous consideration of economics and literature is not without precedent,[4] but what has tended to stand is what James Thompson has recently called 'the discursive or disciplinary separation' between the novel on the one hand and political economy on the other, or 'how it is that the novel tells one kind of story about early modern value and how political economy tells another'.[5] The two stories inevitably overlap or intermingle at moments, and my study of sensibility and economics in the novel is partly a study of such moments – a good example can be found in my discussion, in Chapter 2, of Cynthia's unexpected analysis of contemporary economic life in Sarah Fielding's *David Simple* (1744). However, it is not only such transgressive moments that interest me, but rather the idea that sensibility, as a movement, as a discourse, took part in and partook of the very constructs and values it is conventionally supposed to have abhorred. I wish to examine the conventional division between the novel and economic discourse, but I do so on the specific basis that sensibility itself demands that this division be challenged. In the chapters that follow, the languages of sensibility and economic theory, conventionally deemed to be separate and indeed antagonistic, are shown to overlap and coincide. I shall argue that sentimentalism, despite ostensibly representing a sphere wholly inimical to the concerns of political economy, has, by its very nature, worked in ways analogous to, and involved with, economic processes as presented by contemporary theorists.

If such a fundamental aspect of the sentimental novel has been frequently ignored or glossed over, this is in large part because the genre has always been seen as essentially feminine. Sensibility, whether in women or men, was an inescapably feminine attribute in the eighteenth century, and male writers of the sentimental novel were recognised as dealing in a feminine form.[6] In doing so, men writing sentimental novels contributed to what has been seen as a general 'feminisation' of the novel during the eighteenth century.[7] The apparent concentration in sentimental novels on areas of feeling and response rather than on issues of economic or political importance was seen as entirely appropriate for such a feminine form. Yet an emphasis on feeling is, of course, in itself a politically significant preoccupation. The overt politicisation of sensibility in the final years of the eighteenth century amply demonstrates this, although it is equally, if more covertly, true throughout my period.[8] As a result of this, it is perfectly possible to address 'public' issues of contemporary economic or political debate within the framework of a sentimental exploration of the 'private' world of feeling.[9] This study aims to demonstrate how sentimental novelists of both sexes, using a variety of strategies, addressed such public issues in their work.

Recent work on sentimentalism has been invaluable in retrieving it from the margins of eighteenth-century studies and affirming its importance in the culture of the period. John Mullan's assertion in *Sentiment and Sociability* (1988) that sentimentalism needed to be reassessed, that it is not simply 'a scarcely explicable foible of "major" writers, and a paralysing obsession of "minor" ones', is one with which I entirely concur.[10] But even when critics have undertaken such reassessment, it has never included considering the possibility that sentimental fiction could offer an active critique of economic or political issues. In writing about Sterne's *Sentimental Journey*, Robert Markley certainly recognises the link between sentimentalism and economics; and in his analysis of Yorick's gift of a purse to the chambermaid he makes the fundamental point that money 'becomes the sentimentalist's medium of exchange, a palpable, materialist manifestation of good nature as commodity'. However, he goes on to comment that Sterne's work,

> Like most eighteenth-century sentimental narratives ... suppresses questions about how one acquires the wealth to be able to afford one charitable act after another. The poverty and social inequality that Yorick encounters on the Continent are not described as the result of any specific economic or political conditions, any authoritarian strategies of repression or any conscious malevolence abroad in the world; they are simply presented as opportunities for him to demonstrate his 'natural', innate virtue.[11]

Yet 'most eighteenth-century sentimental narratives' – even, as I argue in Chapter 5, *A Sentimental Journey* itself – do not avoid such issues in the way this suggests. The question 'about how one acquires the wealth to be able to afford one charitable act after another' is considered very clearly in *David Simple* where, for example, the charitable hero quite simply runs out of money and thus cannot afford to carry on fulfilling his role as benefactor – with disastrous results. In many other novels, from Frances Brooke's *Lady Julia Mandeville* (1763) or Goldsmith's *The Vicar of Wakefield* (1766) to Robert Bage's *Barham Downs* (1785) or Agnes Maria Bennett's *Anna: or Memoirs of a Welch Heiress* (1785), the benefactor's source of wealth – whether trade or land, whether honourable or dishonourable – is a subject of considerable significance, as I discuss at numerous points in the following chapters. This study illustrates that, rather than suppressing such factors, many sentimental narratives are centrally concerned with them. Far from distancing itself, in John Mullan's words, 'from any politics of criticism or analysis', the sentimental novel had the capacity to produce just such a politics.[12]

THE MEANINGS OF 'ECONOMY'

In the sentimental scale of value, the ability to dispose of money charitably becomes a measure of personal worth. The more you give, the more you prove your feeling response to the sentimental stimuli of suffering and distress. However, this correspondence between the degree of financial generosity and the degree of proven sensibility immediately raises the possibility of the excessive response – extravagance of both financial and emotional (and often by implication, as I discuss, sexual) kinds. Against this dangerous possibility (as it was commonly perceived) was very often set the virtue of 'economy', and the use of this word in the period is sufficiently diverse to warrant closer attention.[13]

'Economy' (and its derivatives – economic, economical, economist) was used in a variety of contexts during the eighteenth century. The term was essentially in the first stage of a process which was to lead to a major shift in significance and usage, but initially this variety gave the appearance of the acquisition rather than the loss of meanings – a progression typical of the period, according to Erämetsä's assessment: 'It was a characteristic of the eighteenth century that the vocabulary of the period ... adopted a great number of new senses for words already existing, while the number of completely new words remained remarkably small.'[14] Meanings of 'economy' to do with household management were prevalent throughout the century: 'the management of a family; the government of a household' is the first meaning given in Johnson's *Dictionary*.[15] An 'economist' was therefore still as likely to be a woman running a home in the eighteenth century as in the sixteenth century when such usage is first recorded. However, from the early eighteenth century 'economist' began to acquire first a more general application: 'A manager in general; one who attends to the sparing and effective use of anything, especially money' (the *OED* records this meaning from 1710 to 1841). Later in the century, a far more specific meaning emerges: 'One of the school of "Economistes" who flourished in eighteenth-century France.' This heralds the emergence of 'political economy', a phrase used perhaps most famously in Sir James Steuart's *Principles of Political Economy*, published in 1767 and defined by the *OED* as 'the art or practical science of managing the resources of a nation so as to increase its material prosperity'. With political economy evidently a male preserve, by the end of the century an economist could equally well be a man concerned in national affairs as an individual concerned with personal domestic organisation.

During the 1740s, the beginning of the period covered in this study, 'economy' became a crucial element in debates surrounding the desirability – moral and material – of luxury. The emphasis was on economy as 'sparing and effective' management, as in the definition above: Johnson's second definition of economy is 'frugality; discretion of expense; laudable parsimony'. Such frugality had been commonly recommended since the early years of the century, on both a public and a private scale, as a panacea for the country's political and economic ills: in 1721, for example, George Berkeley wrote 'Frugality of Manners is the Nourishment and Strength of Bodies politic. It is that by which they grow and subsist, until they are corrupted by Luxury; the natural Cause of their Decay and Ruin',[16] while in 1740 a booklet was published entitled *An Enquiry into the Melancholy Circumstances of Great Britain: more particularly in regard to the œconomy of private families and persons, gentlemen, clergy...*; and 1746 saw the appearance of *National Œconomy Recommended, as the only means of retrieving our trade and securing our liberties... .*

The concern over luxury was partly class-based, as the rising middle classes gained access to luxuries hitherto confined to the ruling class. Many writers saw this as the corruption of middle-class morality by vicious aristocratic tendencies. Indeed, the identification of excessive consumption, whether material or sexual, with aristocratic degeneracy was strong throughout the period. Oliver Goldsmith, for example, deplored the eager desire of the middle classes to be 'seen in a sphere far above their capacities and circumstances', but far from wishing to curtail their social progress he urged 'every mechanic in London, "Keep your shop, and your shop will keep you." A strict observance of these words will, I am sure, in time, *gain them estates.*'[17] Frugality, in other words, would eventually give the middle classes considerable economic, and therefore political, power; whereas indulgence in luxury goods would dissipate their resources. As *The Economy of Human Life*, an enormously popular conduct book (first published in 1750, it was issued in various forms at least 38 times by 1800), warns: 'Let not thy recreations be expensive, lest the pain of purchasing them exceed the pleasure thou hast in their enjoyment. Neither let prosperity put out the eyes of circumspection, nor abundance cut off the hands of frugality: he that indulgeth in the superfluities of life, shall live to lament the want of its necessaries.'[18]

The use of 'economy' in the title of a conduct book – where it can be read as meaning management and organisation, with definite overtones of that management being 'effective' or 'frugal' – is both indicative of the concept's popularity and quite to be expected, since 'economy' was something regularly recommended in such books, whether they were addressed to women or men. For women, however, effective management was strictly confined to the household. Thus Wetenhall Wilkes, in his *Letter of Genteel and Moral Advice to a Young Lady* (1740) stated confidently: 'Œconomy, or the art of house-keeping, is the most immediate female business.'[19] Here, far from associating generosity with excessive sensibility, economy is recommended as the best way to further any charitable projects: 'frugality is the support of generosity. Constant inquietudes ... and many other inconveniencies, prevent a profuse person to do many noble and generous things; but the table of a good œconomist, is always attended with neatness, plenty, and chearfulness...'[20] Such direct association of economy with female management is found frequently, and in distinctly conduct book terms, in the novels. Clarissa, crucially, was not only good at writing letters but was also 'an excellent ECONOMIST and HOUSEWIFE' and defined generosity as 'the happy medium between parsimony and profusion'. Indeed, her whole complex organisation of time is described in economic terms: she kept 'an account' of time as she would of money and time was a 'fund' to which she could be indebted.[21] In *David Simple* Camilla's father confesses to her that '"altho' with Œconomy I am able to support you and your Brother in a tolerable manner, yet my Fortune is not large; and if I should marry, and have an Increase of Family, it might injure you".'[22] Camilla generously encourages him to follow his inclinations; but it is the new wife herself who causes economic (financial and organisational) havoc, not new children: Camilla and Valentine 'looked with Horror on the Consequences of the expensive sort of Life Livia was drawing her Husband into', and finally 'my Father's House ... was converted by this Woman's Management into my greatest Torment'.[23] Here an economy (the organisation of a household) is being ruined, financially and emotionally, by lack of economy (moderation, frugality) in a woman.

Such a disaster in the novel seems to reproduce and validate conduct literature's recommendation of good economy in both senses of the word. Yet the influence genre may have on discourse is a factor here. Certainly the effects of generic considerations on the construction of sensibility or the presentation of economic arguments cannot be ignored. *David Simple*'s ultimate trajectory, as discussed in Chapter 2, questions the orthodox position of the conduct book through, among other things, its juxtaposition of David's undoubted moderation in material matters with his tragic end. Indeed, features often seen as generically characteristic of the sentimental novel (such as the affirmation of extreme emotion as an indication of moral worth) can also be seen as fundamentally inimical to the project of most conduct books. The different pressures on *David Simple* both as a novel and as a particular kind of novel preclude the possibility of straightforward transference.

This engagement in fiction with a discourse of economy set against extravagance is part of the wider eighteenth-century debate described above. Civic humanist in tendency, these discourses promote civic virtues (prudence, valour, liberty, frugality, etc.) against destructive vices (self-interest, extravagance, corruption, cowardice, etc.) and espouse the belief that the state should be governed according to ethical principles.[24] Stephen Copley identifies two versions of it, aristocratic and bourgeois, in his introduction to *Literature and the Social Order in Eighteenth-Century England*. The conduct books and novels discussed in this book are generally rooted in the bourgeois version of civic humanism. Copley also shows how other discourses were questioning the very meaning and validity of such words as 'luxury', 'superfluities' and 'necessaries'. The narrator of *David Simple, Volume the Last* defines poverty as being, 'with a large dependent Family, in a Situation in Life, that you know not how to go out of, and yet are not able to support; and when you pay *Cent. per Cent.* for every Necessary of Life, by being obliged to buy every thing by retail...'[25] Bernard Mandeville, however, would not allow talk of 'necessaries' even in this situation. In *The Fable of the Bees* (1714–25) he argues, 'If every thing is to be Luxury (as in strictness it ought) that is not immediately necessary to make Man subsist as he is a living Creature, there is nothing else to be found in the World, *no not even among the naked Savages* ...' (my emphasis).[26] Mandeville maintained that man's vices were an integral part of the economic system, providing desires to be gratified and thus products for trade:

> Fraud, Luxury and Pride must live,
> While we the Benefits receive ...
> So Vice is beneficial found,
> When it's by Justice lopt and bound ...[27]

The upper classes had a crucial role to play as conspicuous consumers: their demand for luxury goods lined the pocket of the tradesman – which was arguably good for society as a whole, for it increased the amount of wealth in general circulation. An economic account of society was produced which allowed, as John Barrell puts it, 'disinterested virtue [to be] built on interested vanity'.[28] Such accommodation of private vice for the public good had further support in Pope's *Essay on Man*:

> Better for Us, perhaps, it might appear,
> Were there all harmony, all virtue here;
> That never air or ocean felt the wind;
> That never passion discompos'd the mind:
> But ALL subsists by elemental strife;
> And Passions are the elements of Life.[29]

Mandeville's 'Justice', however, had to intervene when it came to the vices of the lower classes, since 'the Multitude of Working Poor' was 'the Basis that supports all': 'All should be set to work that are any ways able, and Scrutinies should be made even among the Infirm.'[30]

As this comment indicates, the opposing humanist and Mandevillian analyses of economic life extended also to views on charity. Richard Steele approved of education for the poor as helping to recover the present age 'out of its present Degeneracy and Depravation of Manners. It seems to promise us an honest and virtuous posterity.' He also found the Thanksgiving Day procession of boys and girls from charity schools an occasion for sentimental enjoyment: it 'could not forbear touching every Heart that had any Sentiments of Humanity.'[31] Mandeville's attitude to the poor was far more bracing: 'Charity, where it is too extensive, seldom fails of promoting Sloth and Idleness, and is good for little in the Commonwealth but to breed Drones and destroy Industry. The more Colleges and Alms-houses you build the more you may.'[32]

It has been argued that we are not likely to find the new kind of economic analysis in the fiction of the period, and that eighteenth-century literary works largely, if not completely, ignore such analysis in favour of humanist discourse.[33] Examples above of civic humanist positions informing the portrayal of women and economy in the fiction might seem to support this view. Yet it is difficult to see how humanist and newer economic discourses can be quite so confidently separated, particularly when the diverse and gendered implications of 'economy' are taken into consideration. J. G. A. Pocock highlights this discursive interplay when he writes,

> When a diversity of such languages is to be found in a given text, it may follow that a given utterance is capable of being intended and read, and so of performing, in more than one of them at the same time; nor is it at all impossible that a given pattern of speech may migrate, or be translated, from one language to another found in the same text, bearing implications from the former context and engrafting them among those belonging to the latter.[34]

Foucault, of course, also emphasises the complexity of discourse and the way in which discourses constantly break up and recombine depending on diverse situations. Writing of economy and related issues would thus be a task subject to varieties of interpretation and appropriation: depending, in Foucauldian terms, on 'who is speaking, his [or her] position of power, the institutional context in which he [or she] happens to be situated'.[35] The fact that women themselves are implicitly excluded from being subjects in civic humanist discourse, for example, must not be underestimated. I show that, rather than lacking the newer economic vocabularies, eighteenth-century sentimental fiction incorporates and assimilates them in a variety of ways, so that whenever such texts deal with the financial, particularly where it is connected with feeling and with charity, there is a perhaps unexpected but nevertheless crucial conjunction of apparently inimical discourses.

DISCOURSES OF FEMININITY

Discourses of sensibility are bound up with those of femininity. As a feminine attribute, all those characteristics that go to make up sensibility are particularly associated with women: the man who possesses them must, necessarily, be in some degree feminised. Charitable impulses and benevolence, the feeling heart and the speaking body are all the proper attributes of the sensible female and help to set up one of the ways in which sensibility empowered – or appeared to empower – women. During the eighteenth century discourses of sensibility were instrumental in building up the moral ascendancy of women. They asserted women's superiority in matters of finer feeling and discrimination and established their role as a benign reforming influence. Just as, however, virtuous sensibility harboured dangerous possibilities of 'excessive' behaviour, so the creation of the morally ascendant virtuous woman had as its corollary the vicious woman who, by refusing this role, necessarily pollutes her associates. Thus the power afforded to women by the marrying of discourses of sensibility and virtuous femininity is of an admittedly limited kind; nevertheless, it has great importance for my argument in its conjunction with economic discourses.

The working woman, or even the woman with economic ability, has never been a figure associated with sentimental fiction; but she is there, even if her position is precarious. The connotations surrounding the working woman in the eighteenth century, as I examine in Chapter 3, were almost exclusively negative, assuming that her work must necessarily be of a sexually immoral kind. The working woman who appeared in sentimental fiction, then, had to be written as firmly as possible into the mould of the sensible, virtuous female. But as the century progressed, the developing discourses of economics came, if perhaps briefly, to her aid.

Commerce came to be described in terms which emphasised its civilising and morally beneficial effects.[36] In Chapter 6, I illustrate how this development allowed discourses of sensibility, femininity and economics to come together in an unprecedented fashion, and I explore how this manifested itself in sentimental fiction, particularly through the figure of the working woman.

The development of a discourse that argues for the beneficial effects of trade on civilisation is, of course, crucially linked to the issue of class, since it embodies a bourgeois challenge to the 'aristocratic' view that trade is a low occupation in which no gentleman would become involved. Sentimental fiction is essentially a middle-class genre which both creates an idealised aristocracy and deplores the luxury and excess associated with aristocratic vices, while simultaneously exploiting the commercial opportunities those vices afford. On the subject of trade it can be equally schizophrenic, often associating it overtly with mean-minded self-interest, while covertly employing it to strengthen the position of key figures. At other times, while a residual discomfort with the notion of commerce may still be apparent, trade actually becomes the means of a more or less limited female emancipation.

With the development of feminising discourses praising the ability of commerce to civilise and morally benefit society, however, there appears a new figure in sentimental fiction: the British Merchant. Combining the 'aristocratic' virtues of nobility, courage and honour with the middle-class trading qualities of frugality, probity and industry, this figure attempts to unite the best interests of the best aspects of the upper and middle classes by shedding (ostensibly at least) both aristocratic luxury and bourgeois self-interest. While the British Merchant is of course a male figure, the union of these competing class interests is actually exemplified most compellingly through the female body, as my discussion in Chapter 6 of Agnes Maria Bennett's *Anna: or Memoirs of a Welch Heiress* shows.

Discourses of femininity are also crucially involved with those of class. The debilitating, corrupting effects of aristocratic luxury were analogous to those of the vicious female, and degeneracy was a feminising process. As John Brown wrote in his *Estimate of the Manners and Principles of the Times* (1757): 'the Character of the Manners of our Times: ... on a fair Examination, will probably appear to be that of a *"vain, luxurious,* and *selfish,* EFFEMINACY".'[37] The feminised sentimental hero, then, was always in danger of being read not as supremely sensitive, but as supremely degenerate, since ambiguity of gender difference, as Brown asserted and as Harriet Guest has discussed, was the mark of a degenerate society. This led the bourgeois woman into a dilemma: the ideology of her class required her to be virtuously self-effacing, but that same ideology simultaneously needed her to demonstrate this mark of approved femininity publicly through 'virtuous display', to confirm the healthy state of society.[38] One of the problems facing the working woman was that employment almost inevitably involved some kind of public, extra-domestic activity. If this could be seen as virtuous display, employment for women could even be rewritten as part of virtuous femininity. There is evidence that such an attitude is emergent during the period, but the inclination to equate employment with immoral activity remains powerfully operative up to, and beyond, 1800.

WRITERS ON ECONOMICS

During the course of this study I refer to a number of writers on economics including Bernard Mandeville, Sir James Steuart, David Hume, Adam Smith, Thomas Robert Malthus and Jean-Baptiste Say. Of these, Mandeville and Smith are probably the most important.

Central to sentimentalism is the idea of community: community of feelings, ideas and opinions or, as it is expressed in *David Simple*, the 'Union of Hearts'.[39] In such a community, self-interest or selfish behaviour is unknown; the interests of all the individuals comprising it are the same and all wish to promote the happiness of the others. During the eighteenth century, the views of Mandeville's *Fable of the Bees* summarised the antithesis of this ideal. His society, bound together purely by economic self-interest, was based entirely on expedience, with no room for sentimental ties of gratitude and obligation. For years after its publication, *The Fable of the Bees* was held up as an example; its account of the social and economic system was seen as wholly immoral and therefore had to be rejected, as Adam Smith's explicit attack at the end of his *Theory of Moral Sentiments* (1759) demonstrates.[40] For this reason, Mandeville figures fairly frequently in this study as the notorious representative of an ostensibly unpopular but profoundly influential position.

Adam Smith's *The Wealth of Nations* (1776), while not necessarily the overwhelmingly original work it has sometimes been claimed to be, brings together views on economic theory which had been developing at least since the late seventeenth century.[41] His two major works also clearly coincide with the two principal areas examined in this study. While the two can seem at first sight to deal with very different concerns, *Moral Sentiments* actually underwrites much of the later work in its gradual honing down of 'sympathy' until the quality becomes almost indistinguishable from middle-class self-interest. The idea of community is, like the sentimental circle, restricted to those who will understand – that is, to those whose class and economic position dictates that they will experience an analogous sentiment. Smith's merging together of self-interest and social good is, as I discuss in Chapter 4, perilously close to Mandeville's formulations, but couched in less blatant terms; and in a work which explicitly dissociates itself from *The Fable of the Bees* as 'pernicious', the manoeuvre is rendered acceptable.

Smith's work is interesting not only for this reason, however; it is also important in this study for its retention, despite everything, of certain serious reservations about commerce and its effects upon society. Smith may view the propensity to 'truck, barter, and exchange' as fundamental to human nature,[42] but he is by no means convinced that it is an essential good, associating it also with narrow-minded, mean-spirited attention to sordid details which closes the mind to higher considerations such as courage and honour. His worries reveal how far even an advocate of commerce could be persuaded to view commerce as useful but nevertheless unpalatable. The British Merchant of sentimental fiction in the later eighteenth century was specifically designed to answer such charges against the commercial spirit.

The shape of this study is broadly comparative, with each chapter, apart from Chapter 7, devoting a substantial part of its length to a close comparison of two novels, one by a woman, the other by a man. Thus one of the continuing concerns of the book is the extent to which the gender of the author has an impact on the treatment of issues of economics, sensibility and femininity. The comparative structure does not preclude, however, the discussion of further novels, and the aim throughout is to provide detailed analysis of texts – many of which have been rarely, if ever, afforded that treatment – while keeping in view broader debates and dilemmas. Thus in Chapter 7, which covers the 1790s, the complexities peculiar to that turbulent decade demanded that a broader range of novels be considered. The study is also chronological, following the development of the sentimental novel from the 1740s to the end of the century and, approximately at least, taking novels from one decade for consideration in each chapter. Choosing which novels to examine was not always easy, and while I hope that my choices are representative enough to allow me to draw defensible general conclusions from my study of them, I am equally certain that, had I but world enough and time, many other novels could have been profitably included in the discussion. The obvious major omission is Richardson, of course. There is no doubt that a study of discourses of economics and sentimentalism in Richardson's three novels – or indeed in any one of them – would be a fascinating undertaking, but it would also be potentially book-length in itself and needs greater space to do it justice than would be available within such a study as this. I am happy to suggest that the work is still there to be done.[43] The achievement of this book is, I hope, that it establishes the great value of reading the sentimental novel for its use of economic discourse and its engagement with economic debate.

2
Economic Sense and Sensibility in *David Simple, Tom Jones* and *The Countess of Dellwyn*

The Adventures of David Simple (1744; *Volume the Last*, 1753), *Tom Jones* (1749) and Sarah Fielding's later and less well-known novel *The Countess of Dellwyn* (1759) all explore the compatibility (or otherwise) of the commercial world and more idealistic principles: in this case, those of the feeling or good-natured community. But where Sarah Fielding's novels foreground the problem, and suggest in different ways that it is one with which their female characters can most readily engage, *Tom Jones*, in its confident assumption of universality, is more inclined to suppress it. What follows in the first part of this chapter is a reading of *David Simple* and *Tom Jones* that sees them not, as has so often been the case, as exemplifying two entirely distinct genres, the sentimental and the comic, but rather as using the same vocabulary and terms of reference in dealing with similar concerns, although coming ultimately to very different conclusions. *The Countess of Dellwyn* then takes forward the insights achieved in *David Simple*, and proceeds on the strength of these to introduce an unexpected figure into English fiction: the middle-class working wife and mother.

If it is not usually thought of as a 'novel of sentiment', *Tom Jones* nevertheless has important affiliations with works in that genre.[1] *Tom Jones* is addressed to 'the good-natured Reader' (see, for example, the titles of Book VI, chapter vi and Book VI, chapter xi), and in such ways the novel internally projects for itself an extensive, generously sympathetic audience. When the narrator despairs of describing Sophia's state of mind, he tells us: 'Most of my Readers will suggest it easily to themselves; and the few who cannot, would not understand the Picture, or at least would deny it to be natural, if ever so well drawn.'² This appeal to the reader who will understand differs very little from the appeals in novels of sentiment to those with 'feeling hearts'. The narrator of *David Simple* excuses herself from describing David and Camilla's grief thus: 'Words cannot reach it – the sympathizing Heart must imagine it – and the Heart that has no Sympathy, is not capable of receiving it'.³

Between this and *Tom Jones*, there is the obvious similarity that whoever picks up the book becomes one of the understanding readers: the ill-natured and unfeeling are always someone or somewhere else. But these passages share also an assumption of common responses and values; what difference there is between the two appeals lies in the implied size of their internal audiences. In *David Simple*, the sympathetic community turns out to consist essentially of David, Camilla, Cynthia and Valentine, their children, and the sympathetic reader; at the end, the community has been reduced to Cynthia, David's daughter Camilla, their unnamed benefactor and once again the feeling reader. *Tom Jones*, by contrast, has a broad spectrum of understanding hearts. There are villains (Blifil and Thwackum) and heroes (Tom, Sophia, Allworthy), but there are also plenty of characters (of which, significantly, Tom himself is one for much of the book) who are manifestly imperfect but yet can be accommodated into the broad category of the 'good-natured' – Squire Western, Mrs Western, Partridge, Mrs Fitzpatrick, Nightingale, Nancy, Mrs Waters, Molly Seagrim, even Black George – not to mention 'all our Readers', as in the chapter title of XIV, vi. Where true benevolence is rare indeed in David Simple's world, the narrator of *Tom Jones* proposes benevolence as a far more common propensity: 'there is in some (I believe in many) human Breasts, a kind and benevolent Disposition, which is gratified by contributing to the Happiness of others' (VI, i, 270).

At issue, then, is the *size* of the feeling community, but not the *values* by which the community should operate. What we find in looking from *David Simple* to *Tom Jones* are not two different kinds of value, but two views on how easily that value is to be found in this world. This is, of course, one of the crucial factors in the generic difference between comedy and tragedy: comedy posits a majority of right-feeling, right-thinking individuals – that is why there can be a happy ending; tragedy, on the other hand, posits a minority. Jina Politi, following Watt in quite reasonably identifying the novel as 'the art-form expressive of the middle-class ideology which dominated English culture in the eighteenth century', goes on to deduce from this that the English novel takes place 'within the province of humour, sentimentality, analyticity and wit', never extending 'into the regions of the tragic ... of the irrational, and of the instinctual relation to emotion'.[4] This is to ignore the darker side of sentimentalism. In *Clarissa*, the right-thinking, right-feeling minority becomes a single individual, since even the people Clarissa could communicate with – Anna Howe, Mrs Norton – are cut off from her: 'Fellow-feeling in *Clarissa* has a vocabulary tragically divorced from application; there is no confidence in benevolent sociability here.'[5] 'Benevolent sociability' in this case has to look for its fruition in heaven. Politi points out that both Richardson and Henry Fielding resolve the ethical oppositions in their novels by reference to a higher reconciliatory principle – divine love and benevolence – but where Tom Jones finds such a principle in this world, Clarissa, like David Simple, can only hope to find it in the next.[6]

Whether conceived as besieged or broadly available, sensibility and good nature are both inextricably bound up with the economic. The problems encountered by David Simple and his community of friends are essentially financial: the question is not *how* to avert disaster (the answer is, money) but whether or not the means to avert disaster will be forthcoming, which in turn depends on the arrival of a sufficiently benevolent monied individual. In Volumes I and II, David himself is that individual and his reaction to the tragic story of Isabelle, which will not admit of any material reparation, reveals clearly how far the benevolence of sensibility relies on economic solutions: '"How unhappy I am to meet with a Person of so much Merit under a Sorrow, in which it is impossible for me to hope to offer her the least Consolation!"' (IV, ii, 250). Sophia sends Tom 16 guineas, 'being indeed [her] whole stock. ... For tho' her Father was very liberal to her, she was much too generous herself to be rich' (VI, xiii, 319). The degree of generosity is directly related to the degree of sensibility: as the latter increases, so does the former. However, as I suggested in the Introduction, this leads to potentially excessive responses. One of Tom's faults throughout the novel is imprudence; we are told that he had 'naturally violent animal Spirits' which could produce 'most extravagant Effects' (V, ix, 252). On hearing Mrs Miller's account of her poor cousin's family, Tom, who has only just come into funds again, offers immediately this entire sum for their relief (of which she, prudently, will only take a proportion). Even after Allworthy's lecture on prudence near the end of the novel, Tom is still 'kind to Excess' in his behaviour to Blifil (XVIII, xi, 968). David Simple's acute sensibility, taken to the extreme, renders him virtually incapable of any action at all: 'his Sensations were too strong, to leave him the free Use of his Reason, and he stood some time without knowing what to do' (II, ix, 129).

While excessive behaviour in the fiction is certainly not limited to one class, it is often associated with the aristocracy, and such figures as Lord Fellamar and Lady Bellaston, with their literary forebears – respectively, the Restoration rake and Pope's famous line that 'ev'ry Woman is at heart a Rake'.[7] Yet because Lady Bellaston, while sexually profligate, is also coolly manipulative, and because Fellamar is a comic figure who despite his attempted rape has 'honourable' designs upon Sophia, the issue is complicated – excess in one area of life does not necessarily mean excess in all others. The areas of life associated most frequently with 'excess' and 'extravagance' during the eighteenth century are those of feeling, sexuality and money. Any two, and sometimes all three of these can occur together with varying degrees of approval and disapproval.

Excessive feeling and financial extravagance when the result of that feeling – these are the subjects of particular ambivalence. For Janet Todd, the fictional sentimentalist despises 'those who hoard and increase money and [dispenses] his own wealth liberally and with speed ... David [Simple] simply expends'.[8] However, this rapid dispensing of wealth has to be distinguished carefully from the kind of extravagance which David's dissolute brother indulges in. He tells how David periodically relieved him, 'but then that was only enough perhaps to pay some Debt, just to keep me from a Jail; but was nothing to what I wanted to squander in Extravagance' (VI, vii, 287). This extravagance involves vicious self-indulgence, whereas David's household is moderate; after their first financial setback, he rents a house rather than buying an estate and 'they were still possessed of enough to gratify every innocent Desire, and no extravagant Wishes did they ever entertain ...' (V, i, 316). When total destitution stares them in the face, the same adaptation to circumstances applies: David 'changed his small House for a Habitation yet less, redoubled his Diligence, and if ever Poverty and Oeconomy subsisted together, it was in this Family' (VI, iii, 351).

Money in *Tom Jones* tends to be a largely providential commodity. It is inherited, lost, stolen and bestowed, but rarely, if ever, earned.[9] At the beginning of *Tom Jones*, it appears to belong to the natural, providential order of things: Allworthy is 'the Favourite of both Nature and Fortune ... . From the former of these, he derived an agreeable Person, a sound Constitution, a solid Understanding, and a benevolent Heart; by the latter, he was decreed to the Inheritance of one of the largest Estates in the Country' (I, ii, 34). Equally, Tom himself turns out to be the natural successor to this wealth: 'Tom comes to happiness and reward because of his essential virtue but also because of his rightful hereditary claim.'[10] Throughout the novel he is identified as having something in his air 'which distinguished him from the Vulgar' (VIII, viii, 431); he has 'natural, but not artificial good Breeding' (XIII, iv, 699). Thus Tom's essential virtue *is* his hereditary claim – they are inseparable.

By contrast, although wealth in *David Simple* is often portrayed in a similarly providential way, its roots are clearly established at the outset of the novel as in the real world of trade:

> Mr. David Simple was the eldest Son of Mr. Daniel Simple, a Mercer on Ludgate-hill. His Mother was a downright Country Woman, who originally got her Living by Plain-Work ... they were married, and lived many Years together, a very honest and industrious Life; to which it was owing, that they were able to provide very well for their Children. (I, i, 9)

Thus David and his brother are bred up as gentlemen at a public school and 'kept there in a manner which put them on a level with Boys of a superior Degree' (I, i, 9): they are part of that class mobility indicated by Goldsmith as the result of an industrious trading life.[11] It is the industry of David's parents that has 'gained them estates', not the smile of Fortune, as in the case of Allworthy. Virtue plays a part in both acquisitions, but where with Allworthy it is a virtue of an abstract and timeless kind, with David's parents it is a practical virtue which enables them to accumulate but not dissipate wealth.

In the work of Henry Fielding, this kind of class advancement is treated with disapproval, albeit a disapproval based on a certain ambivalence with regard to the place of luxury. The landlord of the inn on the way to Bristol where Tom is wounded is described as having been 'bred, as they call it, a Gentleman, that is, bred up to do nothing, and had spent a very small Fortune, which he inherited from an industrious Farmer his Uncle, in Hunting, Horse-racing, and Cock-fighting ...' (VIII, vii, 428). Here is the same scenario as we find in *David Simple*: the industrious older generation, which keeps to its class position because it is too busy accumulating wealth rather than spending it, sets up the younger generation in a higher station in life. Here it is shown as being a station in which the younger generation cannot maintain itself. The implied criticism is of bringing up a person who was meant in the natural and providential order of things to work, 'to do nothing' – the prerogative of a small élite, as Henry Fielding maintained in a pamphlet of 1751: 'To be born for no other Purpose than to consume the Fruits of the Earth is the Privilege (if it may be called a Privilege) of very few.'[12]

In the same pamphlet, Henry Fielding also wrote of the 'vast Torrent of Luxury which of late Years hath poured itself into this Nation...' and attributed to it the tendency of each level in the social hierarchy to aspire to the one above, since

> it is a Branch of Liberty claimed by the People to be as wicked and as profligate as their Superiors ... the Gentleman will aspire to the proper State of the Nobleman; the Tradesman steps from behind his Counter into the vacant Place of the Gentleman. Nor doth the Confusion end here: It reaches the very Dregs of the People ...[13]

This is in some respects the voice of traditional civic humanism objecting to the overthrow of the established social order, but it is a confused voice. The aristocracy are the source of the torrent of luxury, but Henry Fielding also comments that among them 'Luxury is probably rather a moral than a political Evil', thus separating ethical from social considerations in a Mandevillian move, and he recommends the withdrawal of temptation to 'Voluptuousness' from 'the Tradesman, the Mechanic, and the Labourer' as the solution to the problem. In the end, he concludes, it is the 'Business of the Politician ... to prevent the Contagion from spreading to the useful Part of Mankind ... and this is the Business of Persons of Fashion and Fortune too, in order that the Labour and Industry of the rest may administer to their Pleasures, and furnish them with the means of Luxury.'[14] This is a distinct variation on Mandeville's theory: there, luxury was useful to the tradesman by providing a market for his goods and was only explicitly denied to 'the Working Poor'; here, luxury is the *right* of the upper classes, while it is the duty of all the lower classes to remain in their allotted stations and provide it. The fact that furnishing the upper classes with the means to luxury may well create profits which will enable the manufacturers also to take part in it is not addressed – and yet, earlier in the same pamphlet, Fielding had expressed the essentially Mandevillian opinion that 'as Riches are the *certain* Consequences of Trade, so is Luxury the no less *certain* Consequence of Riches' and thus 'To prevent this Consequence ... of a flourishing Commerce is totally to change the Nature of Things, and separate the Effect from the Cause'.[15]

Between the conflicting discourses of Fielding's prose pamphlet and the text of *Tom Jones* there does seem to exist the divide between the discursive and the literary discussed in Chapter 1. In the novel, Allworthy represents the voice of Augustan temperance: his 'sermon' to Captain Blifil on hearing of his secret marriage to Bridget Allworthy is a model of moderation, distinguishing clearly between luxuries and necessaries, between wants created 'by Folly and Vanity' and those created by nature (I, xii, 71). We are told that though Allworthy 'was too sober to be intoxicated with it, he was too sensible to despise' Sophia's vast fortune (VI, iii, 282). All other ways of dealing with money – Squire Western's parsimony, Tom's own well-meaning profusion – seem eventually to be discarded for the practice of Allworthy's civic humanist virtue of prudence. However, the efficacy of this quality is called into question by the fact that, despite Allworthy's merits, he is not a perspicacious man. Like Parson Adams in *Joseph Andrews*, or indeed like David Simple, he can be, and is, imposed upon by distinctly unworthy characters. The speech in which luxuries and necessaries are so prudently defined is also the one in which he tells Doctor Blifil: 'Your Brother appears to me to be a Man of Sense and Honour' (I, xii, 70). Such undermining occurs in the novel from time to time, as when the narrator comments on Tom's penniless situation: '"Nothing out of Nothing" is not a truer Maxim in Physics than in Politics; and every Man who is greatly destitute of Money, is on that Account entirely excluded from all Means of acquiring it' (VII, ii, 331) – Augustan prudence would not help Tom here, even if he had it. However, owing to the comic structure, the issue is never seriously in doubt since wealth, ultimately, will find its way to the people who have most right to it through birth and virtue.

The question of a person's correct station in life is also addressed in *David Simple*, but since the whole novel is about a man who belongs to the class of gentlemen newly created by the previous generation's success in trade, it is problematised from the very beginning. Of Camilla's three qualities in a gentlewoman, 'Birth, Family and Education' (III, ii, 169), David has only education – an education which has bred him 'to do nothing', thus rendering him incapable of getting his living by trade as his parents did. The instability of his station as a new gentleman is manifest, but whether we are to regard him as an upstart – a Shamela – or as a perfectly legitimate example of social advancement is ambiguous. The Dunsters, a farming family, are noted, apparently approvingly, for the fact that 'although they rented a very large Farm, yet they did not affect to live *above their Station*' (V, i, 321). However, in *Volume the Last* the person most concerned about station, not surprisingly, is Mrs Orgueil, whose use of station to inflict misery on little Cynthia is presented critically, without ambiguity of any kind.

If the narrative does not indicate definitely how we are to regard David's class position, neither does it in any way gloss over it; we are reminded quite definitely of his middling status when, having decided to explore 'High Life', 'as he had never lived at that end of the Town before, kept no Equipage, and was besides a very modest Man, he was under some difficulty how to get an Introduction to Persons of Fashion'. However, Spatter's offer to take him wherever he goes also calls into question the exclusivity of the 'High Life' to which David imagined entrance might be difficult: 'He told him he had nothing to do, but get a fine Coat, a well-powdered Wig, and a *Whist-Book*, and he would soon be invited to more *Routs* than he would be able to go to' (II, i, 77). A little later on, Cynthia defines 'fine Ladies' on David's request, and further breaks down notions of innate class difference. Being a fine lady has nothing whatever to do with being upper class, it is to do with power relations: 'They are not confined to any Station; for I have known, while the Lady has been insulting her Waiting-woman in the Drawing-Room, the Chamber-Maid has been playing just the same Part below stairs, with the Person she thought her inferior, only with a small Variation of Terms' (II, vii, 115). This recognition of the existence of localised power systems – particularly as they are power systems identified with women – offers us a chance to view class-society in the novel in Foucauldian terms: power can cease to be a male, monolithic and all-embracing structure and become 'the multiplicity of force relations immanent in the sphere in which they operate and which constitute their own organisation'.[16]

This example of a reinterpretation of the way in which the dominant system works is reinforced by one particular incident which takes place not long after David, Camilla and Valentine are reunited with Cynthia. The friends decide to spend a day travelling around London, and after they have been out some time Cynthia asks everyone to tell their thoughts to the rest of the group. She herself begins, and the passage is worth quoting in full:

> She said, she was considering, amongst the variety of Shops she saw, how very few of them dealt in Things which were really necessary to preserve Life or Health; and yet that those things which appeared most useless, contributed to the general Welfare: for whilst there was such a thing as Property in the World, unless it could be equally distributed, those People who have little or no share of it, must find out Methods of getting what they want, from those whose Lot it is to have more than is necessary for them; and, except all the World was so generous, as to be willing to part with what they think they have a right to, only for the pleasure of helping others; the way to obtain any thing from them is to apply to their Passions. As, for instance, when a Woman of Fashion goes home with her Coach loaded with Jewels and Trinkets, which, from Custom, she is brought to think she cannot do without, and is indulging her Vanity with the Thoughts of *out-shining* some other Lady at the next Ball, the Tradesman who receives her Money in Exchange for those things which appear so trifling, to that Vanity perhaps owes his own and his Family's Support. (III, vi, 189–90)

Several things are striking about this passage. It is coolly pragmatic, in a way not usually associated with the sentimental novel; and although it still preserves a more traditional humanist attitude to what is a necessity ('necessary to preserve Life or Health') and what is a luxury (things which 'appeared most useless'), its analysis of a commercial society which uses people's private vices, or 'Passions', as a means to profit in trade (and that constitutes, of course, the public good) is a model of Mandevillian new economic discourse. Not only is such discourse quite outside a woman's usual 'economic' sphere, the household, it also involves an argument which removes the moral stigma traditionally attached to vices, here proposed by a woman (and, at another remove, written by one) whose own morality could therefore, potentially, be challenged by opponents. Yet it is spoken by a character with an integral part to play in the novel's sentimental 'Union of Hearts' (V, i, 314), whose credentials as a feeling individual have already been proved.

Compared to the thoughts of the other three, this short homily is even more oddly placed. Camilla and Valentine both give voice to thoughts to do with their own personal preoccupations, while David's thoughts concern a man the group encountered earlier in the day. David replies to Camilla's comments, Cynthia to David's, while Valentine's allusion to his love needs no answer beyond Cynthia's blush. No one, however, comments at all on Cynthia's theory of luxury and necessity. Perhaps this is not surprising, since it highlights the essentially marginal nature of David's entire motivation in life. It is an account of the world where the number of people generous enough to part with material wealth 'only for the pleasure of helping others' (people like David, that is) is insignificant. 'Pleasure' in this analysis is a far more utilitarian quality which helps to make the commercial world go round. In this context, David's way of operating is exposed as amiable but ultimately ludicrous – something which, indeed, has been hinted at more than once earlier on in the novel.

David's unsuccessful courtship of Nanny Johnson is dealt with by the narrator in an ironic tone, which completely undermines the idealistic terms in which the hero frames his desire for a 'real Friend'. Not only does she 'make no manner of doubt, but if [Nanny] had not met with this Temptation, she would have made a very affectionate Wife to the Man who loved her: he would have thought himself extremely happy, with a perfect Assurance that nothing could have tempted her to abandon him' (I, v, 38), but she also affirms that if David had been a little more sophisticated in his assessment of the situation, 'he might have carried her wherever he pleased' (I, vi, 40). Some time later, when David hears from Varnish how Spatter had ridiculed his desire to find a real friend behind his back, the narrator tells us: 'However difficult it was to raise David's Resentment, yet he found an Indignation within him at having his favourite Scheme made a jest of: for his Man of Goodness and Virtue was, to him, what Dulcinea was to Don Quixote ...' (II, v, 96). But Dulcinea the princess, of course, didn't exist; she was really Aldonza Lorenzo, the farm girl, just as Don Quixote was not really a knight but simply a man who 'utterly wrecked his reason [and] fell into the strangest fancy that ever a madman had in the whole world'.[17]

David's fancy produces a world of good and evil, and he behaves accordingly in a world which is actually more often than not shades of grey, as the narrator's apology for Nanny Johnson reveals: 'I hope to be excused by those Gentlemen, who are quite sure they have found one Woman, who is a perfect *Angel*, and that all the rest are perfect *Devils*, for drawing the Character of a Woman who was neither ...' (I, v, 37; emphasis in original). Suddenly, we are closer to the comic world of *Tom Jones*, with its possibility that we can 'censure the Action, without conceiving any absolute Detestation of the Person' (VII, i, 327). But the world of *David Simple* is always darker than that of *Tom Jones*, even if it does sometimes echo with laughter in the dark, for while Nanny is neither angel nor devil, she does reap the reward of her behaviour. With typical brusqueness the narrator dispatches her thus: 'Her Husband, notwithstanding his old Age, died of a spotted Fever; she caught the Infection of him, and survived him but three Days. But I think it now full time to look after my Hero' (I, vi, 44).

If the position of David as an ingenuous and uncomplicated man in a world which operates on quite different principles is occasionally shown to be untenable, the novel as it was published in 1744 was able to resolve this dilemma by reverting to the conventional happy ending which glosses over such tensions. Adherence to one's station in life is both linked back to a monolithic structure, that is, 'the natural order of things', and recommended as the way to real happiness: 'it is in the power of every Community to attain it, if every Member of it would perform the Part allotted to him by *Nature*, or his *Station in Life*, with a sincere Regard to the Interest and Pleasure of the whole' (IV, ix, 304; emphases in original). Here a quotation is used from Pope's *Windsor Forest*: 'Where Order in Variety we see;/And where, tho' all Things differ, all agree.'[18] The use of this quotation here is problematised both by the immediate context and by what has been said earlier in the novel. The narrator prefaces the quotation by telling the readers: 'In the Animal and Vegetable World there would be full as much Confusion as there is in human Life, was not every thing kept in its proper Place' (IV, ix, 304). The previous line in the poem uses the same word: 'as the World, harmoniously *confus'd*'.[19] Where the narrator of *David Simple* places concern for the 'Interest and Pleasure of the whole' in individual men, however, *Windsor Forest* is very definitely written from the same lofty point of view as the *Essay on Man*: in this view of the world, it is confused as far as the inhabitants are concerned because they are never elevated enough to see the divine plan, which is available only to the poet and certain great men.[20] In the service of an appeal to mankind to be *disinterested* participators in society, a quotation is used from a discourse which willingly accepts the interested nature of man on the understanding that 'private vice, public virtue' resolves the moral dilemma.

This then is another instance of a woman dealing in a discourse from which she herself is implicitly excluded on account of her sex. As Cynthia used Mandevillian economics, so Sarah Fielding's narrator here uses a version of civic humanism which proposes an ideal 'gentleman' as able to achieve a position sufficiently lofty to resolve all apparent contradictions in society. The effect of these two appropriations is however rather different. Cynthia's pragmatism allows the possibility of women making a space for themselves in economic discourse and indeed economic activity. The narrator's knowledge that 'The lowly Hedge, and humble Shrub, contribute to the varying and consequently beautifying the Prospect, as well as the stately Oak and lofty Pine' (IV, ix, 304) might represent a fleeting appropriation of power by a woman writer in assuming such a stance at all, but it leaves women as a sex firmly in their place – hedges, but never oaks. *David Simple, Volume the Last* (1753) reversed the happy ending of 1744, and in doing so it also allowed many of the submerged contradictions present then to reappear in ways less easy to accommodate to any comfortably benevolent version of the world, whether relying on an extensive or more select circle of right-feeling individuals. In the process, it is Cynthia, rather than the narrator at the end of Volume II, whose views are borne out.

One of the most significant areas to be questioned by *Volume the Last* is that of the role of the benefactor in the sentimental community. By the unwritten, unspoken rules of such a community, conferring and receiving obligations are part of their way of life, something sacred which are not to be abused. In Volume II, David is afraid to reveal his love for Camilla, 'lest she should be offended, and think he was *mean* enough to expect a Compliance from them both, on account of the Obligations they owed him' (IV, vi, 276; emphasis in original). (Despite Cynthia's sarcastic comment that *'there are very few People, who have any Notion of Obligations which are not pecuniary'* [II, vii, 116; emphasis in original], 'Obligations' in *David Simple* are almost invariably financial at base, unlike, for example, Harriet's obligation to Sir Charles Grandison which is unmistakably sexual.) David's delicacy in this matter reveals him as the ideal benefactor. However, Cynthia's story has already shown the darker side of that role. Her comments on 'fine Ladies', quoted earlier, not only break up power relations into localised struggles, they are also part of her own experience as a companion to a woman who did not scruple to use her position as financial superior to persecute her dependant. Cynthia tells David, 'melancholy Experience has taught me how miserable it is to abandon one's self to another's Power' (II, vii, 117). However, her position as a dependant makes it virtually impossible for her to live in any other way: she has to be rescued from her tormentor by David, who also gives her the money to travel to her cousin's. The fact that David does not abuse the power he has over Cynthia in this transaction does not alter the fact that she is, none the less, most certainly in his power.

It is because the benevolent David is the principal benefactor in the first part of *David Simple* that the disadvantages in the relationship can be smoothed over. However, in *Volume the Last*, David himself must rely on benefactors for support and it is here that the sentimental model breaks down almost completely. Mr Ratcliffe and the Orgueils give more promises than concrete support and David has all the misery of being obliged to continue relations with people who use their power unmercifully (most gruesomely in Mrs Orgueil's treatment of Cynthia's daughter, which ends in the child's death) but from whom, against all the odds, he still hopes to get help. It is only after the death of Camilla that David becomes strong enough to reject Mrs Orgueil's offer to adopt his eldest daughter. The narrator draws a grim picture of the young Camilla's life as it would have been had David accepted, and ends 'Joyfully I write thus that Mrs. Orgueil would have acted, for it was not Camilla's miserable Fate' (VII, vii, 418). Yet ultimately Camilla's fate is to rely on the generosity of a benefactor, an anonymous family near Bath from whom Cynthia had met with 'uncommon Treatment' while taking the waters. From them she receives 'a kind Promise that she and her Niece Camilla should be taken Care of' (VII, x, 428). Quite apart from the fact that this is a *deus ex machina* resolution to the problem of which the reader has had absolutely no warning, it is also, from what we now know about benefactors, a risky undertaking. After all, Cynthia's tormentor 'seemed as if she loved me' (II, vi, 111) at the outset. Yet *David Simple* can propose no other solution to the problem of how an impoverished gentlewoman is to support herself. As Camilla had told David,

Birth, Family, and Education, become Misfortunes, when we cannot attain some Means of supporting ourselves in the Station they throw us into … . If we were to attempt getting our living by any Trade, People in that Station would think we were endeavouring to take their Bread out of their mouths, and combine together against us … (III, ii, 169)

This must not be seen as simply a point about class, however; it is also about gender. For the generational/class shift between David's mother and Camilla is a fictional demonstration of the way that *women as a sex* were being ousted from trades as the eighteenth century progressed. As Ruth Perry writes:

The growth of cities and the beginnings of industrialism caused new divisions of function on the basis of sex as well as class, and this seriously affected the condition of women in the literate classes. These city women no longer were the economic partners of men, for the new, capitalistic modes no longer made public use of their labor, but separated them from the active concerns of life. …[21]

David's mother was precisely the 'economic partner' of her husband, but before she was married she 'got her Living by Plain-Work' (I, i, 9) – she was economically productive both before and after marriage in a way now barred to Camilla by the double handicap of sex and class.

'Simplicity' was a notion much discussed in the eighteenth century, and had connotations ranging from 'Plainness; artlessness; not subtilty; not cunning; not deceit' to 'Weakness, silliness'.[22] The *OED* also records meanings of 'absence of or freedom from luxury' and 'freedom from useless accessories'. Certainly the word was used during the period both as a pejorative term and a term of approval, and it is in the light of this doubleness, ironically, that we should see the character of David Simple. Here I would take issue with Janet Todd, who writes,

In both parts of *David Simple* tenderness is the summary of sentimental philosophy. Occasionally an unwary reader might be tempted to see irony at the expense of the tender and simple David (similar to the self-irony of Sterne's Yorick), but the temptation should be withstood, for all tenderness in so bleak a world is to be respected.[23]

On the contrary, it is precisely the amount of respect due to tenderness that is severely questioned by the events of *Volume the Last*. For if the workings of the commercial world undermine David's stance, so do his own experiences.

At the end of Volume II, the narrator tells us that for this ideal community, 'The very Infirmities ... such as Pain, Sickness, etc., were by their Contrivance not only made supportable, but fully compensated in the fresh Opportunities they gave each Individual of testifying their Tenderness and Care for the whole' (IV, ix, 304). This positive affirmation of suffering as an occasion for sentimental display is modified at the beginning of *Volume the Last*, where financial setbacks are accepted uncomplainingly by the community, who 'could not be ruffled or discomposed, but by a Separation, or seeing any one amongst them afflicted with Sickness, or any other real Calamity' (V, i, 327). From this admission that sickness in a companion is potentially painfully distressing, the narrative develops to show it as literally *insupportable* for the mind of acute sensibility. In his dying speech David acknowledges this: '"I found, even in my Days of Happiness, that, in obtaining my Wishes, I had multiplied my Cares; for, in the Persons of my Friends, I felt, at once, several Head-achs, and every other Infirmity of Body, and Affliction of Mind, to which human Nature is incident ..."' (VII, viii, 431). At the beginning of Volume I, David had been sure that if he could 'find a valuable Friend, in either Man or Woman, he should be doubly paid for all the Pains and Difficulties he could possibly go through' (I, vii, 46): his thoughts at the end of *Volume the Last* give the lie to this pious hope, and prove that the insensitive Mr Orgueil's unpalatable belief that compassion is 'a very great Weakness' (I, xi, 71) is ultimately correct. As Malcolm Kelsall writes, David's

> capacity for love and his springs of inward content remain the same throughout, but now [in *Volume the Last*] his inability to judge character truly, the timidity latent in his gentleness, the stupidity present in his *naïveté* ... are all exposed, as the comforting props of a safe income and a country life retired from the evil of the world are knocked from under him.[24]

Despite the use of the passive here, it should be stressed that David himself destroys the props supporting his way of life. The word 'simpleton' – characterised by Johnson as 'low' – was coming into general usage from the mid-seventeenth century onwards. *OED* gives the meaning as 'One who is deficient in sense or intelligence; a silly or foolish person; a fool'. For Mandeville, 'whoever can subsist and lives above his Income is a Fool'.[25] From the point of view of the world, David qualifies for both these titles, for when his law suit starts he continues '(without an exact provident Calculation) to afford his Family and Friends the Comforts of Life, without one of the Extravagancies' (V, i, 325). Quite apart from the fact that the Mandevillian world would not make any distinction between 'Comforts' and 'Extravagancies', David allows his feelings – his concern for his family and his desire to believe well of Ratcliffe and Orgueil, his 'friends' – to persuade him to continue with a suit his reason soon tells him to give up. David's problem is that he is both 'simple-hearted' and 'simple-minded': he is indeed ingenuous, sincere, unsophisticated; but he is also distinctly lacking in acumen where it matters – which, for all practical purposes, is in the world of business, not the world of feeling. As a father warns his son-in-law in Mary Collyer's *Felicia to Charlotte*: '"Pity has ruined thousands … indeed, men of great humanity, though of the best sense, frequently err in the plainest cases; even, where one, but a degree above a natural, would not be deceived."'[26] David's interview with the money-lender demonstrates this clearly. Nichols will not accept the verbal assurance of a sentimental friendship as security for a loan; David, battling against a system of values he can barely comprehend, let alone compete within, tells him, 'You don't talk our Language, Sir' (VI, vii, 369). Here, communication between the sentimental and the commercial is portrayed as frankly impossible.

If David is viewed at the end of the novel as a Mandevillian fool rather than a sentimental hero (arguably the same thing by a different name, from a different standpoint), the status of *David Simple* as typifying 'the serious plot of male sentiment'[27] is brought into question. Although I do not think it is necessary to choose to view him solely in one way or the other, in its employment of different discourses, and in its ultimately unhappy ending, the novel does demonstrate how difficult it is to propose an easy co-existence of the sentimental community and the early modern commercial world. It also problematises the practicability and desirability of the sentimental system of conferring and accepting 'obligations' as a means of financial support; *Tom Jones*, on the other hand, employs principally the discourse of humanist morality, which, bolstered by the traditional happy ending, can effectively bypass these issues, thus endorsing a far more conservative ideology.

In Sarah Fielding's *The History of the Countess of Dellwyn* (1759), the problems surrounding the sentimental community in a commercial world are explored once again, with a rather different result. The main plot of the novel, describing the downfall of the Countess, is related using terms and opinions straight from contemporary conduct literature. The heroine is seduced initially not by love, but by luxury. Miss Lucum's early distaste for London life is attributed to her being 'accustomed to early Hours, constant Employment, and a regular Manner of Life'.[28] She has obviously been leading an 'economical' existence in the country, of the type approved by Wetenhall Wilkes: 'Always be employed in somewhat innocent, or useful; for various, and beyond description, are the inconveniencies which besiege the mind in vacancy of employment.'[29] Once the bourgeois country girl has been corrupted by urban aristocratic pleasures and has become the vain, finery-loving Countess of Dellwyn, her fate is sealed – as she herself would know, had she paid more attention to conduct book advice which identified 'the vanity of conquests' as

the most dangerous companion that can lurk in a female bosom. It softens her sentiments; makes her fond of being politely addressed; curious of fine speeches; impatient of praise; and exposes her to all the temptations of flattery and deceit ... even to listen to compliments, and gay addresses, may betray [ladies] into weakness and indiscretion.[30]

Wilkes's homily provides a neat summary of the main plot of *The Countess of Dellwyn*. Against this tale of aristocratic vice is set a counter-tale of bourgeois virtue. This is not in itself surprising; it is the form which that virtue takes which lends the novel its particular interest.

Mrs Bilson's reaction to her husband's neglect is as exemplary, in conduct book terms, as Lady Dellwyn's behaviour is deplorable. 'Meekness and complacency, are the only weapons wherewith to combat an irregular husband,' cautions Wilkes.[31] But Mrs Bilson does not need to consult books on such matters, for her 'good Sense convinced her, that she might, with greater Ease, render Home detestable to her Husband than renew the Delight he once took in it; therefore her great Study was not to convert his Indifference into Aversion. She always received him with Affection ...' (I, 164). While Mrs Bilson has sense, she is also imbued with a 'tender Sensibility' (I, 157), and is described in terms which mark her out as a sentimental heroine. Yet when disaster strikes and her husband is thrown into the Fleet prison for non-payment of debts, she does not adopt the expected attitude of 'virtue in distress'. Camilla told David, 'there is no Situation so deplorable, no Condition so much to be pitied, as that of a Gentlewoman in real Poverty' (III, ii, 169). Mrs Bilson, however, does not, as Camilla does, reject trade as a means of financial support, and she sets out, without literary precedent (except, of course, the unacceptable one of Defoe's Roxana) to earn her family's living. Thus, as a female member of the middle classes, she reappropriates the earning power possessed by David Simple's mother, but severely eroded by the changing modes of production resulting from pre-industrial capitalism. Suddenly too, sentimental virtues are allowed to be compatible with economic sense; more than that, they *make economic sense*. For Janet Todd, in *David Simple* sentiment is 'a surplus in the economy with no exchange value'.[32] For Mrs Bilson sentiment is commercially viable and crucial to the success of her millinery business: 'her Business was constantly increasing ... . The Novelty of the Case rendered it a Fashion to buy of her' (I, 187); one of Mrs Bilson's customers 'immediately shewed her Compassion by the many Purchases she made' (I, 190). In 1798 Priscilla Wakefield urged women of the upper classes to 'countenance, in an especial manner, the industry of their own sex, in every department in which they can be employed; and to use the most strenuous efforts to remove those prejudices which have a tendency to continue women in a state of ignorance, dissipated sloth, inactivity, and helpless dependance',[33] but nearly 40 years before that appeal, Mrs Bilson was already taking part in just such a female, if fictional, network. Even the contradictions inherent in Wakefield's argument are also inherent in *The Countess of Dellwyn*. Both disapprove strongly of luxury in the civic humanist manner in one breath, while lauding it, in ways reminiscent of Mandeville, as a source of income for women in the next. Luxury is the downfall of the eponymous heroine, but the saviour of her virtuous counterpart.

The Countess of Dellwyn does not, however, as the previous paragraph may at first suggest, escape the issue of benefactors and the conferring and receiving of obligations, so severely questioned in *David Simple*. For, while Mrs Bilson herself is firmly bourgeois, she has, unlike David, aristocratic connections. One of these, Lady Dently, becomes her principal customer. She requests Mrs Bilson's company for whole days, taking her reluctantly from her family; she complies through 'Poverty, but not her Will', being also 'extremely sensible of the Honour conferred on her ...' (I, 194). From this beginning it is possible that Mrs Bilson may find herself in a situation similar to that suffered by Cynthia, but this possibility is averted by an alteration in the balance of power: when Lady Dently offers Mrs Bilson and her children an apartment in her house, Mrs Bilson refuses; she cannot leave her husband. Lady Dently is 'sensibly mortified by this Refusal, yet her Esteem for Mrs Bilson was increased by it' (I, 197). She is also further guilt-ridden by the fact that she has not yet, through snobbery, confessed her relationship to Mrs Bilson. Eventually, when she reveals it and takes the entire family, including the reformed Mr Bilson and his illegitimate daughter, into her household, we are to understand both sides of the transaction as equally obliged: 'This Family, equally happy in obliging and receiving obligations ...' (I, 202). Money earned is once again subsumed into money inherited, when Lady Dently leaves her fortune to the Bilsons on her death. In a reversal of the pattern in *David Simple*, the Bilsons themselves become benefactors, having been destitute. While the story does not seriously question the social hierarchy, it is significant that when first offered an 'obligation' Mrs Bilson can *choose* what to do: the money she earns gives her a measure of freedom.

On becoming independently rich, the Bilsons immediately free 'all such Prisoners in the Fleet as deserved it' and, in good conduct book fashion, 'settle the Œconomy of their House within very moderate Bounds' in order 'to make their Fortune extend to the Relief of as many as possible'. Theirs is the charity of a meritocracy; sentiment has become answerable to a set of criteria: the objects of its mercy must be 'deserving' – a status ascertained by 'inspection' and 'enquiries' – and 'œconomy' is of paramount importance (I, 206–7). Unlike David Simple, who failed to make 'an exact provident Calculation' (V, i, 325) when it mattered, the Bilsons do just this to render their charitable deeds economically and emotionally efficient. This version of charity is a strange hybrid of the two represented by Richard Steele and Bernard Mandeville, as described in Chapter 1. The reforming zeal of Steele seems to have become somewhat muted, since rather than pulling anyone, let alone an entire age, out of 'Degeneracy and Depravation of Manners', charitable aid is only given to those previously identified as deserving it. Seemingly aware of the possible Mandevillian jibe that charity only promotes 'Sloth and Idleness', the charity of the Bilsons – like that of Sir Charles Grandison – is of a relentlessly active kind. Sarah Scott's *Millenium Hall* (1762), which describes a benevolent community run by women, articulated this imperative as to do with the donor's idleness rather than the recipient's, but the net effect is the same: 'By giving [the poor] my money I may sacrifice my covetousness, but by doing it negligently I indulge my indolence, which I ought to endeavour to conquer as much as every other vice.'[34] There are no negligent effusions of bank notes from either Scott's Miss Mancel or the Bilsons, but rather setting people up in their respective callings, providing incentives to save, and educating.

The Countess of Dellwyn looks in this light as if it is trying to provide the fictional sentimentalism of earlier years with what it lacked: a credible social programme, a way to work within this world, not the next. As a literary movement largely initiated by the emerging middle classes, it could be seen as important to link its virtues with economic activity rather than paralysing incapacity. Published in the same year as *Dellwyn*, Adam Smith's *Theory of Moral Sentiments* articulated similar concerns through the medium of moral philosophy rather than fiction, asserting for example that 'Man was made for action ... .He must not be satisfied with indolent benevolence, nor fancy himself the friend of mankind, because in his heart he wishes well to the prosperity of the world.'[35] John Mullan has discussed the way in which Smith's 'sympathy' differed materially from Hume's, involving not 'a direct reproduction of the "passions" of "others"', but rather the production of an 'analogous emotion' in the breast of every 'attentive spectator'.[36] Sympathy thus becomes far closer to the possibility of objective assessment – to the kind of 'inspection' and 'enquiries' the Bilsons undertake before parting with their money for charitable purposes. Again, Smith writes that 'General lamentations, which express nothing but the anguish of the sufferer, *create rather a curiosity to inquire into his situation*, along with some disposition to sympathise with him, than any actual sympathy that is very sensible' (my emphasis).[37]

Thus charitable gestures are no longer simply the result of a moment of intense feeling, but are programmatic, much as in life the individual donor was increasingly supplemented by collective activity.[38] The small and ever-shrinking union of hearts of *David Simple* is expanded in *The Countess of Dellwyn* to 'some Hundreds, besides the much greater Numbers, who felt occasional Blessings from their Benevolence ...' (I, 206). For David Simple, compassion is shown to be a 'weakness'; Mrs Bilson's sensibility is rewritten as strong, in total accord with the active moral life, just as for Smith 'Our sensibility to the feelings of others, so far from being inconsistent with the manhood of self-command, is the very principle upon which that manhood is founded.'[39] The sex of the 'sensible' protagonist is, however, clearly relevant here: as the conduct books show, a woman's virtue is crucially involved with both her sensibility and her economic (domestic managerial) activity. If not firmly connected to the moral domestic life, a woman's sensibility could be swiftly connected with an immoral sexual one. Sensibility in women fell either side of the moral divide: 'Women are more inclined to criminal Excesses of that kind, than Men, when they are left without Restraint: And ... they are infinitely more chast than Men, if they are educated with proper Care.'[40] 'Feeling' was therefore always sufficiently morally dubious to need clear definition. Mary Collyer's *Felicia to Charlotte* is also concerned to locate feeling firmly within the morally acceptable, as Felicia's description of her aunt shows:

> everybody that sees her must immediately think (I should rather say *feel*) her a very good [lady]. In short, she is a woman of great prudence, and a perfect œconomist, and therefore her thoughts seem equally divided between the management of her own family, and a generous care for the welfare of those who apply to her for assistance.[41]

What is different about Mrs Bilson, however, is that her activities go beyond the domestic – or at least, they enlarge the domestic sphere so far as to enable a woman to be dealing with problems at a considerable remove from her immediate, personal responsibilities.

If David Simple can be viewed either as a Mandevillian fool or a sentimental hero, Mrs Bilson is that most unlikely combination, a sentimental, Mandevillian heroine. What this means in effect is that her position is essentially contradictory: luxury is both deplorable and useful; obligations are both something you do not have to accept and something you must be suitably 'sensible' of; sensibility and business sense – mutually exclusive to the archetypal sentimentalist – are united. *David Simple* problematised the co -existence of the sentimental community and the commercial world: *The Countess of Dellwyn* attempts to offer a solution by conflating sensibility and commercial instinct and recruiting the resulting combination in defence of the middle classes. Where David Simple finds vice in all the sections of society he explores (high, middling and low), vice in *The Countess of Dellwyn* is very much an aristocratic affair, to be morally disapproved of, but economically exploited. The combining of sensibility and commercial instinct within a female figure, while perhaps unexpected, is also an increasingly significant feature of sentimental novels in subsequent decades of the century, as the following chapters explore.

So where does this leave the orthodox divide between Sarah Fielding's 'novel of sentiment' and the comic novel of Henry Fielding? I do not want to draw any rigid line between the two Fieldings: not only are their novels discursively rich, the influence and constraints of genre must also be taken into account – not only, as discussed before, comedy and tragedy, but romance and satiric social commentary. *Joseph Andrews* and *Tom Jones* are both ultimately framed by a love story in the traditional manner, ending in marriage – a pattern which almost inevitably puts a definite, optimistic closure on events. Neither *David Simple* nor *The Countess of Dellwyn* belongs to that pattern. My reading of the works suggests that Sarah Fielding's novels, generally labelled 'sentimental', not only question the 'universality of social understanding',[42] but also actually identify and examine many of the practical, economic problems inherent in the whole sentimental system, often ending in ways which leave the system seriously discredited (*David Simple*) or strategically modified (*The Countess of Dellwyn*). By contrast, the comic romance structure tends to validate the sentimental reliance on 'right-feeling' by proposing a world where such feeling triumphs, thus precluding any need for rigorous analysis or change.

3

Sexual Innocence and Economic Experience: the Problems of *Amelia* and *Ophelia*

David Simple and *The Countess of Dellwyn* demonstrate how criticism and modification of the sentimental system can take place via an economically able, but still sensible, woman. This pattern becomes, in slightly different ways, a crucial feature of both Henry Fielding's *Amelia* (1751) and Sarah Fielding's *The History of Ophelia* (1760). In this chapter, I explore ideas of femininity and the nature of their relation to economic activity. As these novels illustrate, the relation between these two is not only complex, it is also in the early stages of a process of change – a process which will, as the century progresses, enable connections to be made between areas where previously none was possible, thus altering the dynamics of the relationships among femininity, sensibility and economic activity.

When Mrs Bilson stepped out of the domestic sphere to earn her family's living and pay their debts, she helped to forge a new connection in fiction – between herself, as sensible female, and economic (that is, business managerial) activity. In order to do this, as has been noted, it was necessary already to have placed her carefully as an exemplar on the other, domestic, economic front. Lack of domestic economic ability could render a woman's virtue questionable: in her *Narrative* of her life (1755), the actress Charlotte Charke attributes much of her later 'oddity' to this lack when she admits that, had she paid more attention to her needle, it 'would have rendered me less troublesome in a Family, and more useful to myself, and those about me'.[1] Her adult life of morally dubious 'Vagabondizing' is the inevitable result of a masculine education involving, among other things, Latin and the use of guns. However, as this indicates, it is not simply her inability to perform the domestic tasks conventionally

allotted to women that condemns Charke, but also her pursuit of
extra-domestic activity *per se*, which was generally seen as inherently
immoral in a woman. As James Fordyce warned young women: 'if a
young person ... will always be breaking loose through each domestic inclosure, and ranging at large the wide common of the world,
those destroyers [i.e. 'the worst men'] will see her in a very different
point of light. They will consider her as lawful game...'[2] Any activity
beyond the 'domestic inclosure' becomes, by definition, immoral
activity, and automatically deprives the woman of any of the protection supposedly afforded by her rightful sphere.[3]

Thus one of the most obvious kinds of extra-domestic activity,
earning money in 'the wide common of the world', was not the
province of a respectable female; on the contrary, the economic role
of such a woman lay within the home, dutifully 'improving and
securing' her husband's fortune.[4] Correspondingly, I want to argue
that in much eighteenth-century writing it is possible to discern an
inherent identification of the woman who either chooses or is
forced to be financially independent with the sexually immoral
woman.

Historical accounts of women and work have found the area one
of great difficulty. Chris Middleton has written that

> It is one of the curiosities of historiography that ... women's
> contribution to economic life appears to be perpetually on the
> wane. Histories of every period (at least until the present
> century) depict women as undergoing a process of rapidly
> advancing economic marginality, yet those of subsequent periods
> attest with equal conviction to women's economic vigour and
> importance at the start of their own age.[5]

In *Women, Work and Sexual Politics in Eighteenth-Century England*
(1989) Bridget Hill agrees that there is a need to review some of the
conclusions drawn by Ivy Pinchbeck, the pioneer in eighteenth-
century women's history. Nevertheless she maintains with
Pinchbeck, and in fulfilment of Middleton's pattern, that, 'In the
eighteenth-century as strictly defined, there seems little doubt that
women lost out as far as opportunities for work are concerned.'[6]
Whatever the historical reality, there is at least evidence for a contemporary *perception* that employment possibilities for women were
becoming scarcer as the century progressed. For example, in
support of her view that London in particular saw a rise in crime

(especially prostitution) and suicide in the wake of female un-employment, Pinchbeck cites Henry Fielding's *Covent-Garden Journal* for 26 June 1752. Fielding noted that, while a number of female suicides had been reported recently, there had been no reports of men resorting to such action and he commented, 'Perhaps the distress to which some females have been lately reduced may in some measure account for it.'[7] When the Lock Hospital for venereal disease opened in 1746 it was found that 'the men when discharged resumed their former employment, but the women, it was acknowledged, had usually no other resource than to go back to prostitution'.[8] Towards the end of the century, Mary Wollstonecraft was deploring the fact that 'an attempt to earn their own subsistence' sunk women 'almost to the level of those poor abandoned creatures who live by prostitution', and asked, reveal-ingly, 'are not milliners and mantua-makers reckoned the next class?'[9] Forty years earlier this supposition is already implicit in *Amelia*, where the mother of the morally corrupt Trent 'carried on the Trade of Milliner in *Covent-Garden*'.[10]

A contemporary belief that the prospects of respectable employ-ment for women were shrinking would certainly be consistent with a view that the working woman must therefore be earning her living immorally. As Camilla discovered in *David Simple*, men could be found to provide a woman with money, if she, in her turn, were willing to pay the price: 'they severally entertained me with the Beauty of my Person, and began to talk to me in a Style, which gave me to understand they were not silly enough to part with their Money for nothing.' For Camilla, this was 'a Price I thought too dear for any thing they could do for me',[11] but eighteenth-century fiction does not lack examples of women who decide to take up such offers, and (in contrast to most of their historical coun-terparts who sought help at the Lock Hospital) turn them to their own advantage.

In discussing *Roxana* (1724), for instance, Jane Jack writes of the '*bourgeois* air of substance and ... unshakeable determination to get on in the world' of Defoe's protagonists;[12] getting on in the world for a deserted middle-class wife such as Roxana inescapably involved sexual liaisons, since the alternative was starvation: 'nor had I any thing to subsist with, but what I might get by working, and that was not a Town where much Work was to be had.' Roxana accepts her landlord's offer, deciding in effect 'to lye with him for Bread', and thus begins her successful career as a high-class prostitute. The moral ambiguity of *Roxana*, however, is complete. The doubt as to whether a woman really 'ought rather to die, than to prostitute her Virtue and Honour', or whether Roxana's poverty (as Amy argues) justifies her action, is not solved by the darkening of the prospect in the later part of the novel, nor by the assertion of the Preface that not all Roxana's prosperity could 'abate the Reproaches of her Conscience'.[13] The most telling aspect of the novel's final third is the untimely return of her daughter Susan, which admittedly adds to the negative implications of Roxana's career, as James Thompson has shown.[14] Yet her success has been detailed in 300 pages, while her ultimate downfall is referred to in a few lines: it is arguably the former, rather than the latter, which endures. Vice and profit are still undoubtedly, if ambiguously, linked.

In *Memoirs of a Woman of Pleasure* (1748/9), more commonly known as *Fanny Hill*, this link seems much less problematic. In this male fantasy, the heroine leads a largely enjoyable life as a prostitute, remarkably neither contracting venereal disease nor becoming pregnant. Moreover, she takes good care of her earnings, benefiting from the advice of her bawd and friend Mrs Cole, and has a reserve of £800 laid by when she meets and agrees to live with a wealthy elderly gentleman. He, dying after a short time, leaves her his sole heiress:

> and that this unexpected elevation did not turn my head, I ow'd to the pains my benefactor had taken to form and prepare me for it, as I ow'd his opinion of my management of the vast possessions he left me, to what he had observ'd of the prudential œconomy I had learned under Mrs. *Cole*, of which the reserve he saw I had made, was a proof, and encouragement, to him.[15]

In addition to this material good fortune, Fanny soon meets Charles again, her first and only true love, who is returning penniless from an unsuccessful journey to the South-Seas. They marry, produce 'fine children'[16] and live happily ever after in virtue and prosperity – all owing, of course, to Fanny's profitable life of vice. Such a tale, with its use of both sentimental and conduct book vocabulary ('benefactor', 'prudential economy') at the moment at which traditionally defined vice gets its greatest financial reward, lends a nice irony to earnest rhetoric such as Adam Smith's in *The Theory of Moral Sentiments* (1759): 'What is the reward most proper for encouraging industry, prudence and circumspection? Success in every sort of business. And is it possible that in the whole of life these virtues should fail of attaining it?'[17]

Using *Roxana* and especially *Fanny Hill* as examples obviously has further implications of kinds that I shall only touch on here. The female narrators of both texts are, of course, the creations of male authors, and as such can be seen as offering examples of how, in Philip Simmons's view, the 'voyeuristic narrative can serve as means of constructing and controlling representations of female subjectivity'.[18] *Fanny Hill* has been read by women critics both as a text which exploits and ultimately exhibits a dislike for women, and as a cheerful celebration of healthy physical love.[19] Either way, I would argue, there is no justification for Simmons's further conclusion that the text 'makes every attempt to mask its transgressions'.[20] On the contrary, the panegyric on virtue with which the book ends, however it is read, cannot and does not seriously try to efface the overt connection between economic success and a sexually immoral life, a connection which expresses plainly the dangerous creed that economy, prudence and good management – those conduct book virtues associated apparently exclusively with the chaste woman – can be attained and exploited by the woman who should, on the evidence of her sexual profligacy, be constitutionally unable to exercise the control necessary to have access to such qualities. Furthermore, the novel demonstrates the irony that the conduct book virtues possessed by Fanny make a woman economically powerful when exercised beyond the paternal or matrimonial home, just as the approved use of them within the home renders her effectively powerless. This representation of the economically powerful woman is, of course, predicated upon the distinctly disempowering assumption that she will be available to any man who can pay; if this is unpalatable, it nevertheless illustrates clearly a connection I believe to be of great importance in the fiction of the period.

This connection between extramarital sexual experience and financial expertise is a significant factor in both *Amelia* and *The History of Ophelia*. Lady Palestine, Ophelia's unlikely chaperone, was left a young widow in less favourable financial circumstances than she had anticipated, and so decided to use her wit and beauty to make 'those for whom she relinquished the Esteem of Mankind, give her the Means of purchasing their Civility, and outward Respect'.[21] She is not punished for her collusion in the plot against Ophelia's virtue, nor does she lose her position in society on account of her unorthodox way of maintaining herself. The narrator, the older Ophelia, comments on the situation sardonically: 'If a Woman has Assurance enough not to be ashamed of Infamy, and a Fortune to afford every fashionable Expence; the World may blame her ill Conduct, but it will not desert her, while they censure her Behaviour they will court her Acquaintance ...' (I, 154). There is no denying, however, that Lady Palestine's decision was, economically and socially, a successful one. Ophelia finds Lady Palestine lacking in prudence, but since her imprudence does not seem to have distressed her nor made her life in any way irksome to her, the criticism is undermined. On the contrary, since Lady Palestine's 'greatest Happiness was a general Acquaintance, a Blessing to which she had attained' (I, 151), the actions labelled 'imprudent' by the narrator can be seen as highly prudent in the circumstances and suitably successful.

If Lady Palestine chooses a sexual fall in order to maintain her material expectations in life, Mrs Bennet in *Amelia* has no such freedom to choose. Raped while drugged, like Clarissa, her nightmarish experience seems at first to have only disastrous consequences. Her husband dies, as does her son, and she is reduced to accepting a small annuity from the noble lord, author of her misfortunes. But, as Terry Castle has noted,[22] as the novel progresses the curve of Mrs Bennet's fortune begins to rise once more, first with her marriage to Serjeant Atkinson and then with her successful attempt to secure a promotion for her husband. Her experience enables her to go where the innocent Amelia dares not: she uses the masquerade to conduct a financial negotiation from which she emerges victorious. The Serjeant's promotion is assured and so, accordingly, is the couple's financial security. While Mrs Atkinson is, of course, free from vice,[23] the connection between sexual experience and economic dexterity still holds good.

In both novels, the heroines, sexually pure and innocent, are set against these compromised women as the absolute standard. The young Ophelia has no concept of sexual vice and thus she has no idea how to recognise a sexual threat – or even to realise that such a thing exists. She is completely unaware 'that there ever was known any criminal intercourse between man and woman' (I, 24) – in other words, she apparently possesses a prelapsarian innocence, befitting her upbringing in Edenic isolation. Amelia, although allowed slightly more awareness than Ophelia on account of her status as a married woman, is presented by Booth in similar terms as he relates his history to Miss Mathews:

> 'Poor dear Love! how should the sincerest of Hearts have any Idea of Deceit? for with all her Simplicity I assure you she is the most sensible Woman in the World.'
> 'It is highly generous and good in you,' (said Miss Mathews, with a sly sneer) 'to impute to Honesty what others would perhaps call Credulity.'
> 'I protest, Madam,' answered he, 'I do her no more than Justice...' (II, ii, 70–1)

'Simplicity' is a key word in relation to both heroines. Both have to be warned of their precarious positions by the sexually experienced. Mrs Atkinson warns Amelia against both the specious noble lord and the treacherous 'friend' Colonel James; Ophelia is enlightened as to Dorchester's intentions by a rival for her attentions, the rakish Lord Larborough. Yet 'simplicity', as has been discussed in the previous chapter, is by no means an unproblematic quality – as Miss Mathews' sour rejoinder above demonstrates. While in *David Simple* the irony of the word's double meaning (artlessness, not deceitful/weakness, foolishness) worked to expose the dubious desirability of the quality, in *Amelia* and *Ophelia* the irony emerges from the possible unreliability of the word – whether it means artlessness or foolishness – as a suitable epithet for either heroine.

One reason for this is, of course, that the virtue and sexual innocence of women was a controversial subject, which many writers of conduct literature found themselves entangled in: women were creatures of sensibility, but as Jean Hagstrum has written, sensibility could be either 'fine excess or deplorable excess'.[24] Were women innately chaste or innately lewd? And if the former, how were they supposed to recognise the perils of a lewd world? One solution used by writers of both conduct books and novels was that the innocent and virtuous woman possessed a kind of sexual early warning system: 'A sweet timidity was given them to guard their innocence, by inclining them to shrink from what ever might threaten to injure it.'[25] So Ophelia, embraced roughly in the dark by a man she believes, wrongly, to be Dorchester, already feels the impropriety of such a gesture: 'without knowing the reason for it, I was disturbed at this address. I could not think such violence the necessary consequence of love' (I, 30). Yet such a shrinking, or undefined disturbance, implies innate carnal knowledge as much as – if not more than – innate innocence. The pure simplicity – artlessness – of women is always already compromised since some art is essential if they are 'to guard their innocence'. The same applies, in different circumstances, to Amelia. Despite Booth's eulogy, Amelia is not as transparently simple as she seems. In fact, she spends the greater part of the novel 'keeping a secret' from her husband, the secret that she has known all along about his brief affair with Miss Mathews. She can practise deceit (albeit of a benevolent kind) as well as anyone else. Her stratagem to avoid attending the second masquerade – and thus avoid the unwelcome attentions of Colonel James – is another instance of art protecting 'innocence'. Practically speaking, innocence in women has to be innocence of the deed, not innocence of the danger, of sexual misdemeanour. The irony that conduct books themselves recommended such benign deceptions, while simultaneously requiring women to be transparently good, further demonstrates the contradictions of the position from which they were writing.

If simplicity as artlessness is not entirely appropriate to these heroines (or, implicitly, any heroines), neither is simplicity as foolishness. For while neither woman becomes a startling economic success in the way of Roxana or Fanny Hill (or indeed Mrs Bilson) each possesses economic ability in a variety of ways. Both novels offer a number of different economic possibilities (by contrast, for example, with the overarching providentiality of *Tom Jones*), with which the heroines seem better able to engage than any of the other characters. In their capacity as exemplary virtuous women, this does seem to reinforce the connection made through Mrs Bilson between the sensible female and economic activity. But given the 'always already fallen' condition of even the most virtuous woman, the link between economic activity and sexually immoral behaviour cannot be severed completely, a point which is underlined in both novels, in different ways, as later discussion will show.

Ophelia has been brought up in idyllic economic self-sufficiency with her aunt. They have their cottage deep in rural Wales and possess a few animals, having no contact with the outside world beyond seeing 'a few Times an old Man ... on Occasions necessary to our rural life' (I, 15). The Miltonic vocabulary emphasises the prelapsarian nature of their life:

The vernal Beauties of the finer Seasons charmed our Eyes, the tuneful Choir of Birds enchanted our Ears, and both united to raise our Contemplations to their Creator; we were grateful for general Blessings, not less esteemed by us for being common to all Mankind, we wanted no partial Favours; we saw much to admire, much to rejoice in, and nothing to Envy. (I, 13)[26]

The two women are indeed very close to living in 'that original state of things' described by Adam Smith in *The Wealth of Nations* (1776), 'which precedes both the appropriation of land and the accumulation of stock', when 'the whole produce of labour belongs to the labourer. He has neither landlord nor master to share with him.' In their closed system of production and consumption, no money is necessary; even the fundamental Smithian 'propensity to truck, barter, and exchange one thing for another'[27] is unknown to Ophelia. She is shocked to learn, on arriving at an inn for the first time, 'that their Hospitality was a mere Trade, by which they gained a Subsistence' (I, 39). Thus she arrives in the mid eighteenth-century economic world as an outsider – and an outsider who has no need to take part in this strange system on her own account since she has been provided with everything she could want by the man responsible for abducting her from her Eden. As an observer, she comes to conclusions which combine both sentimental and Mandevillian insights in a complete rejection of a money-based system.

Like Mandeville, she 'soon perceived that Luxury was universal', but unlike him, she can refer to a world in which that is not so: 'even the poorer People enjoyed such a Share of it, as surprized me, when I compared it with the plain Simplicity in which I had been bred.' Coming from Eden, Ophelia is in a position to object to 'the Invention of Coin', something Adam Smith was to identify as the crucial step on the road to a successful commercial society,[28] and to see it as 'equally a Spur to Avarice and an Incitement to Luxury' (I, 76). The problem of how a sufficiency – as against deficiency or surplus – is defined is side-stepped by the use of a character who can claim, from first-hand experience, to know. When Ophelia writes, 'People, whose Desires are inspired by Reason alone, can soon say, "I have enough of every Thing"' (I, 76), it is not the assertion of a theorist, but the comment of someone whose mind has been nurtured by such 'Reason'.

If her upbringing gives Ophelia certain privileges in her analysis of the economic system, it also leads her to find strange other aspects of the world she enters. The notion of correct station in life, undermined in *David Simple*, comes under attack once more from Ophelia, since she knows a world where there is neither 'landlord nor master'. Her first surprise is at the church on Lord Dorchester's estate, where elaborate tombstones on the one hand and wooden monuments on the other indicate the divergent social status of the deceased: she is 'shocked at this distinction of Ranks; and to find that here the Rich and the Poor do not lie down together ...' (I, 59). Later on, when Ophelia has been in London for a little time and is becoming socially more sophisticated, she attends a masquerade. The snobbish Lady Cambridge is of the party, and Ophelia's solemn mockery of aristocratic precedence lays open both her companion and the system she upholds to contempt:

> Lady *Cambridge* was as new to the Entertainment as myself, never having been at a Masquerade before; and I could see the great Familiarity with which every one accosted her, with as little Distinction as they could the lowest Plebian, greatly offended her Pride, and she could scarcely prevail on herself to conceal so much Nobility under a Mask. That I might be sure of the Cause of the Disturbance I perceived in her, I observed, that, 'this Diversion seemed an Emblem of Death; it laid all Hearts open, and put an End to all Dissimulations and Pretence... . That, like the Grave too, it levelled all Distinctions, and brought high and low upon an Equality.' Upon thus touching the tender Point, her Ladyship answered, that, 'indeed she thought Masquerades could never long meet with Encouragement from Persons of Rank, unless they could find out a Method of distinguishing their Conditions.' I proposed a Coronet on the Mask, as the easiest Method of fixing the Stamp of Rank and Fashion on those who could claim it. She was charmed with the Thought, and declared, 'She would endeavour to bring her Friends into it; and if it once became general, she should be a constant Person at those Diversions, since, in every respect, but that levelling Quality, she liked them extremely.' (I, 221–2)

The episode of the masquerade demonstrates in little many of the tensions which animate *The History of Ophelia* as a whole. The older Ophelia's account of the event seems in many respects to conform to what Terry Castle identifies as the archetypal response of the eighteenth-century satirist: 'the real world, with all its chicanery and bad faith, was ultimately indistinguishable from the masquerade; both resolved, pathologically, into a *mundus inversus*, where all pretended to be what they were not.'[29] Ophelia sees the masquerade as an inevitable, even necessary, mirror-image of the corrupt and insincere society she has been introduced to; if in everyday life members of that society mask their minds but not their faces, at the masquerade they dress fantastically, masking their faces (along with all signs of social status), and thus they are enabled to lay 'aside those Parts, which Interest, the Love of Power, or Fame, induced them to act in publick' (I, 221). She observes with gentle contempt, 'I should imagine some Relaxation from the painful Exercises of Dissimulation and Flattery necessary ...' (I, 218). Yet still 'the Divine Countenance of Truth' is to be found no more easily at the masquerade than in everyday life: 'Accustomed to Excesses, People lose the Relish for the true Medium, and make but one Step from Flattery to Abuse' (I, 220).

This is the voice of Augustan temperance, that enemy of all excess. Here it is heard, as are Ophelia's observations on economic life, in the knowledge that the speaker is supposed to have had intimate, inaccessible (and thus unverifiable for the reader) experience of 'the true Medium'. Her position, from that point of view, is unassailable. Yet her views on rank are potentially anarchic from the perspective of the hierarchical Augustan, and threaten that balanced position: while the masquerade in *The History of Ophelia* is clearly not available as a joyful 'English Saturnalia',[30] neither is it solely in the hands of the archetypal satirist. The heroine evidently relishes the discomfort of Lady Cambridge; rank can be ridiculed, and even dismantled. That the 'lowest Plebian' and the aristocrat cannot be distinguished is not an occasion for censure, but for amusement.

The prelapsarian economic model, with its ideal of sufficient production and consumption untarnished by money or exchange, is not, as suggested earlier, the only model explored by *Ophelia*. Despite the heroine's distaste for her discovery that the innkeepers make a 'trade' out of hospitality in order to gain a subsistence, the ways and means (or lack of them) of earning a living occupy a significant place in the novel. They occur most tellingly in the story of Traverse, a half-pay officer whose problems are very similar to those of Booth in *Amelia*. His wife, Caroline, is 'so good an Œconomist' (I, 240) that the family – growing in size year by year – manage well enough until Traverse hears 'the fatal news of the

Reduction of our Regiment', thus rendering their income 'insufficient for the Support of so large a Number' (I, 243–4). Traverse, too ill physically and mentally to earn a living, has to rely on his wife, who

> 'As fit to struggle with bad Fortune, as to grace good ... soon, by various Kinds of Work, found Means of increasing our Income ... . Thus, by my *Caroline*'s Ingenuity and Industry, we were supported; nor, was I ever, for a Moment, able to perceive, that she either repined or grieved at being obliged to give this Assistance; on the contrary, she appeared to take greater Pleasure in it, than in any Amusements she had ever enjoyed.' (I, 244–5)

Momentarily we see the return of Mrs Bilson; but here the construction of a economically productive and successful woman is set up only to be destroyed almost immediately. One day Caroline Traverse returns home wet through 'from a Place where her Business had called her' (I, 245), and is struck down by an illness which permanently deprives her of the use of her hands. In the light of Fordyce's warning to women who break through 'domestic inclosures', this deprivation could be looked on as a punishment. Practically, in the novel, it forces the Traverse family back to a reliance on benevolence: a consequence which will be examined in more detail later on.

Like Caroline Traverse, Amelia is, in approved conduct book manner, mistress 'of every Œconomical Office, from the highest to the lowest' (XI, viii, 488). Her position as wife and mother is constantly stressed, and it is within this framework that she tells Booth that he has 'a Wife who will think herself happy with you, and endeavour to make you so in any Situation'; he is not to worry, for 'Industry will always provide us a wholesome Meal' (IV, iii, 162). While this is obviously at one with the duties of the 'perfect-wife-and-mother', it is also the first of three occasions on which Amelia makes what Sheridan Baker sees as her 'surprising offer to work with her hands'. He further refers to it as 'the romantic urge toward love in a cottage expressed by Amelia'.[31] It can be seen as a rather more practical suggestion, however, made by the undeniably more practical partner in the Booth marriage. Carolyn Williams recognises this when she comments that 'Amelia has discretion enough for two – which for Will Booth's wife is the necessary ration'.[32] Indeed Booth himself recognises his wife's superior managerial skills. He has 'already lost every Farthing they were worth' (X, vi, 436), when Amelia pawns her picture to get money to buy food; Booth – not realising how she came by the money – insists that Amelia take all but one guinea, 'saying she was the safest Treasurer' (XI, viii, 489). Booth is not merely a bad treasurer, however; he is also very bad at making money in the first place. This is partly to do with his attitude towards it. Unlike Amelia, he dismisses trade as quite impossible: 'all Business required some Knowledge or Experience, and likewise Money to set up with; of all which I was destitute' (III, xii, 145). Clearly Booth's idea of business is not the same as Amelia's when she later suggests that the small sum left to them might possibly put them 'into some mean Way of Livelihood' (X, vi, 436). When attempting to become 'Farmer Booth', he makes a bad bargain almost immediately, and after two years is £40 in debt.

With all her common sense, financial and otherwise, Amelia is a subservient wife, telling Booth she will 'always submit to [his] superior Judgment' (XI, v, 479), although this confidence in Booth's judgment becomes less and less tenable as the novel progresses. Her offers to help repair the family finances are never taken up, and of course ultimately are not needed, but her bid to enter the world of production – to do what Mrs Bilson and Caroline Traverse later succeed in doing, however briefly – is none the less significant, particularly as it is accompanied by both a definition of wants which derives more from Mandeville than from civic humanism, and a levelling tendency which prefigures Ophelia's undermining of rank. Amelia asserts, '"I can level my Mind with any State... . How many Thousands abound in Affluence, whose Fortunes are much lower than ours! for it is not from Nature, but from Education and Habit, that our Wants are chiefly derived"' (IV, iii, 162). Later she cries, '"Am I of a superior Rank of Being to the Wife of the honest Labourer? Am I not Partaker of one common Nature with her?"' (XII, viii, 527). *Amelia* does not rely solely on its heroine to question the meaning of rank, however. Mrs Bennet, in becoming Mrs Atkinson, marries below her station – an act which the novel affirms in sentimental style, eschewing rank based on social status and claiming instead a hierarchy of goodness (VII, x, 304–5). The sarjeant's subsequent promotion, a literal improvement in rank, advances him to a point beyond that which his social status would have dictated, but which is more suited to his intrinsic worth. In this respect, *Amelia* is an archetypal sentimental novel,[33] substituting emotional for material methods of evaluation; but where in other novels this substitution becomes the site on which the tragedy takes place,[34] in *Amelia* it results in an unorthodox but successful marriage. Station in life is not helplessly deplored as a cruel obstacle of fate, but actually and happily surmounted.

If in this instance *Amelia* uses sentimental values to positive effect, at other times they themselves are found wanting. This applies most significantly to the sentimental model of benevolence ultimately validated in *Tom Jones*, but criticised so severely in the action of *David Simple, Volume the Last*. In *Amelia*, its treatment is riddled with irony from the moment Booth and Amelia find themselves in need of money.[35] Fellow officers who believe Booth to have married 'a great fortune' offer him money with great generosity when he has no need of it; when he goes to them in real need, they have regrettably ordered their affairs in such a way that the money is no longer available (III, vii, 122). The title of 'benefactor', which belongs to Allworthy in *Tom Jones*, is transferred to the undeserving James and the vicious noble lord, and the narrator can only wonder that pride 'should so seldom hint to us the only certain as well as laudable way of setting ourselves above another Man, and that is by becoming his Benefactor' (IV, iv, 170). Thus a benefactor is no longer one of the kind and good, but simply one of the powerful; the worst motives are far more likely to encourage apparent generosity than the best. Amelia, although full of gratitude to those whom she believes – usually wrongly – to be showing generosity for its own sake, does attempt to break through the imprisoning cycle of benevolence and obligation. She tries to persuade Booth that they are 'little obliged' to someone who has been good to them in the past but is now just as determined to make them miserable (IV, v, 175). One of her arguments in favour of taking up some 'mean Livelihood' is that little can be expected from any other source: Booth's dependence on Colonel James 'is all vain, I am afraid, and fallacious' (X, vi, 435). Booth himself, when given some hint of the noble lord's ulterior motives for helping his family, begins to see the danger of this form of support, telling Amelia that he sees obligations as 'the worst kind of Debts', having 'observed that those who confer them, expect to be repaid ten thousand fold' (VI, ii, 236).

That the moral as well as the financial power is on the side of the benefactor rather than the recipient is evident from the language used to describe these transactions. Booth speaks of James having 'oppressed me ... with Obligations' (IX, iv, 368), while Adam Smith asserts that we are 'shocked beyond all measure' if recipients of largesse 'appear to have little sense of the obligations conferred upon them'.[36] *Amelia* rebels against this weighty moral pressure in that it depicts all benefactors (apart from Dr Harrison, who is not rich enough to solve the Booths' problems) as acting from dishonourable motives and thus abusing all the moving and tearful gratitude of the recipients.

In *The History of Ophelia*, on the other hand, both the heroine and Dorchester play the role of benefactor, and in the process structures that were set up in *The Countess of Dellwyn* are questioned. *Ophelia*, like *David Simple*, furnishes examples of both amiable and unamiable benefactors. In the latter category comes the Marchioness of Trent, Ophelia's rival for Lord Dorchester's affections, who abducts Ophelia and imprisons her in an ancestral castle in one of the book's more bizarre – even Gothic – developments. Ophelia's keeper during her imprisonment is Mrs Herner, the Marchioness's dependent relative and resident slave, who is never for a moment allowed to forget 'the Weight of the Obligation' upon her. However, the narrator's sympathy for Mrs Herner is limited, both because her dependence is the result of lack of economy earlier in life ('by a strange Fatality, she spent to the last Shilling before she attempted to lessen her Expences') and because she submits to her miserable situation not through necessity but through being 'too proud to take any other Means of gaining a Support' (II, 4–5). The narrator is not specific as to what other means Mrs Herner should rather have taken, but with the examples of both Mrs Bilson and Caroline Traverse before us, we can imagine more honourable ways to earn a subsistence. Yet the example of Caroline Traverse is no sooner cited than doubted: her industry and ingenuity cannot conquer illness, and the family are rescued from poverty through the benevolence of Dorchester. This, then, is the limit of Bilsonian self-help: the middle-class working woman, while a revolutionary development, is of course subject to the same liabilities as the working man. As Charlotte Charke wrote, 'I was as liable to Death or Infirmities as any other Part of the Creation, which might have disempowered me from getting my own or my Child's Bread.'[37] In a world without state sickness benefits, benevolence is the incapacitated worker's only hope.

Henry Fielding had addressed this question in a pamphlet of 1753, and asserted that society 'is so far from being at Liberty to punish a Man for involuntary Idleness, that it is obliged to support him under it'.[38] But the pamphlet referred to the working classes, proposing to keep all idle proletarians out of mischief and in productivity by forcibly confining them to a workhouse; having stated society's duty, it does not make clear where those who 'labour under any utter Incapacity' to work, such as the old and the sick, are to go.[39] In any case, the author clearly did not formulate his proposals with any idea of middle-class penury in mind. Perhaps this is because middle-class penury is more likely to excite sympathy than working-class squalor and thus theoretically will have no difficulty finding private charity. As Adam Smith wrote,

> The mere want of fortune, mere poverty, excites little compassion. Its complaints are too apt to be the objects rather of contempt than of fellow-feeling. We despise a beggar... . The fall from riches to poverty, as it commonly occasions the most real distress to the sufferer, so it seldom fails to excite the most sincere commiseration in the spectator.[40]

Compassion in this passage begins to seem more like enlightened self-interest than disinterested pity. The 'we' who despise a beggar, 'the spectator' who feels sincere commiseration, are evidently literate, financially secure, unable to experience fellow-feeling for 'mere poverty' because they have never known it. The sympathy they feel for the sufferer who has fallen from prosperity to poverty is a result of class solidarity: middle-class people in financial distress should be able to rely on other middle-class people to relieve them. Here again, as we saw in the previous chapter, the limits of Smith's 'sympathy' become clear. Far from promoting the view that the operation of sympathy ensures mutual understanding within society whatever the situation of individuals, sympathy is shown to be strongly tied to class position, unable to function beyond the limits this dictates.

This construction of a benevolent community based on barely disguised self-interest certainly finds some echoes in the fiction. In spite of her distaste for rank as it displays itself in the graveyard or in the snobbery of Lady Cambridge, Ophelia stays to listen to a poor woman's story because she is 'moved by an Appearance superior to such a Degree of Poverty' and accordingly discovers that the woman 'was reduced by Misfortunes from easy

Circumstances' (I, 73–4). Although Henry Fielding urges the readers of his pamphlet to feel compassion, not abhorrence, for the poor, the protagonists of his novel are inevitably a middle-class couple with some social grace, not the physically repulsive Blear-Eyed Moll. While they may have bad experiences of charity within the plot, the reader is evidently supposed to feel charitably disposed towards them.

In *Ophelia*, the heroine sets out to distribute money given her by Dorchester 'among Persons who were in real Want of it' (I, 62). Her inexperience, however, leads her in her first donation to contribute unknowingly – but as Mandeville would argue, inevitably – to 'the increase of Vanity and Laziness' (I, 63). Another visit results in her giving money to a woman who turns out to be so miserly that the distress Ophelia sees in her family is entirely self-imposed. Charity in the hands of naïveté becomes a hit-and-miss affair, easily abused in these instances by the recipients rather than the donor, and very much in need of the kind of investigation and control practised by Mrs Bilson. Later on, Dorchester's relief of the Traverse family is preceded by action aimed at just such control, evidently with the approval of the older narrator:

> Lord Dorchester made very diligent Enquiry after our Captain, to know the Reality of what he said; for People who would not mis-apply their Bounty, must be on their Guard against what they hear, lest Truth should be disguised by Falshood, or clouded by Partiality. (I, 250)

But while he then confers boundless obligations upon the Captain and his family, Dorchester also frees Mrs Herner from her burden-some obligation to the Marchioness (thus giving her a lighter one, to himself) by insisting that the latter should settle on her an 'Independency' (II, 95).

It is, then, in the nature of benevolence to be resolutely contradic-tory. In some hands it leads to inequality and misery; in other hands it is presented as the only way of releasing people from dependence or poverty and distress. *David Simple* recognised this, but laid the emphasis, in *Volume the Last*, on the former, destructive, possibility; *Ophelia*, culminating in a happy ending, can lend the latter possibility more credence. The revelation of the unknown benefactor at the end of *Volume the Last* seems threatening as much as promising; here, we know the Traverse family are in safe hands as they receive Dorchester's bounty. This leads to certain questions regarding the structures of the novels. Does the romance structure inevitably produce a less critical text? Does *Ophelia*, despite the heroine's thoughts about economics and rank, ultimately gloss over these tensions in the same way as the 1744 ending of *David Simple*? And what conclusions do these thoughts prompt concerning the generically unstable *Amelia*?

Looking first at Henry Fielding's novel, it is clear that critics have always had problems defining it generically. For David Blewett, the novelist has relinquished the comic mode of his earlier works in favour of 'a new social realism'; this is in line with George Sherburn's view of the novel as in the 'tradition of private history done with fidelity to the facts of everyday life'. Sheridan Baker, by contrast, sees *Amelia* as 'a final and domesticated version of the old day-dream of recognition and fairy treasure'. Baker's opinion would probably be one with which Terry Castle would sympathise, if not fully concur. For her, this 'least ingratiating and accountable' of Henry's novels is radically disrupted by the presence of the masquerade: 'the drastic mystique of the carnival world pervades those works that try to domesticate it, bringing about their own lapse away from the cherished paradigms of purity, coherence and legibility.'[41]

In my view, Baker and Castle provide the most useful accounts of *Amelia*: the 'realism' of the prison scenes is undeniably at odds with the disguise, transgression and transformation of the masquerade; the domestic concern with where the next penny is to come from is unexpectedly and romantically resolved, through recognition – of Amelia's picture at the pawnbroker's – and the discovery of a forged will. In some respects this could be seen as linking back, rather improbably, with the notion in *Tom Jones* that wealth will always ultimately find its way to those who most deserve it through birth and virtue. But where the dénouement is carefully set up from the beginning of *Tom Jones*, the joyful ending of *Amelia* is not in the least inherent in the Booths' cycle of debts and dashed hopes. But that is not to say the romance ending has no logic to it whatsoever. What logic it does have is provided by two related things: the novel's complete rejection of benevolence as a feasible means of support, and the need to reinforce the heroine's position as pure, domestic and wifely. This latter need is made more pressing by the fact that Amelia actually undergoes a directly sexual 'fall' from paragon status when she goes to the bedside of the sick Atkinson; for she feels for him 'a momentary Tenderness and Complacence, at which *Booth*, if he had known it, would perhaps have been displeased' (XI, vi, 483). Significantly this lapse has connections with Amelia's egalitarian outlook, her heart having 'stood firm as a Rock to all the Attacks of Title and Equipage', but being softened by 'the plain, honest, modest, involuntary, delicate, heroic Passion of this poor and humble Swain' (XI, vi, 482). As Terry Castle writes, Amelia does not actually transgress, but 'such a narrative development now seems possible in the fictional world in a way that it did not before'.[42] Mrs Bennet had after all told Amelia earlier that it was her steadfast opinion 'that the Woman who gives up the least Out-work of her Virtue, doth, in that very Moment, betray the Citadel' (VII, vii, 295).

If *Amelia* comes to the same conclusion as *Volume the Last* on the subject of benefactors, it accordingly has a similar dilemma in formulating an ending. The choices available are essentially these: first, Booth and Amelia are relieved from their worries by a wealthy benefactor; second, Amelia's offer to work with her hands is accepted and she attempts to restore, or at least maintain, the family's fortunes in the style of Mrs Bilson or Caroline Traverse; third, there is no 'ending' in that Amelia and Booth continue to struggle unsuccessfully, perhaps sinking through illness to squalor such as that experienced by Camilla and Valentine in *David Simple*; and finally, Sheridan Baker's 'fairy treasure' appears and solves all difficulties.

The fourth option is, from various points of view, the only real possibility. The first choice would have all the instability of the ending of *Volume the Last*: having demonstrated the disastrous consequences of accepting 'obligations', the reader can have no confidence in the durability of such an ending. On the other hand, to allow Amelia to become productive is clearly unacceptable if her status as domestic (household) paragon is to be re-emphasised and maintained. The events of the novel and indeed Amelia herself undermine that status, as both the preceding pages and Terry Castle point out in different ways; but to validate such a falling off would be remarkable: Amelia is to be the prototype of the Victorian leisured wife, busily consuming, not of the Thatcherite business woman. The third choice could only be the product of a far more sustained exercise in the 'new realism' than *Amelia* ever presents. 'Fairy treasure' successfully bypasses all these problems: the money is the Booths' and they owe 'obligations' to nothing but justice; they as a family unit will be wholly independent, while Amelia as wife and mother will be suitably dependent upon her husband.

If the possibility of female economic productivity is voiced in *Amelia*, it finds an oblique outlet only in the subplot, in the 'ruin' and subsequent rise of Mrs Atkinson; the heroine's claims to the right to labour are ultimately incorporated as part of her paragon status. On hearing her last assertion that she is able to work for her living, Booth cries,

> 'My Angel ... it delights me to hear you talk thus, and for a Reason you little guess; for I am assured that one who can so heroically endure Adversity, will bear Prosperity with equal Greatness of Soul...' (XII, viii, 539)

Amelia thoroughly undermines any system of benevolence, but the potentially radical discourses involving economic production and station in life which surface as a consequence of this at moments during the action of the novel, are effectively contained and neutralised by the romance ending.

In *Ophelia*, where the success of benevolence is still given some credence, the romance ending can seem to reinforce a comfortably benign view of life. However, two points in particular need to be emphasised here, not least of which is that if *Ophelia* validates benevolence it does so on the strictly sentimental basis that that quality is not to be found with ease in a largely vicious world. This novel, quite as much as *David Simple* – or indeed *Amelia* – presents the best people as being under siege. Society is corrupt; it has tainted even the benevolent Dorchester, as his formulation of a dishonourable scheme against Ophelia illustrates. While he is ultimately led to eschew his former opinions, the Lord Larboroughs of the world, for whom there is no hope of redemption, still exist in plenty. The second point is this: despite the fact that Ophelia loves Dorchester from the very beginning, she does not immediately sink into his arms at his belated proposal of marriage; for the novel has effectively set up such standards for the heroine as make it impossible for her ever to do so, while maintaining those standards.

If Ophelia's opinions on rank and economics in eighteenth-century society stem from her upbringing in Eden, where there were neither Duchesses nor money, so too do her opinions of morality. When she discovers Dorchester's deceit, the duplicity she has noted in society, at first with disbelief and then with disapproval, touches her personally. Her heart and actions correspond: she cannot conceive – as David Simple could not – that others (particularly others in whom she has placed her trust) should behave otherwise. She tells Dorchester that she has lost all confidence in him and in the society he inhabits; she will go away to where 'Virtue makes every Action open and intelligible', since his heart is not 'made like' hers and is beyond her judgement (II, 237). At this point the novel is, logically, all set for an unhappy ending; for were Ophelia to marry Dorchester now it would amount to a deliberate abandonment of principles. To confirm this point, when Ophelia finally agrees to marry him, she regards her compliance as a 'Weakness' (II, 279), despite the assurance of her aunt that he has genuinely recanted. Neither does her opinion of her conduct change when time has shown her that all is well, as she tells her unnamed correspondent: 'mine was a dangerous Trial, and, I think, my Imprudence in making it, deserved a Punishment rather than a Reward; which has increased my Gratitude to Heaven for a State of Happiness I by no Means merited' (II, 283). This can be read in two ways. On the one hand, it is the voice of prudence cautioning the reader against such 'dangerous trials', which, it is implied, cannot always be expected to end so happily. But on the other hand, it is, quite simply, a validation of imprudence. The heroine has followed her inclinations, not her reason, and the result is unalloyed happiness – sanctioned, moreover, by the highest authority. The romance ending thus becomes perhaps the most radical aspect of the work, and allows Bilsonian values to be questioned in the novel on two counts: the illness of Caroline Traverse exposes the vulnerability of the seemingly strong position of Mrs Bilson as a working woman, whilst the heroine's successful flight into imprudence at the end of the novel undermines the very basis of the Bilsons' prosperity. Crucially, however, *Ophelia* does not question the extra-domestic economic ability of women *per se*: Caroline Traverse is just as cheerfully able as Mrs Bilson until illness prevents her from continuing to work; Ophelia herself is perfectly able when it comes to analysing the workings of the economic world around her, albeit from the unassailable position of one who has known Eden.

Both *Amelia* and *Ophelia* forge some links between economic ability and the virtuous woman: by comparison with the women in fiction previously allowed economic skills, they are sexually irreproachable. By comparison with the highest standards, however, both heroines fail to measure up. This is partly because all women have always already failed, as discussed earlier; but it is also because of specific falls on the part of each heroine – Amelia's, in her momentary feelings for Serjeant Atkinson, and Ophelia's, in her self-confessed imprudence. The link between economic ability and sexual immorality, while not overtly made in the figures of the heroines, cannot be entirely broken. It is only for Ophelia, however, that any degree of the freedom enjoyed by Fanny Hill becomes available. Her transgressive step is made as an integral part of the novel's embracing romance resolution; that same resolution, by contrast, neutralises Amelia's.

4

'Godlike benefactors': Patriarchal Patterns in *Lady Julia Mandeville, The Vicar of Wakefield* and *Humphry Clinker*

Sir James Steuart's *Principles of Political Œconomy* (1767) opens with a resolutely orthodox definition of economy: 'in general ... the art of providing for all the wants of a family, with prudence and frugality.' This standard formulation nevertheless seems to offer momentarily the possibility that an 'economist' can be either male or female. Given the pervasive conduct book model of the exemplary female housekeeper, the latter could even be thought to be the more likely choice. This fleeting impression vanishes, however, with the subsequent sentence: 'The whole œconomy must be directed by the head, who is both lord and steward of the family.' The private economist in this case is male, and it becomes evident why this must be so when Steuart moves on to his main subject with the statement that 'What œconomy is in a family, political œconomy is in a state ....'[1] In making an analogy between the private and the public, it is clearly impossible for the controlling representative in the private sphere to be a woman, since there is no analogous position for her to occupy in the public sphere.

In the process of making economy a male preserve, Steuart's formulation also seems to imply that a well-regulated economy and patriarchal government go hand in hand. Whether as head of a family or as Steuart's ideal 'statesman', it is the benign but stern father-figure who dominates the organisation. Although anxious to distinguish government and political economy – 'the first [is] the power to command, the second the talent to execute' (I, 149) –

practically speaking Steuart's treatise unites the qualities required for the two within the single figure of the statesman.

However, not only does Steuart use a patriarchal model of government as the condition for a well-ordered economy, his discourse of political economy also reveals affinities with certain aspects of the workings of the sentimental community. Steuart defines credit, for example, as 'no more than a *well established* confidence between men, in what relates to the fulfilling their engagements' (emphasis in original). This confidence, he goes on, needs two aids – laws and manners: 'By laws the execution of formal contracts may be enforced: manners, alone, can introduce that entire confidence which is requisite to form the spirit of a trading nation' (II, 105). The assumption of a 'well established confidence between men' is precisely that made by the members of a sentimental community in their dealings with one another and with the world. The conferring and receiving of obligations is carried out, ideally, in a situation where both parties know that neither side will abuse its position – either by asserting power or by failing in gratitude. The exchange of obligations is mutually beneficial. Thus, as was seen in Chapter 2, David Simple is an ideal benefactor, just as Camilla and Valentine are ideal beneficiaries. Theirs is a system needing only 'manners'; laws are not necessary. Translated into economic terms, the recognition that exchange could be mutually beneficial is identified by Louis Dumont as an indicator of the development of economic ideology, as opposed to the 'primitive idea' of pre-commercial societies that 'in trade, the gain of one party is the loss of the other'.[2] But however benign, Steuart makes clear that exchange in the economic sphere cannot be left to the management of manners alone, just as David subsequently discovers – as do Amelia and Booth – that the sentimental system of exchange becomes nightmarish when in the wrong hands: credit, whether of the financial or sentimental variety (and the two regularly coincide) needs controls. It is as the source of such control that the novels discussed in this chapter, no less than Steuart's *Principles*, look to the patriarch.

Although it is not true to say that the sentimental community is inevitably patriarchal – consider, for example, David Simple's community of friends or *Clarissa*, where the patriarchal family is what the heroine has to challenge – there are ways in which the sentimental system particularly lends itself to such an organisation. One of its most important tenets – the conferring and receiving of obligations – is predicated upon the protection of those who are weak (usually in financial or sexual ways) by those who are strong. Individual benefactors are not always male, and recipients not always female, but to be a benefactor is to assume a masculine role, while the recipient is pressed into a feminine position of dependency. The representation of a woman such as Mrs Bilson is so challenging precisely because of the explicit separation of the female individual from a culturally defined feminine position, and the role of omnipotent benefactor is far more usually taken by a conventional male authority-figure, by a Squire Allworthy or a Grandison. Yet in Frances Brooke's *Lady Julia Mandeville* (1763), despite the strongly patriarchal nature of the community described, the peculiarly female combination of sentimental virtues and economic ability becomes a prominent feature once again, via the key figure of Lady Anne Wilmot. As a result, although *Julia Mandeville* ends tragically and Goldsmith's *The Vicar of Wakefield* (1766) happily, it is Brooke's novel which provides the more positive conclusions of the two, along with the more scathing critique of the patriarchal system both novels explore. Smollett's *Humphry Clinker* (1771) then shows by its anxious reinscription of patriarchal patterns the extent to which the kind of threat to established order embodied by Anne Wilmot could be both recognised and determinedly (but never totally) defused.

Set beside the contrasting communities of right-feeling individuals already examined, the society over which Lord Belmont presides in *Julia Mandeville* has far more in common with that found in *Tom Jones*. In the management of his estate Belmont 'seems a beneficent father surrounded by his children, over whom reverence, gratitude, and love, give him an absolute authority'.[3] Colonel Mandeville (Belmont's friend and relative) extols Belmont's virtues to his son Harry, commenting that he has 'enlarged his own circle of happiness, by taking into it that of all mankind, and particularly of all around him' (p. 29). Belmont's estate represents no besieged minority then, but a broad, potentially all-inclusive community headed by a man with high social and political status. This strong identification between the estate and the man – strengthened by the way that both are referred to as 'Belmont' – is conspicuously lacking in the central benefactor of *The Vicar of Wakefield*, however. Sir William Thornhill, far from using his estate as the base from which all his bounties flow, allows his nephew Squire Thornhill to live there, and 'content with a little himself … chiefly resides in town' (iii, 29). In disguise as Mr Burchell for most of the novel, Sir William is presented as a 'humourist' (iii, 30) who prefers eccentric methods to fulfil his beneficent inclinations. The extent of his bounty is theoretically as great as that of Lord Belmont, but its organisation is less obvious. As Sir William finally reveals his 'native dignity' and 'truly majestic' air in the nick of time to resolve *The Vicar of Wakefield* happily,[4] so it is only at the end of the novel that his full force as a patriarchal figure comes into play.

Neither Belmont nor Sir William is unique in his position as patriarch. Writing of theories of patriarchy such as that described in Robert Filmer's *Patriarcha*, H. T. Dickinson points out that 'with obedience to kings went reverence and submission to parsons and squires, to fathers and employers'.[5] A patriarchal society replicates reliance on the father-figure at all levels and in accordance with this, both novels provide 'doubles' whose characteristics both mirror and significantly diverge from those of the senior figure.

Harry Mandeville is in love with Belmont's daughter Julia, but lacks a fortune to match his birth and education. While Lord Belmont has offered help in finding a career, Harry confesses to Mordaunt (his chief correspondent) that he 'would be rich independently of [Belmont's] friendship' (p. 109). Here, Harry is aiming to break out of the patriarchal orbit of Belmont, to become a patriarch in his own right. Indeed this potential in Harry is what Julia, unsurprisingly, has fallen in love with: 'it was not easy to find a lover equal to that idea of perfection my imagination had formed: he alone, of all mankind, rises up to it; the speaking grace, the easy dignity of his air, are the natural consequences of the superiority of his soul. He looks as if born to command the world' (p. 98). What neither Julia nor Harry – nor indeed the reader – realises at this stage is that their futures have already been mapped out by their fathers: Harry is to be Belmont's heir, and to marry Julia. Far from needing to forge his own dynasty, Harry is already destined to take over as the paternal overseer of the Belmont inheritance. The intention, at least, is that all should end up as in *Tom Jones*, with wealth in the hands of those who have most claim to it through birth and virtue.

While Harry is the intended ideal patriarch of the future, Lord T——, to whom Harry goes hoping for help in his career, is a misguided landowner who serves to confirm more emphatically Lord Belmont's wisdom. Lord T——'s estate, by contrast with Belmont, is 'a scene of desolation', depopulated and falling into ruins. Where Lord Belmont is universally blessed, Lord T—— suffers 'the curse of thousands' (p. 107). Also misguided is Mr Westbrook, 'a plump, civil cit' beginning to acquire land in the country near Belmont. As the obverse of all the ideal patriarch should be, Lord T—— and Mr Westbrook share a function with the different but equally undesirable Squire Thornhill in *The Vicar of Wakefield*. Squire Thornhill eschews the benevolent rule of the enlightened patriarch for quasi-feudal rights, carrying off most of the young women in the area, including Primrose's two daughters, and bullying his tenants.

The other patriarchal figure in *The Vicar of Wakefield* is of course Dr Primrose himself. The 'Advertisement' for the novel explains that in its hero can be found united 'the three greatest characters on earth', namely, 'a priest, a husbandman, and the father of a family' (p. 14), and Primrose accordingly describes his family as the 'little republic to which I gave laws' (p. 33). But the instability of the vicar's position in the text is becoming a commonplace of Goldsmith criticism, and John Bender recognises this difficulty when he describes Primrose as 'at once the apparent narrator, the chief actor, the possessor of considerable foresight, and a laughably erroneous good soul'.[6] As patriarch, then, we find the vicar occupying a space which encompasses both caricature and affirmation.

Julia Mandeville and *The Vicar of Wakefield* include two other patriarchs: the monarch and the creator. Through references to these ultimate benefactors, we are able both to recognise the 'god-like' qualities of Lord Belmont and Sir William and to see the wider justifications for the patriarch as ideal governor. God in *Julia Mandeville* is, in terms reminiscent of the introductory descriptions of Lord Belmont, 'that beneficent Being, to whose bounty we owe the full reward of our toil, the plenteous harvest, and who rejoices in the happiness of his creatures' (p. 133), while Primrose declares that, 'if there be any thing sacred amongst men, it must be the anointed sovereign of his people, and every diminution of his power in war, or in peace, is an infringement upon the real liberties of the subject' (pp. 102–3). It is quite in keeping, then, that Belmont's bounty to his dependants should appear not in any prosaic way but rather descend 'silent and refreshing as the dews of heaven' (p. 30), and that Sir William's arrival at the conclusion of *The Vicar of Wakefield* should constitute a *deus ex machina* resolution to the plot. Thus both novels contain what amounts to a hierarchy of patriarchs, from the abusers of patriarchal responsibility in Squire Thornhill and Lord T——, through to its aspirants and parodists in Harry and Primrose, its rightful exercisers in Belmont and

Sir William, and finally its perfect earthly and heavenly realisations in the monarch and in God.

A divine father has no need to worry about the material base of his power, but this is not the case with earthly ones. The source of the patriarch's wealth is significant in both novels; and while Lord Belmont and Sir William would appear to share the same source of income – the landed estate – their relations to that source are rather different, if equally ambiguous. Furthermore, these relations render their status as ideal governors uncertain.

Sir William, as we learn early in the novel, lost one fortune through imprudent benevolence and, realising the error of his ways, determined to restore his squandered wealth. As Mr Burchell, he explains that 'For this purpose, in his own whimsical manner he travelled through Europe on foot' – and with success, since now 'his circumstances are more affluent than ever' (p. 30). Precisely how travelling through Europe on foot can restore a vanished fortune is not revealed, and this is then explicitly challenged when Primrose is reunited with his 'philosophic vagabond' son, George: '"Why, aye, my son," cried I, "you left me but poor, and poor I find you are come back; and yet I make no doubt you have seen a great deal of the world." – "Yes, Sir," replied my son, *"but travelling after fortune, is not the way to secure her*; and, indeed, of late, I have desisted from the pursuit"' (p. 106; my emphasis). The real source of Sir William's recovered wealth, then, is rendered mysterious, even disreputable. Perhaps such a mystification of Sir William's material standing is in keeping with his position as a miraculous figure at the end of the novel – his wealth is arguably more akin to the 'fairy treasure' Sheridan Baker finds at the end of *Amelia*.[7] Yet unlike that fairy treasure, this wealth has always been at its rightful owner's disposal. Its presence throughout the narrative in the unworthy hands of Squire Thornhill, who constantly abuses the power it gives him, is due to Sir William's own whimsicality. His status as fairy godfather is therefore tainted by his blood relationship with the Squire and by his giving control of so much of his fortune to such an unscrupulous individual in the first place. The source of his wealth thus remains open, simultaneously including unwritten possibilities as diverse as manna from heaven and successful gambling.

Similarly, the source of Lord Belmont's wealth is compromised. He is initially associated with 'old money', living 'with all the magnificence and hospitality of our ancient English nobility' (p. 4), and sharply distinguished from Mr Westbrook, whose 'genealogy in the third generation loses itself in a livery stable' (p. 21). This 'new money equals low birth' equation is unsettled, however, when it is revealed that Belmont owes his wealth not to a simple process of inheritance but to a combination of chance, 'the partiality of an ancestor' and 'the military talents of his father'. Harry explains that he comes from the elder branch of the family, who lost their wealth 'in endeavouring to support the throne, when shaken by the rage of faction and narrow-minded bigoted enthusiasm'; Belmont, by contrast, is descended from the younger branch, which 'escaped the storm, by having a minor at its head' (p. 67).

Ironically, then, Harry's forebears lost their patriarchal status in defending the ultimate earthly patriarch, while Belmont's ancestors held on to their wealth because they were conveniently unable to take part in that defence. While there is no suggestion that Belmont's birth is anything but thoroughly noble, the contingent nature of his position and the hints of something in the past that did not quite accord with fair play (through such words as 'partiality' and, a little further on, the stronger 'injustice' [p. 68]) make the fitness of his filling the role of patriarch questionable. That 'partiality' should have any part in his family history is in itself damning since, as will be discussed at some length below, disinterest is a defining feature of the patriarch: God in *Julia Mandeville* is 'the impartial Lord of all' (p. 27). The source of Belmont's wealth, that undefined 'partiality', could thus be as disreputable as Sir William's, although in both cases it is left to conjecture rather than certain knowledge.

While the patriarch relies on material wealth as the basis of his authority, the sentimentalist must deny its primary importance and assert, as Colonel Mandeville does in a letter to his son, that 'Health, peace, content, and soft domestic tenderness' are 'the only real sweets of life' and available to all alike (p. 27). This conflict between patriarchal and sentimental values becomes the site of many and various negotiations in both novels, as they are made to seem compatible on the one hand and demonstrated to be mutually exclusive on the other. In the process it is prudence, that essential civic humanist virtue so popular with conduct book writers, which becomes the most crucial site of negotiation. As already discussed, 'excess' is the point at which sensibility and prudence diverge. Prudence is by definition always moderate, but sensibility, while at the same time an essential attribute for women and a desirable one for men, is constantly in danger of indulging in excessive responses.

Those who represent the reconciliation of sentimental and prudential views in the novels are necessarily the principal patriarchal figures of Sir William Thornhill and Lord Belmont, since they are the only characters who occupy positions which are, potentially at least, all-inclusive. Sir William's ability to unite prudence and sensibility derives from his personal experience of having 'carried benevolence to an excess when young' due to 'a sickly sensibility of the miseries of others' (p. 29). As his means to assist dwindle, so does his once numerous circle of 'friends'. This has the desired educative effect on the young Sir William who restores 'his falling fortune' and learns to keep 'his bounties ... more rational and moderate than before' (p. 30). Although he 'preserves the character of an humourist' and illustrates this by his use of disguise, that disguise also becomes the means by which he conducts Bilson-like 'inspection' and 'enquiries' concerning the merits of his people, as his revelation to George that he has 'long been a disguised spectator of [his] father's benevolence' demonstrates (p. 168). His assessments of worth are now the result of much rational observation, not the impulsive reactions of an uncontrolled sensibility.

Lord Belmont, on the other hand, seems to have always possessed the ideal prudent benevolence, the organisation of his estate being the outward manifestation of his inner moderation. The 'economy' of the house – overseen by Lady Belmont – is 'magnificent without profusion and regular without constraint' (pp. 5–6), while the lives of his tenants also conform to this ideal, his farms being 'not large, but moderately rented', able to keep their families with ease and yet 'none rise to exorbitant wealth' (p. 29). The doctrine of self-control is summed up by Lord Belmont in a letter to Harry: 'The passions of every kind, under proper restraints, are the gentle breezes which keep life from stagnation; but let loose, they are the storms and whirlwinds which tear up all before them, and scatter ruin and destruction all around' (pp. 106–7). This implicit rejection of the *Essay on Man*'s maxim that 'ALL subsists by elemental strife/And Passions are the elements of life'[8] neatly divorces Lord Belmont from any Mandevillian views on the utility of vice and anchors him firmly, it would seem, to a civic humanist espousal of virtuous moderation. There is a flaw in Lord Belmont's prudence, however, which he shares with Colonel Mandeville. In planning to unite their children, they agree on the form their educations are to take: Harry should be educated in the world as befits a man, while Julia should be kept firmly within the auspices of the 'household gods' (p. 173). Yet the results of these educations are curiously inconsistent with their parents' professed ideals.

This becomes obvious from the very opening of the novel, as Harry sings the praises of the 'liberal education' his father's 'unsparing bounty lavished on [him]' (p. 2). 'Unsparing' and 'lavish' are surprising words from a young man educated in moderation, and this initial impression is confirmed when Lady Anne Wilmot observes that Harry has 'a habit of profuse expence' (p. 23). Harry's father writes to him that he has only one fear: 'inured to a habit of profuse expence', he dreads his being 'unable to practise that frugality which will now be indispensable' (p. 72). And yet ironically, Colonel Mandeville had himself to exercise 'economy' in order to afford Harry's extravagant education in the first place (p. 174). The intended transience of the ludicrous position Harry is in – unwitting heir to a fortune, while being exhorted to exercise indispensable economy – does not alter the fact that his education has evidently been an imprudent one if such exhortations are necessary at all. The tragic dénouement of the novel thus becomes inevitable: Harry has not learnt prudence, and the inability to control his passions, with the concomitant scattering of ruin and destruction, is the consequence. Belmont, with his failure to see that Harry received the appropriate education, thus becomes responsible for the collapse of his own plans.

Similarly, Julia's education at home has apparently not equipped her with the qualities required to produce another Lady Belmont. Lorraine McMullen describes Julia as a 'courtesy-book heroine',[9] but this takes into account only some of the virtues such books demanded. She has modesty and chastity, but she lacks the moderation and practical abilities which conduct books found equally necessary. Harry notes with approval that, 'As her mind has been adorned, not warped, by education, it is just what her appearance promises; artless, gentle, timid, soft, sincere, compassionate; awake to all the finer impressions of tenderness, and melting with pity for every human woe' (p. 3). This last phrase, reminiscent of Sir William Thornhill's excessive 'sickly sensibility', demonstrates that her education has failed to endow Julia with a proper degree of restraint; she could not fulfil the requirements of the economical existence demanded by such writers as Wetenhall Wilkes: 'The nicest rule in œconomy, is to make our being, one uniform and consistent series of innocent pleasures, and moderate cares; and not to be transported with joy, on occasions of good fortune, or too much dejected, in circumstances of distress.'[10]

Harry and Julia seem, then, to illustrate a signal failure of patriarchal rule to pass on its prudential standards to the next generation and thus perpetuate itself; and yet the issue is more complicated than this. The lovers independently arrive at the conclusion that they themselves are to blame for the tragedy that overtakes them because they have failed to fulfil their *sentimental* obligations to the patriarch. Harry's attempt to break out of the patriarchal orbit is finally abandoned when he meets Mr Herbert, who advises him from his own experience to 'be content with your paternal fortune, however small' (p. 145). This advice to accept the provision of the father is finally, but too late, taken by Harry when he determines to write to Lord Belmont confessing his love and throwing himself 'entirely on his friendship' (pp. 161–2). Julia, meanwhile, laments after Harry's death, 'I have been to blame: not in loving the most perfect of human beings; but in concealing that love, and distrusting the indulgence of the best of parents' (p. 193). From the sentimental point of view, Harry and Julia have been guilty of lacking the frankness that should obtain in all sentimental relationships, including that with the patriarch, and thus pursuing, as Harry admits, 'a conduct unworthy of [his] heart' (p. 162). Although he may appear to unite prudence and sensibility in the management of his estate, Lord Belmont yet fails to pass this on to those intended to come after him, while they in their turn show that even the sentimental side of their education was lacking.

If *Julia Mandeville*'s bringing together of sentimental and prudential values in the person of Lord Belmont proves not wholly successful, Lady Anne Wilmot represents another figure with the potential to unite these qualities. Anne's letters to her lover Colonel Belville share with those of Harry to Mordaunt the main burden of the novel's narrative. Her observation of Harry's 'profuse expence' is paid back to her in kind since Harry himself observes to Mordaunt that Anne 'is elegant in her dress, equipage, and manner of living, and rather profuse in her expences' (p. 7). In spite of this extravagance, however, and Anne's own assertion that 'prudence was never a part of my character' (p. 112), she nevertheless has far more talent for prudent management than either of the lovers. McMullen is right to observe that Anne, 'more than anyone else in the novel … is governed by right reason as well as elegant manners'.[11] Her relationship with Belville is, as Harry's with Julia appears to be, the victim of unpropitious material circumstances. As a widow her substantial jointure only continues if she remains unmarried, in which case she can leave her fortune to whom she pleases on her death. If she remarries, however, it goes immediately to her late husband's niece. Added to this, Belville's own fortune is 'extremely moderate' and Anne has no intention of marrying under such conditions: 'If I marry him at present ... his income will remain *in statu quo*, with the incumbrance of an indigent woman of quality, whose affairs are a little dérangé, and amongst whose virtues œconomy was never one of the most observable' (p. 121). Rather than marry in such inadequate circumstances, or rail against fortune for its cruelty to lovers as Harry and Julia are inclined to do, Anne determines to come to a private agreement with the niece, dividing the fortune equally. Her lack of 'œconomy' in the sense of frugality is none the less combined with an 'economic' ability to organise and manage – and to be prudent in so far as the recognition of her extravagance prevents her from ever entering into a situation where it would prove ruinous. Since Belville unexpectedly (if predictably) comes into a fortune, she is never called upon to put her plan into action. This does not, however, detract from the plan's prudence.

More prudent than the lovers, Anne also has a self-confessedly less trembling sensibility. When Miss Westbrook, daughter of the 'civil cit', falls in love with Harry and threatens to kill herself if her love is unrequited, Harry and Julia lament the hard case in all seriousness. Anne, who has assessed Miss Westbrook far more accurately as 'having a servile passion for quality' rather than any lasting passion, loses her patience with them: 'The whole scene is too ridiculous to be conceived, and too foolish even to laugh at. I could stand it no longer; so retired, and left them to their soft sorrows' (p. 59). Yet while Anne lacks the 'too tender heart' (p. 98) of Julia, she is by no means insensible. After the deaths of the lovers, Anne writes, 'I lament, I regret: but am enough myself to reason, to reflect' (p. 200). This ability to lament and yet reason is far closer to the conduct book requirement for a controlled sensibility (the kind possessed by Mrs Bilson, for example) than are Harry's overflowing passions or Julia's fainting-fits. Anne partakes of the delights of Belmont and admires the companionate marriage of its owners, telling Lady Belmont that to a sensible mind 'there is no cold medium in marriage: its sorrows, like its pleasures, are exquisite' (p. 119). In doing so she ensures her rightful place in the sentimental circle while at the same time combining her sensibility with that unlikely pair of qualities, extravagance and prudence. In her ability to combine supposedly disparate qualities successfully, Anne clearly has affinities with Mrs Bilson, with Cynthia, and with Amelia and Ophelia, and this ability – whether it be to combine prudent economic ability with sexual chasteness, or both these with financial extravagance – is thus becoming a peculiarly female ability of some significance in its suggestion that the sentimental and the economic are not as widely divided as they are usually represented as being.

Combining sentimental and prudent qualities is an equally complicated matter in *The Vicar of Wakefield*. Sir William's patriarchal 'doubles' render any such unity highly unstable. Primrose's relation to prudence is an ever-shifting one, and on at least two occasions of structural importance in the novel he appears to advance the plot through a deliberate rejection of its dictates. The first of these occurs as preparations are going on for the marriage of his son George and Arabella Wilmot. Mr Wilmot and Primrose are at loggerheads over the subject of monogamy when a relation calls Primrose away from the room to tell him that his fortune has been lost. This relation then advises Primrose to give up the argument, assuming that his 'own prudence will enforce the necessity of dissembling at least until [his] son has the young lady's fortune secure' (p. 16). Primrose's reaction to this is immediate and decided:

> 'Well,' returned I, 'if what you tell me be true, and if I am to be a beggar, it shall never make me a rascal, or induce me to disavow my principles. I'll go this moment and inform the company of my circumstances; and as for the argument, I even here retract my former concessions in the old gentleman's favour, nor will I allow him now to be an husband in any sense of the expression.' (p. 24)

Mr Wilmot's ready agreement to call off the match on hearing the news prompts Primrose as narrator to comment, 'one virtue he had in perfection, which was prudence, too often the only one that is left us at seventy-two' (p. 25). The second pivotal incident occurs when, later on, Primrose refuses to give his consent to the imminent marriage of Squire Thornhill and Arabella Wilmot. As it becomes clear that the Squire intends to punish Primrose's 'insolence' to the full, his family beg him to 'comply upon any terms, rather than incur certain destruction' (p. 138). Primrose once again refuses to sacrifice his principles and as a result of this principled imprudence ends up in jail.

In both these cases Primrose associates prudence in worldly affairs not with self-control or moderation but with a materialist self-interest. Prudence is thus rewritten: from being a necessary quality in the disinterested man of moderation, it becomes a quality more suitable for a self-serving individual blinkered to all considerations but his own best interests. This is further confirmed at the end of the novel when even the dastardly Squire can be admitted by Sir William to have acted 'prudently' in refusing a duel (p. 170). Such a rewriting of this virtue obviously renders its desirability suspect, but the vicar's relation to prudence is more complex than this. If on two occasions he refuses to be bound by its dictates, his story, like that of David Simple, nevertheless inexorably shows that he cannot live without it. When Sophia is thrown from her horse into a river and nearly drowns, Primrose tells the reader: 'My sensations were even too violent to permit my attempting her rescue: she must have certainly perished had not my companion, perceiving her danger, instantly plunged in to her relief' (pp. 30–1). Like David, Primrose has excessive reactions which leave him unable to act. Unlike David, Primrose has the patriarchal figure of Sir William to rescue Sophia and make up for his deficiency. Thus the entire shape of Primrose's tale is in fact prefigured in one significant event near the beginning of the novel. It is only because of the presence of Sir William that *The Vicar of Wakefield* does not end in the same tragic way as *David Simple*.[12] Primrose is only able to reject prudence with ultimate impunity because he receives the protection of a prudently benevolent patriarch. Put another way, with his feminine dependency as recipient he can only exist if supported by Sir William's manly virtue as benefactor.

That Primrose needs such protection in a commercial world is emphasised by the two occasions on which he and his family try to make money by selling horses at market. The first time, Primrose sends his son Moses to the fair, only to see him return with the bargain of 'a groce of green spectacles' (p. 67). On the second occasion, Primrose determines to go himself. His narrative voice is at this point aware of the limitations of his fictional self:

Though this was one of the first mercantile transactions of my life, yet I had no doubt about acquitting myself with reputation. The opinion a man forms of his own prudence is measured by that of the company he keeps, and as mine was mostly in the family way, I had conceived no unfavourable sentiments of my worldly wisdom. (pp. 71–2)

Primrose is gulled too, however, and for essentially the same reason that David Simple made such a bad financial manager. Just as David mistakenly assumed that his verbal assurance of friendship with Valentine would suffice as security for a loan, so Primrose asserts that 'A draught upon my neighbour was to me the same as money' (p. 75) and is consequently fooled out of both his money and his horse by the plausible Jenkinson. To use Sir James Steuart's terms, both Primrose and David rely solely on 'manners' without realising that 'formal contracts' are the only possible guarantees in a commercial world. John Bender's comment that Primrose's trials 'seem impelled by an impersonal, brutal force'[13] is only partly true. The commercial world could perhaps be seen as that force, but the vicar's trials arise as a result of the interaction between his values and those of the world; to this extent both the vicar and David invite their own calamities.

These incidents in *The Vicar of Wakefield*, as in *David Simple*, illustrate the 'primitive idea' referred to above that 'in trade, the gain of one party is the loss of the other'. For Dumont, this is 'a basic ideological element, an "ideologeme"' of the pre-commercial period and should be seen

> in relation to the general disparagement of trade and money that is characteristic of traditional societies in general. To think of exchange as advantageous to both parties represented a basic change and signaled the advent of economics. Now this change occurs precisely in the mercantilist period, not suddenly, but progressively ...[14]

Julia Mandeville displays such a 'general disparagement of trade and money' in many ways. The characters frequently disclaim the need for money – which, as noted, befits also their role as sentimentalists – and find distasteful the 'exchange-broker' mentality of Mr Westbrook. Yet there are also aspects of the novel which are arguably part of Dumont's progressive change of attitude. For, despite the disparagement, trade underlies the entire patriarchal structure over which Lord Belmont presides, as a result of his own deliberate strategy. He explains to Harry that, when he first arrived to take possession of his estate,

I found my tenants poor and dejected, scarce able to gain a hard penurious living; the neighbouring gentlemen spending two-thirds of the year in London, and the town which was the market for my estate filled only with people in trade, who could scarce live by each other. I struck at the root of this evil, and by living almost altogether in the country myself, brought the whole neighbourhood to do the same. I promoted every kind of diversion, which soon filled my town with gentlemen's families, which raised the markets, and of consequence the value of my estate: my tenants grew rich at the same rents which before they were unable to pay; population increased, my villages were full of inhabitants, and all around me was gay and flourishing. (pp. 43–4)

This is a world in which exchange is thought of as advantageous to both parties: everyone benefits from Belmont's policy. There are complications, however. In promoting 'diversion' Belmont comes close to accepting the utility of vice, from which ideologically dubious opinion his previous condemnation of uncontrolled passions seemed to exempt him. Although he remains vague about the nature of these diversions, the very fact that they 'raised the markets' by appealing to 'gentlemen's families' implies that they probably bear some resemblance to the kind of diversion enjoyed by Cynthia's 'Woman of Fashion' in *David Simple*: the purchasing of trinkets and finery in order to keep up with, and eclipse, other women of fashion.[15] The easy connection between this and the Mandevillian maxim 'private vice, public virtue' is one which Belmont would clearly wish to avoid, and this dissociation is partly achieved in the novel by the distinction between Belmont on the one hand and Mr Westbrook and Viscount Fondville on the other. Fondville, like Westbrook, is an upstart, his nobility being only of the third generation and his wealth coming from a blatantly suspect source, as Anne Wilmot tells Belville: 'He owes his fortune and rank to the iniquity of his father, who was deep in the infamous secret of the South Sea bubble' (p. 37). Appropriately, Fondville eventually marries Miss Westbrook, the pair embodying the very essence of conspicuous consumption; in Anne's words, 'Yes, we are to be Lady Viscountess Fondville; all is agreed, the clothes bespoke, our very garters interwoven with coronets' (p. 149). Belmont's rational taste – in effect his prudent sensibility, in spite of the way in which it is undermined by the behaviour of his heirs – is presented as the very antithesis of this vulgar display.

This differentiation looks forward to the attempts in Steuart's *Political Œconomy* to redefine 'luxury' by dividing it into two carefully distinguished categories. On the one hand there is *'luxury* as it affects our different interests, by producing hurtful consequences', while on the other there is *'luxury*, as it regards the moderate gratification of our natural or rational desires' (I, 307; emphasis in original).[16] This yoking together of 'luxury' and 'moderate gratification' is an obvious rupture of the discursive divisions set out in the Introduction, and *Political Œconomy* also attempts the explicit separation of 'luxury', 'sensuality' and 'excess'. Writing that a 'sober man may have a most delicate table, as well as a glutton' (I, 310) allows Steuart to define 'excess' as 'an abuse of enjoyment' (I, 311). Luxury becomes defined not by its material manifestations – the delicate foods on the table – but by the manner of their enjoyment.[17] What matters is not that Belmont is less rich than Fondville but that he is less ostentatious. Steuart's rejection of Mandeville's system, albeit tacit, recalls Adam Smith's more direct attack in his *Theory of Moral Sentiments*, where Mandeville's ideas are seen as removing all distinction between virtue and vice and being 'upon that account, wholly pernicious'.[18] All these refutations need to be seen, of course, in the light of the eighteenth-century reaction to Mandeville's work. Gertrude Himmelfarb explains how the views expressed in *The Fable of the Bees* were universally rejected:

> So far from being representative of its time, [it] profoundly shocked contemporaries, provoked a frenzy of attacks, and resulted in a presentment handed down by the grand jury of Middlesex condemning it as a 'public nuisance'... . [Its] new ethic subversive of traditional morality and utterly hostile to the poor [was] ... profoundly unpopular.[19]

What Himmelfarb does not consider is that it is perfectly possible to condemn Mandeville in one breath while taking up his ideas, with modification, in another. It is the very delicacy of this operation, whether performed by Lord Belmont, Sir James Steuart or Adam Smith, which makes the protestation of utter distaste necessary and leads to so much definition and redefinition in *Political Œconomy*.

This anxious negotiation around such words as 'luxury' and such problems as the legitimate place of pleasures stems partly, then, from the desire to avoid being branded with accepting vice as an inevitable, indeed necessary, part of any system of society. It also stems, however, from a related desire to maintain the credibility of the disinterested man. For if the maxim 'private vice, public virtue' allows once frowned upon activities to be productive of public good, it also expects everyone to pursue his or her own self-interest, which is deemed ultimately to be the same as the public interest. And if this is so, what practical future is there for the role of the man who oversees and reconciles all – that is, in the terms of this chapter, for the patriarch? Indeed, the very possibility of his existence is doubtful, since even differentiating between self-interest and public interest becomes a problem.

As I have already argued, just that ability to differentiate – and thus to remain impartial – is an essential attribute of the patriarch. Lord Belmont prides himself on this quality in his 'government', explaining to Harry that he never interferes in elections as 'a point both of honour and conscience'; his tenants are left free to vote as they wish; Belmont only insists 'on their keeping themselves as unbiassed as I leave them' (p. 47). Belmont is not a man 'of party'; others may pursue certain interests, but he rises above all that. Equally, when Sir William brings everything to a satisfactory conclusion at the end of *The Vicar of Wakefield*, he does so as a judge, weighing up evidence as it comes to him, willing to accede that the Squire's actions might have been 'equitable' until fresh revelations make his villainy plain (p. 171). This is the role of Steuart's 'statesman', whom he supposes to be 'impartially just' (I, 149); it also looks back to the position of Hume's 'governors' who, 'being satisfied in their present condition, and with their part in society, have an immediate interest in every execution of justice, which is so necessary to the upholding of society.'[20] Hume further maintained that all men have such an 'immediate interest in the execution of justice', and that this is, moreover, 'palpable and evident, even to the most rude and uncultivated of the human race.'[21] Governors are needed, not because men cannot recognise theoretically that self-interest and public interest coincide but because they have a propensity to prefer in practice the contiguous to the remote – to prefer, in other words, immediate self-interest to the long-term self-interest which inevitably coincides with the public good. Lord Belmont can thus be seen as providing a Humean answer to this problem, at least on his estate, by stepping in as the disinterested governor.

John Barrell has shown how the ownership of land could be seen as a guarantee of such disinterest: ideally, it represented a stake in the stability of the nation and also the freedom from engaging in any trade, and thus being tainted, politically or linguistically, with the jargon of any special interest group.[22] The importance of the estate in *Julia Mandeville* is then no surprise, and early in the novel Belmont's position as a gentleman whose wealth is based in land is focused upon in a brief but significant exchange of letters. Barker, a fellow landowner in financial difficulties after an unexpected disaster has followed 'a too careless economy', writes in the hope that Belmont will purchase his estate. Alternatively, he could sell to Mr Westbrook, who is waiting 'with the merciless rapacity of an exchange-broker' to buy the estate of every declining gentleman in the neighbourhood. But Barker has his tenants in mind, knowing that he cannot ensure their happiness other than 'by selling to your lordship' (p. 32). Belmont then lends Barker what he needs in order to recover, so long as he will 'enter on so exact a system of economy as will enable [him] to repay ... in seven years'. The motivation behind this action is the value Belmont sets upon 'the independent country gentleman', and he funds Barker from his '"bank of friendship," on which it is [his] rule to charge no interest' (p. 33). What Belmont seems to be trying to forestall here is the development Barrell sees as inexorably taking place during the eighteenth century: 'the ownership of land was inevitably and increasingly involved in an economy of credit, where values and virtues were unstable, and where man was estimated not by an "objective" standard, but in terms of an opinion of his credit worthiness which was liable to fluctuate whatever the source of his income.'[23] Belmont is determinedly working on an estimation of creditworthiness based on an opinion of a man's correct station in life, according to an 'objective' standard. The qualification for assuming the patriarchal role, that of governor to an area of land and its people, is to be 'an independent country gentleman'. Mr Westbrook, as a cit, can never qualify.

There are two problems here, however. One is that Mr Westbrook, whatever attempts Lord Belmont may be making to the contrary, has already qualified by default. He owns land in the country and since some landowners are Lord T——s and not Lord Belmonts, some Barkers are bound to be swallowed up by the increasing number of Westbrooks 'watching like harpies' for similar opportunities. The other problem is Lord T—— himself, who, despite having all the qualifications of birth Lord Belmont desires, is as much a 'bad' landowner as the upstart Westbrook. Thus it seems that owning land is not of itself guaranteed to create a disinterested man: Westbrook still represents city interest despite his 'stake' in the country, while equally the correct qualifications for his station do not guarantee that Lord T—— will be a disinterested landowner – on the contrary, he pursues a 'narrow selfish plan' (p. 107), mistakenly preferring, to use Hume's terms, the contiguous to the remote. As a result of this, Belmont's own status as disinterested can no longer be relied upon simply by virtue of his ownership of land. On the contrary, owning land puts him firmly on one side of a debate, protecting country interest against city values.

Steuart, however, defines the role of the disinterested man in a self-interested society rather differently from Hume by asserting that, for the governed, public spirit is unnecessary: every man 'ought' to act for his own interest. Self-interest is acknowledged to be the soul of trade and an industrious people; and Steuart asks, in Mandevillian tones, 'Were people to feed all who would ask for charity, what would become of industry?' Public spirit is required only in the governor, and 'Self-interest, when considered with regard to him, is public spirit' (I, 162). Belmont, by virtue of his practical success in imparting the greatest happiness to the greatest number on his perfectly organised estate, is ultimately the only true patriarch in *Julia Mandeville*. All the others fail because of their practical inability to separate immediate self-interest from long-term self-interest, the latter being the public good. In other words, they follow the propensity of the majority of ordinary men. The man who oversees and reconciles all contradictions enables society to be organised on lines that everyone recognises as right in theory but only the few are able to put into action. Belmont can never selfishly promote his own private interest above that of the public good, for in him they become one in practice, as they are in theory for all men.

This is, of course, an argument which has a refutation of all possible disagreements written into it. If Belmont's self-interest, unlike that of anyone else, is synonymous with public interest, his promotion of country values against those of the cits becomes not the action of a biased man of party but the concern of a man who knows what is ultimately needed for everyone's well-being. And since by definition only he can see this, the rest of the population have no base from which to challenge him. This is the way in which both Belmont and Sir William, and presumably Steuart's statesman and Hume's governors, can promote certain specific interests while simultaneously and inevitably promoting the public good.

The undermining of land ownership as the guarantee of disinterest makes it perhaps less surprising that Sir William Thornhill leaves his estate in the hands of the Squire and puts about the belief that he 'chiefly resides in town' (p. 29). The landed estate, while a useful physical manifestation of patriarchal success in impartial distinction between the contiguous and the remote, is no longer the absolute indicator of that success. On the other hand, Sir William does reside in the country a great deal as Mr Burchell, providing the humourist's version of Belmont's determination to live 'almost altogether in the country' (p. 43), and both *Julia Mandeville* and *The Vicar of Wakefield* are novels of the country. The town (meaning more often than not London) in both novels is the undesirable 'other', where George Primrose finds no decent employment and which Belmont visits briefly and reluctantly, hurrying back home to his rural bliss. If owning land ceases to be a definite indicator of virtue, land as a rural 'locus for moral and economic values that provides a challenge to the commercial ethic'[24] continues to have great resonance in both novels.

When Primrose and his family move away from Wakefield, the 'place of [their] retreat' is

> a little neighbourhood, consisting of farmers, who tilled their own grounds, and were equal strangers to opulence and poverty. As they had almost all the conveniencies of life within themselves, they seldom visited towns or cities in search of superfluity. Remote from the polite, they still retained the primaeval simplicity of manners, and frugal by habit, they scarce knew that temperance was a virtue. (pp. 31–2)

The description of this neighbourhood has much in common both with the life Ophelia leads before being deprived of her Eden and the Smithian 'original state of things' discussed in relation to this in Chapter 3. In this instance, the farmers tilling their own grounds recalls that in this state 'the whole produce of labour belongs to the labourer', and he has 'neither landlord nor master to share with him'.[25] The virtual self-sufficiency, the arcane knowledge of what constitutes 'enough' implied by their being 'equal strangers to opulence and poverty' and their 'primaeval simplicity' all contribute to the establishment of this community as Edenic. Primrose himself, however, is implicitly excluded from this Eden, for unlike these self-contained farmers the vicar has a landlord.

This, combined with Primrose's idealistic imprudence, is what leads to his eventual incarceration. Unlike *The History of Ophelia*, where the main protagonist's personal experience of Eden gave her an authoritative position from which to observe and comment on the commercial world, in *The Vicar of Wakefield* Primrose can only observe Eden from the outside, that is from within the very commercial world whose dealings he is so unsuited to master.

The relationship between Eden and the commercial world is rather different in *Julia Mandeville*. The estate of Belmont is itself Eden, providing scenes of rustic festivity which recall 'the fabulous pleasures of the golden age' (p. 9) and 'maintaining as much as possible the natural equality of mankind'. The cottagers, like Primrose's farmers, 'are strangers to all that even approaches want', while no one on the estate gains 'exorbitant wealth' (p. 29). These features – the knowledge of sufficiency, the natural equality – mark Belmont as Edenic. But this is a contradictory Eden, an Eden with a lord and master, an Eden moreover which incorporates a market for its products in the local town, which itself is full of gentlemen's families busily consuming 'diversions'. The estate figures as an attempt to reconcile two states of society which are essentially consecutive rather than contemporaneous, and thus has characteristics of both: the simplicity and sufficiency of the 'original state of things' on the one hand, and the commercial world's flourishing trade based on pleasure on the other.

This attempt at reconciliation is due, appropriately enough, to the deliberate effort of Lord Belmont. As he reconciles prudence and sensibility, so he brings together prelapsarian rural bliss and commerce; and just as he fails to pass on his synthesis of prudence and sensibility to the next generation, so it is the next generation that proves the fragility of Belmont's commercially successful Eden. The deaths of Harry and Julia signal the end of the Belmont dynasty's union of prudence and sensibility, while the marriage of Fondville and Miss Westbrook, the 'cittadina' as she is dubbed by Anne Wilmot, gives an idea of the form the future will take. After the funeral of the lovers, Anne sees Fondville and his bride go past 'in all the splendour of exulting transport' and exclaims, 'Scarce can I forbear accusing Heaven! The worthless live and prosper; the virtuous sink untimely to the grave!' (p. 207). An old order of moderation is passing away and a new one of superfluity is taking its place. Primrose's rewriting of prudence becomes prophetic in this scenario: what prudence there is in the new world will certainly be, as far as the old order is concerned, self-serving rather than a sign of moderation.

Yet if at the end of *Julia Mandeville* Belmont's hopes have failed to materialise and the values of men such as Fondville are in the ascendant, one character is left to salvage at least some aspects of the ideal patriarch. Theoretically disqualified from such a role straight away on account of her sex, as Steuart's definitions at the beginning of this chapter made clear, Anne Wilmot is nevertheless left to conclude the narrative. Her bringing together of prudence, sensibility and extravagance can now be seen as going some way towards effecting the reconciliation between the values of the old world and those of the new, which Belmont finally fails to accomplish. The possibility of her carrying this through from her own private sphere to the public arena is not expressed, however, and it is appropriate that Anne should close her final letter with an appeal to the ultimate patriarch whose ability to be all-inclusive cannot be challenged: 'Certain of the paternal care of our Creator, our part is, submission to his will' (p. 212).

This implied inability to attain Eden, or anything like it, in this world is a suitable theme for a clergyman, and Primrose pursues this theme in his final address to the prisoners, just before his fortunes begin to change for the better. To reach Heaven will be, he tells them, to 'fly through regions unconfined as air, to bask in the sunshine of eternal bliss, to carrol over endless hymns of praise, *to have no master to threaten or insult us, but the form of goodness himself for ever in our eyes* ...' (p. 163; my emphasis). This expectation uncovers a paradox which is inherent in the promotion of patriarchy as the ideal form of government in *The Vicar of Wakefield*. God, 'the form of goodness', is the ultimate patriarch, the heavenly father. Yet to reach him means to escape patriarchal authority. As a distortion of the ideal, an abuser of patriarchal responsibility, the Squire's occupation of that position demonstrates how unsafe it is. Sir William's reappropriation of the patriarchal role cannot efface this – just as the existence of the Belmont estate proves impossible to perpetuate in the face of increasing numbers of Westbrooks and Fondvilles. Indeed Primrose's deliverance by Sir William only goes to illustrate yet again how dependent the weak are on the character of their benefactor. The wealth that gives the Squire and Sir William their power comes from precisely the same source: as in *Amelia*, the benefactor is one of the powerful, and whether that power is used for good or ill depends entirely on who happens to be wielding it.

Through the failure of Lord Belmont and the figure of Anne Wilmot, *Julia Mandeville* questions the desirability of patriarchal rule and, if tentatively, offers an alternative. The joyful ending of *The Vicar of Wakefield*, on the other hand, is achieved only at the cost of turning away from the insights into the weaknesses of patriarchy offered by the body of the novel. In the final part of this chapter, I want to explore through *Humphry Clinker* the ways in which a novel with a clearly conservative agenda attempts to negotiate the disruptive potential represented by Anne Wilmot.[26] This potential – of bringing about a union between sentimental, prudential and commercial values – and what has been argued to be its peculiarly feminine nature, is present in *Humphry Clinker*, but it is manifested in a way quite different from my earlier examples and, indeed, from later ones. Mrs Bilson, Amelia, Ophelia and Anne Wilmot find an unlikely successor in Tabitha Bramble. Precisely how this comes about, and its wider significance, forms the core of my argument about *Humphry Clinker*.

While he is as much the central patriarchal figure as Lord Belmont and Sir William Thornhill, Matthew Bramble nevertheless fills the role in a somewhat different style. That he is himself, in a key episode, the rescued rather than the rescuer (the danger is drowning, as in *The Vicar of Wakefield*), may in itself be taken as an indication of this.[27] Bramble is simultaneously both patriarch and sentimental hero, where in *Julia Mandeville* and *The Vicar of Wakefield* these roles are split – Belmont versus Harry and Julia, Sir William versus Primrose. The collapsing of the two functions into a single character necessarily alters the presentation of the patriarch, and our first introduction to an ailing figure, 'equally distressed in mind and body' and plagued by his family responsibilities (p. 7), may seem far from the apparently Olympian qualities of Sir William and Belmont. The distance, however, seems negligible on closer examination. Bramble too can be defined in terms of the well-managed and prosperous estate, and when he tells Dr Lewis that at home in Brambleton-hall he takes 'pleasure in seeing my tenants thrive under my auspices, and the poor live comfortably by the employment which I provide' (p. 122), this only confirms what has already been implicit in the narrative. Brambleton-hall is, like Belmont, an Eden with a lord and master, and the desired patterns exhibited by both Brambleton-hall and the Dennisons, for example, can be seen as 'a nostalgic invocation of a golden, patriarchal age'.[28] Unlike *Julia Mandeville*, however, and more like *The Vicar of*

Wakefield, the ending of *Humphry Clinker* is both determinedly conservative and politically pessimistic – which means to say that the
ending is happy in a typically sentimental style, whereby an inner
circle of feeling hearts is able to rejoice in each other and in shared
values, despite or in the teeth of a cruel, selfish world beyond. To
quote Sekora:

> At the opening of the novel Smollett pits a luxurious England at
> the peak of its material strength versus a Bramble family at its
> psychological nadir. Faced with such omnivorous vice, Bramble
> is vexed, Jery callously amused, Liddy bewildered, Tabby and
> Win beguiled. In rapid succession at Bristol, Bath, and London,
> we hear of other decent families who against their wills are
> pulled into the vortex or pushed into the hinterlands. Uniting
> around Bramble, this family will not be drawn or divided. At the
> close it is bound together as never before. It is moreover trebled
> in size and worth, having attracted Humphry, Lismahago, the
> three Dennisons, the Wilsons, Baynard, Miss Willis, and Archy
> M'Alpin. The family that had been Bramble's bane becomes his
> blessing, the source of his distress transformed into the spring of
> his joy ...
>   The political despair with which the novel concludes is thus
> balanced by the glow of personal renewal.[29]

The ending of *Humphry Clinker* thus represents a form of triumph
for Bramble, being essentially a sentimental fantasy, in which an
expanding circle of personal contacts provides the bulwark against
a world whose values seem fundamentally inimical.

If Bramble's status as patriarch is underlined by the ideal organisation of life at Brambleton-hall, it is also confirmed by his management of his family. As rapidly becomes clear, Bramble's
complaints are no evidence of an inability to control his dependants: his ward Liddy's imprudent love for a strolling player is
efficiently dealt with, as is his sister Tabitha's insubordination.[30] As
is the case with so many of the key events in *Humphry Clinker*, this
latter incident is reported to us by two of the correspondents – by
Bramble himself, but first by Jery.

In Jery's account, Tabitha's hostility to the penniless foundling
Humphry Clinker and attachment to her unappealing dog
Chowder finally provoke Bramble to anger: 'his eyes began to
glisten, and his teeth to chatter.' To Tabitha's challenge that

Bramble should choose between herself and Clinker, Bramble proposes his own ultimatum:

'Either discard your four-footed favourite, or give me leave to bid you eternally adieu – For I am determined that he and I shall live no longer under the same roof; and now *to dinner with what appetite you may –*' Thunderstruck at this declaration, she sat down in a corner; and, after a pause of some minutes, 'Sure I don't understand you, Matt!' (said she). 'And yet I spoke in plain English – ' answered the 'squire with a peremptory look. 'Sir (resumed this virago, effectually humbled), it is your prerogative to command, and my duty to obey. I can't dispose of the dog in this place; but if you'll allow him to go in the coach to London, I give you my word, he shall never trouble you again –'

Her brother, entirely disarmed by this mild reply, declared, she could ask him nothing in reason that he would refuse; adding, 'I hope, sister, you have never found me deficient in natural affection.' Mrs. Tabitha immediately rose, and throwing her arms about his neck, kissed him on the cheek: he returned her embrace with great emotion. Liddy sobbed, Win Jenkins cackled, Chowder capered, and Clinker skipped about, rubbing his hands for joy of this reconciliation. (p. 88)

Bramble's own account is far briefer:

In our journey from Bath, my sister Tabby provoked me into a transport of passion; during which, like a man who has drank himself pot-valiant, I talked to her in such a stile of authority and resolution, as produced a most blessed effect. She and her dog have been remarkably quiet and orderly, ever since this expostulation. (p. 93)

The interest of these accounts lies both in the way that Tabitha, in common with many literary 'viragos', simply needs to be handled firmly in order to be brought to heel (rather as if both she and Chowder, as Bramble's version hints, were recalcitrant hounds), and in the way that the incident culminates, in Jery's version, in a scene of sentimental reunion. Generally speaking, the presentation of Tabitha is inimical to the requirements of sensibility in just about every way. Neither her appearance ('a maiden of forty-five', she is 'tall, raw-boned, aukward, flat-chested, and stooping' [p. 62]), nor her temperament ('she is proud, stiff, vain, imperious, prying, malicious, greedy and uncharitable' [p.63]) allow much room for recuperation. Indeed, in the terms of this study, attempting to find reconciliation between sentimental and economic values in the figure of Tabitha would seem to be a particularly thankless task. Yet it is precisely Tabitha's almost total failure to accommodate the ideals of sensibility that renders her interesting and, ultimately, accommodating to my broader argument.

The way in which *Julia Mandeville* and *The Vicar of Wakefield* furnish 'doubles' to underline the replication of father-figures required by patriarchal government has already been discussed. This can also be seen in *Humphry Clinker* – in fact, this replicative or doubling process could be described as rampant in Smollett's novel, which provides doubles far too numerous for detailed discussion. Among the most prominent are Jery, Lismahago, Baynard and Dennison, and the kind of 'hierarchy of patriarchs' described as operating in Brooke's and Goldsmith's novels certainly functions in *Humphry Clinker*. Jery, as Bramble's heir, moves fairly rapidly from an initial lack of appreciation of his uncle's qualities to a whole hearted adoption of his views and outlook, while Lismahago both parodies and reinforces Bramble's attitudes and opinions, clinching his position by declaring towards the end of the novel that 'he should think himself the happiest man on earth to be connected with [Bramble's] family' (p. 287).[31] Baynard's re-education, and the reclamation of his estate for prudent management, as well as Dennison's ideally organised domain, provide further evidence of the necessity and efficacy of patriarchal rule. The theme is all-pervasive in *Humphry Clinker* and these examples simply establish its importance – there is no question of exhaustive coverage.

If, then, 'doubling' is rampant in *Humphry Clinker*, the most compelling example of this process is provided by none of those mentioned briefly above but rather, however strangely at first sight, by Tabitha. Having described Tabitha in reasonable detail and in terms that render her the least likely companion to a man of feeling, or member of a sentimental circle, Jery goes on to relate how he 'once told my uncle, I was surprised that a man of his disposition could bear such a domestic plague, when it could so easily be removed'; his account continues as follows:

The remark made him sore, because it seemed to tax him with want of resolution – Wrinkling up his nose, and drawing down his eyebrows, 'A young fellow (said he) when he first thrusts his snout into the world, is apt to be surprised at many things, which a man of experience knows to be ordinary and unavoidable – This precious aunt of yours is become insensibly a part of my constitution – Damn her! She's a *noli me tangere* in my flesh, which I cannot bear to be touched or tampered with.' I made no reply; but shifted the conversation. He really has an affection for this original; which maintains its ground in defiance of common sense, and in despite of that contempt which he must certainly feel for her character and understanding. Nay, I am convinced, that she has likewise a most virulent attachment to his person; though her love never shews itself but in the shape of discontent; and she persists in tormenting him out of sheer tenderness … (p. 64)

This passage is central to an understanding of Tabitha's position in the text, and offers an interpretive key to the novel as a whole. Tabitha seems here to be Bramble's *alter ego*: apparently representative of all that he abhors, she is also somehow necessary to him. Despite her unappealing qualities and resistance to sentimental recuperation, she must be included in Bramble's inner circle, and can even, in key instances, take part in sentimental scenes of reconciliation and sympathy.[32] When the qualities represented by Bramble and Tabitha are considered more fully, the wider significance of their inextricability becomes more clear.

A sentimental hero, Matthew Bramble also represents a particular type; he is not 'simple' in the style of Sarah Fielding's protagonist, nor good-natured and impetuous as is Primrose. Nor is he, as the following chapter will illustrate, a man of feeling in the mould of either Henry Mackenzie's hero or Sterne's Yorick. Thomas R. Preston's 1964 essay on Bramble as an example of the 'benevolent misanthrope type' presented a genealogy that still holds good: Preston argues that Bramble crucially combines both acute sensibility and the qualities of the railing satirist, and Bramble, like Goldsmith's Man in Black, 'harbors a Swiftian rational hatred for mankind while he overflows with compassion for individual men'.[33] The combination of sentiment and satire is not in itself surprising – as Preston recognises, the very grounds of sentimental philosophy set up the conditions for satire, in the inevitable clash between the ideal and the world its adherents encountered.

Bramble's role allows him both to dispense liberal charity to worthy individuals at various points in the text and also to carry on throughout the narrative, personally and through Jery and Lismahago, attacks on all those things he abhors, unrestrained commercial expansion and all its damaging consequences coming high up on the list. Bramble refuses to be bound by purely commercial considerations if the requirements of benevolence need to be considered. In his very first letter, he advises Dr Lewis, 'Tell Barns to thresh out the two old ricks, and send the corn to market, and sell it off to the poor at a shilling a bushel under market price', as well as counselling him, 'Let Morgan's widow have the Alderney cow, and forty shillings to clothe her children: but don't say a syllable of the matter to any living soul – I'll make her pay when she is able' (p. 7). In true sentimental style, there is never any doubt but that he can afford endlessly to make such uncommercial decisions and it is precisely the deleterious effects of commerce on benevolence that come under fire in Lismahago's later attack: 'He observed, that traffick was an enemy to all the liberal passions of the soul, founded on the thirst for lucre, a sordid disposition to take advantage of the necessities of our fellow-creatures' (p. 209). The notion of commerce 'taking advantage' of others returns us to the idea referred to earlier that, to quote Louis Dumont once again, 'in trade, the gain of one party is the loss of the other', and the corresponding disparagement of trade and money is indeed a feature of *Humphry Clinker*. But *Humphry Clinker* also, like *Julia Mandeville*, shows signs of the progressive change of attitude Dumont identifies, and commerce is by no means represented as an unmitigated evil in the novel. This is most clear when the party reach Scotland, which by comparison with England receives a remarkably positive response from the irascible Bramble. Glasgow, for example, is not only 'one of the prettiest towns in Europe' but is also 'a perfect bee-hive in point of industry' whose people 'have a noble spirit of enterprise' (pp. 251–2). The yoking of 'noble' with 'enterprise' almost takes us forward to the kind of promotion of commerce we shall find in the novels discussed in Chapter 6.

Commerce can be a blessing as well as a curse, then, and it becomes clear that for Bramble – and Lismahago – the key to reaping the good rather than the damaging effects of commerce is found in regulation. Lismahago argues that 'Commerce is undoubtedly a blessing, *while restrained within its proper channels*; but a glut of wealth brings along with it a glut of evils ...', to which Bramble's response is, 'I am one of those who think, that, *by proper regulations*, commerce may produce every national benefit, without the allay of such concomitant evils' (p. 287; my emphasis). This response clearly divorces Bramble from a Mandevillian promotion of free trade (notwithstanding the hive analogy above!), but it allows him always to reject as the result of lack of regulation what he sees as the undesirable effects of unrestrained commerce – such as luxury, a constant target of Bramble's invective, more particularly in its most feared role as destroyer of social hierarchies. This is observable especially in London, where the 'poorest 'squire, as well as the richest peer, must have his house in town' and where 'there is no distinction or subordination left' (pp. 90–1). Bramble represents, then, a traditional allegiance to established hierarchies and an abhorrence of the luxury that would threaten these, alongside a willingness to promote commerce within certain bounds. In this respect, *Humphry Clinker* could be seen as echoing the attempts of Belmont to reconcile within his estate old and new, an attempt with which Tabitha is closely concerned.

Included firmly within the sentimental circle, Tabitha Bramble is yet a constant source of friction. Her role as critic of her brother's benevolence is early established over such matters as the Alderney cow (whose profitable sale Tabitha was eagerly awaiting) and the widow at the Hot Well (pp. 8, 22–4).[34] That the Biblical Tabitha is described as 'full of works and almsdeeds'[35] only goes to underline Tabitha Bramble's unsentimental lack of feeling for the unfortunate. Alongside and consistent with this, Tabitha's ability not only to save but to make money on her own account is recorded by Jery:

> Her fortune was originally no more than a thousand pounds; but she gained an accession of five hundred by the death of a sister, and the lieutenant left her three hundred in his will. These sums she has more than doubled, by living free of all expence, in her brother's house; and dealing in cheese and Welsh flannel, the produce of his flocks and dairy. At present her capital has increased to about four thousand pounds; and her avarice seems to grow every day more and more rapacious. (p. 63)

By others, Tabitha's management is only ever represented in the novel as a kind of meanness, but she herself, in the argument with Bramble over Clinker and Chowder, accuses her brother of 'a bad return for all the services I have done you; for nursing you in your sickness, for managing your family, and keeping you from ruining yourself by your own imprudence' (pp. 87–8). Tabitha represents the unacceptable face of prudence – the prudence that is self-serving rather than self-controlled, materialistic rather than moderate. Yet unlike *The Vicar of Wakefield*, where Primrose simply rejects (to his cost) such prudence, or *Julia Mandeville*, where Belmont attempts to effect a reconciliation between versions of prudence, *Humphry Clinker* suggests that the prudence of self-interest can only be contained: by keeping Tabitha within the inner circle of right-feeling, right-thinking individuals, the potential impact of her values can be confined. The world beyond the circle is of course dominated by such self-interest; the inclusion of Tabitha within it, and her subservience to her brother, represents a fantasy of control, an inversion of the real state of affairs. As Bramble's *alter ego*, Tabitha is necessary to enable him to perform this operation of containment.

To give the situation a further twist, Tabitha has her own double: Win Jenkins, her maidservant. Jery notes the similarities between them, unlikely though these parallels seem:

> Win, to be sure, is much younger, and more agreeable in her person; she is likewise tender-hearted and benevolent, qualities for which her mistress is by no means remarkable, no more than she is for being of a timorous disposition, and much subject to fits of the mother, which are the infirmities of Win's constitution: but then she seems to have adopted Mrs Tabby's manner with her cast cloaths. She dresses and endeavours to look like her mistress, although her own looks are much more engaging. – She enters into her scheme of œconomy, learns her phrases, repeats her remarks, imitates her stile in scolding the inferior servants, and finally, subscribes implicitly to her system of devotion. (pp. 212–13)

The similarities between Win and Tabitha allow an intriguing connection to be made between prudence and extravagance. While Tabitha is not free from excess – her attempts to trap a husband and her adoption of Methodism, for example, both result in excessive behaviour – extravagance, in the sense of inappropriately conspicuous consumption, is never one of her sins. Indeed, one of the jokes of the novel is Tabitha's determined refusal to bring her wardrobe up to date, remarked particularly by her London friend Lady Griskin, and by Jery when Tabitha marries Lismahago (pp. 97, 355).

As Tabitha's double, Win arguably becomes by definition guilty of extravagance, since to attempt to look like her social superior is to wear clothes and adopt styles inappropriate to her station. More than this, however, Win is shown throughout the novel to succumb easily to temptation, whether it be a French hairstyle or the bland-ishments of Jery's Frenchified manservant, Dutton. The 'flood of luxury' (p. 59) so deplored by Bramble clearly has no difficulty in carrying Win along with it, and the devastating effects on social order he fears are comically confirmed in Win's correspondence: 'I now carries my head higher than arrow private gentlewoman of Vales. Last night, coming huom from the meeting, I was taken by lamp-light for an iminent poulterer's daughter, a great beauty ...' (p. 112). The threat to Bramble-esque values Win represents is, however, contained, as is Tabitha's. Her outing with Dutton to the theatre at Newcastle (with her 'hair dressed in the Parish fashion' and just a 'trifle of paint') ends with the people, having heard 'infor-mation of their real character and condition', calling her a painted Jezebel and ruining her finery with mud.[36] Her marriage to Humphry Clinker – by now discovered to be Bramble's natural son – becomes part of the novel's effort to absorb all threatening features into its utopian ending, as John P. Zomchick so convincingly argues:

> with the surprising discovery of relation where no relation was to be expected, the narrative suggests that the Bramble/Clinker or the master/servant relation is a natural one. Class relations are naturalized into family relations.
> ... The traditional lower order in the form of Clinker-Loyd is reabsorbed into a paternalist Utopia, taking with it the more threatening person of Winifred Jenkins, who dares to dress like her betters.[37]

If Tabitha is Bramble's *alter ego*, and Win is Tabitha's double, however, the limitations of containment become apparent. Win, like Anne Wilmot, is allowed the task of bringing the narrative to a close, and as Zomchick says, 'Bramble's fears and Jenkins' undi-minished ambitions are real, even more real perhaps than their solutions.'[38] Bramble cannot hope to overcome or expunge the values Tabitha and Win represent, he can only hope to keep them under wraps, for the time being. The prospects for the future do not look good, for all the determined resolution of the ending. One of the ways in which this is made clear is the limited extent to which Bramble can rescue failing squires. Here there is an obvious parallel with Belmont in *Julia Mandeville*, but there is also a difference. Barker, the failing landowner rescued by Belmont, attributes his problems to a 'too careless economy' whose specific cause is unknown. *Humphry Clinker*, by contrast, knows exactly who is to blame in almost every case of grief: women. Baynard is saved, but the competition in which his wife was engaged will continue:

> [The ladies] vied in grandeur, that is, in ostentation, with the wife of Sir Charles Chickwell, who had four times their fortune; and she again piqued herself upon making an equal figure with a neighbouring peeress, whose revenue trebled her own. Here then was the fable of the frog and the ox, realized in four different instances within the same county: one large fortune, and three moderate estates, in a fair way of being burst by the inflation of female vanity.... (p. 301)[39]

Statistically, then, the reclamation of Baynard from a life of extravagance is a drop in the ocean. Finding room for Tabitha and Win within the charmed circle of the ending cannot magically reconcile conflicting value-systems beneath the patriarchal ambit, it can only seem to do so. And the very need of a novel such as *Humphry Clinker* to *show* such containment of its female figures only confirms more securely the continuing association between women and the new economic order.

5

'Above œconomy':
The History of Lady Barton,
The Man of Feeling and
A Sentimental Journey

In her *Essays Addressed to Young Married Women* (1782), Elizabeth Griffith issued what was by then a standard caution to her readers on the subject of economy: 'Neither rank nor riches can place any person above œconomy; and perhaps those who possess such advantages in the highest degree, have the greatest occasion for the practice of this humble virtue.'[1] The diverse uses to which the word 'economy' is put during the course of the eighteenth century, however, makes interpretation of the phrase 'above economy' a necessarily complicated task, a fact that Griffith herself acknowledges to some extent in her characterisation of the subject as a 'cameleon [*sic*]' which must 'take its hue from the surrounding objects'.[2] As previous chapters have shown, the range of meanings attached to 'economy' is wide. It includes management of the private household, of public finances and national resources; it also encompasses frugality and 'laudable parsimony' of the kind approved by conduct books, which meanings lead on to associations with prudence, chastity and propriety. Yet in certain cases economic dexterity in women becomes virtually synonymous with sexual experience, while in others 'economy' and patriarchal government can be written as apparently inseparable.

To be 'above economy', then, would be to inhabit a space where the management of financial resources, private or public, was unnecessary or irrelevant. It would also be to be free from all conduct book constraints of prudential behaviour in either sexual or financial situations. The kind of knowledge and analysis economically adept women employ would not be needed in this realm; neither would the sound judgment of the patriarch. The admonitory voice of the *Essays*, however, would clearly regard such speculation as pointless. No one can be 'above economy', no matter what their apparent qualifications for such a position: there is no space available in which to take it up. Nevertheless, it is precisely this non-existent space that I am interested in examining in the chapter which follows. For despite the assertion in her *Essays*, both Griffith's own novel *The History of Lady Barton* and Henry Mackenzie's *Man of Feeling* supply protagonists of whom the description 'above economy' seems peculiarly appropriate.

Both novels were published in 1771 in what Janet Todd calls 'the middle of the high period of sensibility'.[3] In reaching the 1770s, this study has arrived at the last decade that Todd feels able to include in the 'heyday' of the literature of sensibility. From the late 1770s onwards, doubts and criticisms of sentimentalism's literary and moral pretensions were voiced with increasing vehemence although this did not prevent the continued appearance of sentimental novels and poetry for some years to come – nor, indeed, the incorporation of sentimental elements into works which ostensibly eschewed all links with the discredited genre. Mackenzie's novel, immediately popular, has gone on to become the literary historian's representative sentimental text. In broad agreement with Todd's chronology, for example, John Mullan finds in *The Man of Feeling* the crucial turning-point of the sentimental genre's literary life. This sense of generic crisis he expresses as follows: 'With the publication of Mackenzie's *Man of Feeling* in 1771, the sentimental novel has evolved into a terminal formula precisely because, with all its talk of virtue, it cannot reflect at all on the problems of conduct, the practices of any existing society.'[4] This view of the sentimental novel as ultimately possessing an inevitable irrelevance, an utter inability to deal with any concrete social or political issue and thus an inbuilt capacity for self-marginalisation, is certainly compatible with an interpretation that sees the sentimental protagonist as being 'above economy', in a fantasy world in which the feeling individual is untrammelled by any considerations other than those of the heart. Such a fantasy is undoubtedly an element of sentimentalism which is given particular prominence in the novels to be considered. In this chapter, then, I am principally concerned to examine the way this fantasy operates in two works situated at a significant moment in the history of the sentimental novel, as that history has recently been constituted. Does such a fantasy indeed confirm the inapplicability of sentimental fiction to any practical dilemma? Can this moment, on the evidence in and around these two novels, indeed be seen as initiating 'a terminal formula' in the history of the sentimental novel? Close comparison of *Lady Barton* and *The Man of Feeling* suggests that both questions must be answered with a negative; a coda, in the form of a brief discussion of Laurence Sterne's *A Sentimental Journey*, confirms this conclusion.

The heroine of Griffith's novel *The History of Lady Barton* possesses both rank and riches, but despite the author's subsequent conduct book advice it is hard to find any obvious signs of the 'practice of this humble virtue' of economy in the activities of Lady Barton. Unhappily married to Sir William Barton, her confessional letters to her unmarried sister Fanny Cleveland are curiously devoid of the kind of household detail so evident in earlier novels in this study. Unlike Mrs Bilson, Amelia, Lady Belmont or Mrs Primrose, we have no idea whether Louisa Barton is a good domestic economist. The dearth of such information in her story is further accentuated by the pressing nature of financial considerations in the novel's three interpolated narratives. Olivia, seduced by the libertinous Colonel Walter; Maria, forced into a loveless marriage; and Mrs N——, suffering parental cruelty, all experience economic hardship and must deal with what Olivia calls 'the common concerns of life' in a way which never touches Lady Barton. Thus the very organisation of the novel seems to suggest precisely the opposite of Griffith's conduct book assertion: Lady Barton is 'above economy' and 'this humble virtue' plays no part in her life. Sir James Steuart's *Principles of Political Œconomy*, examined in Chapter 4, might tempt an interpretation which sees this as inevitably the situation of every woman: 'The object of [œconomy], in a private family, is therefore to provide for the nourishment, the other wants, and the employment of every individual. In the first place, for the master, who is the head, and who directs the whole; next for the children, who interest him above all other things; and last for the servants...'[5] Lady Barton, in the same way as the woman who is fascinatingly absent from this construction of the 'private family', inhabits that space where management of resources is not an issue. It becomes a rarefied world where her sentimental distresses can exist in a pure state, unsullied by such economic considerations.

Similarly, the hero of *The Man of Feeling* contrasts quite sharply with the male protagonists of earlier novels discussed in this study.

David Simple and Primrose were economic failures. Each tried to support his family by dint of personal effort and each ended up in the utmost deprivation. In trying, however modestly, to engage with the commercial world, their inadequacy was exposed. Harley, on the other hand, is an economic cypher. As far as possible he does not involve himself with the workings of the economic world. This withdrawal is not an acknowledgment of inadequacy – although clearly Harley is never destined for material success – but rather the result of his whimsicality and comparative security. For, while he is never admitted to the ranks of the wealthy, Harley never experiences abject poverty of the kind suffered by David Simple or Primrose; unlike them he remains independent to the last, the dispenser of alms rather than the recipient of them, while none of his financial losses seems to lead to any economic difficulty. With household management in the capable hands of his aunt, and economic considerations such as how to earn and secure a living left to those on whom he bestows his charity, the novel effectively diverts all practical and financial matters away from the hero, enabling him to exist, in the same way as Lady Barton, in a world where money simply becomes the sentimentalist's token of sympathy and gratitude. If it is also, as Robert Markley puts it, 'the sentimentalist's medium of exchange, a palpable, materialist manifestation of good nature as commodity',[6] this is set up in ostensible opposition to, or replacement of, an unfeeling commercial world.

Harley and Louisa Barton thus share a freedom from any financial responsibilities or worries which enables them to rise above economy in at least one of its senses. This apparent pursuit of a deliberate policy of irrelevance to a harsh world seen as rarely hearing, let alone attending to, the dictates of the heart accords well with the view of sentimentalism put forward by critics such as John Mullan. But being above economy, as I indicated would be the case in my opening paragraph, has further implications which construct the position in rather different ways. To begin with, its effects on gender are far from simple.

In *Lady Barton*, more complex aspects of being above economy reveal themselves, ironically, in the one scene in the novel in which money explicitly becomes the site of marital discord between the heroine and Sir William. As Lady Barton is about to give ten guineas to a tenant whose house has been destroyed by fire, Sir William stops her and with the most supercilious air imaginable, took hold of my hand, bid me put up my money, and not meddle with matters that I did not understand – said I was rather too young for a Lady Bountiful yet; and that if I went on at that rate, they would fire every cottage on his lands, and he should be run into a goal [sic] by my generosity.[7]

Subsequently, Lady Barton secretly sends 10 guineas to the family and discovers that Sir William has already given them £30. Her complaint to her sister on this occasion is not that Sir William should think her unable to control her generosity economically, but that he should restrain her 'from the virtuous pleasure of bestowing charity' and try to persuade her 'that he was totally devoid of it himself' (I, 69). In restraining her benevolence Sir William has implicitly insulted her status as sensible female, since such distress is precisely what women do understand.

This scene pinpoints the essential disaster of the marriage: Sir William's boorish action prevents his wife from exercising a vital component of a woman's moral economy, the essential charity and benevolence which belong in so many eighteenth-century definitions of virtuous femininity. In her Dedication to the second edition of *A Series of Genuine Letters Between Henry and Frances* (that is, between Richard and Elizabeth Griffith), Frances addresses herself 'To My Sex', telling her female readers: 'It is your charms, virtue and decorum, which inspire mens [sic] hearts, refine their minds, and polish their manners ...'[8] The exhortation functions at least in theory as a rallying cry, an attempt to discover power in the circumscribed position of women. Thus when Henry makes some sarcastic comments about women, Frances leaps to their defence with an argument of moral superiority:

I have, indeed, sometimes heard such an arbitrary distinction made, as virtues masculine, and virtues feminine; but the antients, who first classed all human properties, were of a different way of thinking, and tacitly confessed, that all virtuous qualities belonged more properly to our sex; for I have heard you say a very flattering thing, that, 'in all the learned languages, the moral excellencies were nouns of the feminine gender.'[9]

The terms of Frances's exhortation and defence, however, inevitably raise more problems than they solve; while they set up

female moral ascendancy, they reinforce the potent figures of the
virtuous woman as irresistibly reforming influence and her corollary, the vicious woman who necessarily pollutes her associates. As
Lucan remarks to Hume, men have to undergo a 'quarantine, after
the contagion of an abandoned' woman (II, 205). In these terms,
Louisa Barton's palpable failure to bring about a benign alteration
in Sir William's behaviour renders her effectively 'fallen' even at
the outset of the novel. The miscarriage which follows the visit of
the would-be seducer Colonel Walter to her bedside can then be
seen as confirmation of her lapsed state: as Tony Tanner writes, 'an
unfaithful wife' is 'usually by implication a bad mother'.[10] As far as
Sir William is concerned, she has deprived him of 'his heir', 'his
boy' (I, 159–60), thus failing in her primary wifely duty. To be
'above economy' in this sense is to be outside the prescribed moral
sphere allotted to women, to be unsexed. Louisa's mortified exclamation, 'I am, I am a criminal!' (II, 93), her conviction that mental
acquiescence might as well be physical transgression, echoes this
punitive attitude towards feminine duty.

However, the question of woman's influence is not easily settled
in *Lady Barton*. In her Preface, Griffith herself explicitly rejects any
possibility of attempting to reform readers through her fiction.
Happy to form or inform the young and innocent, 'the task of
reforming' she leaves to 'greater geniuses and abler pens' (I, xi). By
embracing another feminine desideratum – modesty – the woman
writer hopes to escape the requirement of salutary influence over
the reprobate expected of her sex. Within the novel, meanwhile,
Lord Lucan simultaneously reinforces and subtly undermines the
notion of woman as the crucial moral factor in the education of men:

> when the object of our affection has a distinct interest rather to
> extinguish, than inspire [virtue], the general bias of our passions,
> aided by the natural indolence of dissipation and debauchery,
> suffer the plant to wither in its bloom, and thus obliterates the
> truest character of manhood.
>
> On the contrary, let the most vicious man become truly
> enamoured of a virtuous woman, and he will at least assume
> the semblance of those virtues he admires in her... (I, 110)

The moral character of the woman is still undeniably influential,
but in this account male agency has a greater role to play – and this,
if only partially and certainly unusually, favours the woman. It is

only when the man has invested 'affection', has 'become truly enamoured', that feminine influence can take any effect. Lady Barton has not 'found in Sir William an object to awaken' her sensibility (I, 49); he has failed to make it clear to her whether his pleasure in her social acceptability arises 'more from vanity, than affection' (I, 4), and whether in his eagerness to marry her he was 'more enamoured, or more artful, than the rest' of her suitors (I, 65). In this version, Sir William is more responsible than his wife for the failure of the marriage. In the three articles of 'love, honour, and obey', Louisa asserts, the first two are dependent upon Sir William; 'the latter only, rests on me; and I will most sanctimoniously perform my part of the covenant' (I, 3). The idea of freedom from 'the common concerns of life' which characterises the way in which Lady Barton and Harley are above financial economy here becomes transmuted into a release from blame; Sir William's failure to draw out his wife's virtuous femininity leaves her, through no fault of her own, with this essential fund of feeling untapped:

> O! why am I debarred the chaste indulgence of a virtuous passion? why must a heart that overflows with tenderness, have all its currents dammed? like a poor river forced from its natural course, am I to blame if it should steal away in useless, nay improper channels? (I, 130–1)

The answer Louisa's censorious sister Fanny gives to this final question is, of course, yes. Fanny is also unhappily in love, but as an unmarried woman 'the weakness which may in [my position], not only be pardoned, but pitied, becomes criminal in yours' (II, 74) – a view which Louisa, as indicated above, comes rapidly to accept. The answer given by the dynamic of the novel, however, in which the boorish – and blameworthy – Sir William is constantly set beside the sympathetic and gentlemanly Lucan, is not necessarily consonant with her view.

The two opposing effects of Lady Barton being above, or outside, women's prescribed moral economy exist together in the novel. On the one hand, she fails to prove her virtuous femininity, and is rendered fallen; on the other, that virtue is denied her by the very figure whose duty it is to draw it out, and the blame is thus displaced on to Sir William. Neither of these effects allows Louisa to disregard this moral economy: it remains the standard by which she is judged to be lacking and it is the question of responsibility for that lack which is at stake. There is a space beyond economy which Louisa perforce inhabits, and yet at the same time there is no possibility for her, as the *Essays Addressed to Young Married Women* asserted, of being above that economy. This paradox is one crucially connected to gender, as an examination of *The Man of Feeling* will show.

Harley's position both echoes and diverges from that of Lady Barton. In *A Series of Genuine Letters*, Frances tells Henry that 'custom, though not ethics, or religion, has put courage in your sex, and chastity in ours, upon the same footing'.[11] If courage for men is morally analogous to chastity for women, then Harley fails to fulfil the requirements of his prescribed moral economy as surely as Lady Barton does hers. *The Economy of Human Life* describes a man of fortitude as he who 'meeteth the evils of life as a man that goeth forth unto battle and returneth with victory in his hand', whereas a timorous man is he who 'by tamely bearing insults ... invites injuries'.[12] *The Man of Feeling*, by contrast, recounts how as Harley approached 'the great man's door, he felt his heart agitated by an unusual pulsation' – a reaction belonging more to what John Mullan refers to as 'the massively sensitized, feminine body' than to a masculine economy of courage.[13] Harley's confrontation with Miss Atkins' father perhaps illustrates the feminisation of his reactions most graphically: 'The blood ran quicker to his cheek – his pulse beat one – no more – and regained the temperament of humanity!' (p. 66). The impulse to respond to Atkins' drawn sword with comparable masculine vigour gives way to the feminine 'temperament of humanity'; the code of masculine honour invoked by the sword is rejected in favour of a feminine declaration of sympathy: 'my heart bleeds for you!'

Lady Barton's failure to conform to a feminine moral economy puts her in a space beyond economy, however problematic that space may be. Harley's rejection of a masculine economy of courage, on the other hand, enables him both to occupy an analogous space and to embrace the very aspects of the feminine moral economy Lady Barton is unable to fulfil. Situated in his space 'above economy', Harley can shrug off the necessity for worldly prudence in a fashion never achievable for earlier sentimental heroes. Advice such as 'grave and prudent friends' can offer is quickly spurned (p. 10), while the suggestions of 'the colder homilies of prudence' which assail him the morning after his first meeting with Miss Atkins are soon rejected with the exclamation, 'to calculate the chances of deception is too tedious a business for the life of man!' (p. 53). While Primrose questioned the desirability of prudence, his story, like that of David Simple, demonstrated its absolute necessity in everyday life; Harley's story, by contrast, does no such thing. While the demise of David Simple is both metaphorical and actual (his sensibility renders him unfit for the world; starvation as a result of worldly imprudence thus takes him out of it), Harley's decline is purely metaphorical. Ample food and shelter, which he always has, cannot save him – this kind of prudence is not a consideration.

Meanwhile, as a feminised man, Harley is able to embrace and exercise precisely that charity and benevolence required of the virtuous woman. This feminisation is not absolute, however: Harley is not bound by all aspects of the feminine moral economy. The specifically feminine aspects of prudence, for example, are irrelevant to him as they can never be to a woman – as Miss Atkins' story, which proves the disastrous consequences for women of lacking prudence, shows. She fails to see through her lover's 'ardent' protestations, whose sincerity 'prudence might have suspected' (p. 58). To have prudence, as I have already discussed in Chapter 3, implies sexual knowledge which a virtuous, innocent woman was not supposed to possess. In making Miss Atkins lack prudence, the narrative preserves her ideal innocence intact while practically leading her to her ruin. 'Calculating the chances of deception' may be 'too tedious a business for the life of man', but it may be vital for the sexually secure life of woman. Even 'feminised', Harley can still throw away this kind of prudence with the impunity of a man; Miss Atkins lacks it at her peril.

Thus Harley can have the best of both worlds, retaining the advantages of being male while taking on selected aspects of femininity. Being 'above economy' is a position imposed on Lady Barton, whether it is she or Sir William who is to blame for this state of affairs. Harley, on the other hand, chooses the state himself: he is the 1770s version of a dropout, who has opted out of particular systems for particular reasons. As the narrator tells us, 'He did few things without a motive, but his motives were rather eccentric' (p. 84). The paradoxical situation of Louisa Barton, outside feminine moral economy but nevertheless unable to escape its dictates, is one only a woman of feeling can suffer; the man of feeling as he appears in Mackenzie's novel is able to sustain a position above economy with considerably more success.

If being above economy has diverse effects on gender for the protagonists of *Lady Barton* and *The Man of Feeling*, it also has implications for their class positions which become inseparable from questions of gender. The apparent superiority of Lady Barton in being above 'the common concerns of life' is intimately related to her rank, on which she herself puts no small valuation. She offers the persecuted Olivia 'any assistance that is in the power of an individual of your own sex, of some rank and consideration in this country' (I, 190). This consciousness of social superiority is invoked even more clearly near the outset of the novel when, *en route* for Ireland, Lady Barton and her companions are rescued from their sinking vessel and carried to a small offshore island, uninhabited bar 'a few goats, and some fishermen, who are almost as wild as they' (I, 15). Louisa continues:

> the hospitable cottagers received us with that sort of surprize, which I imagine we should feel, if an order of higher beings were to descend by miracle to visit us. – But be their kindness never forgot by me! and may their beds of straw, and smoaky rafters, yield them such soft and balmy sleep as they afforded to my harrassed [*sic*] frame! and let them never envy those that toss on down. (I, 15–16)

The passage neatly encapsulates an attitude popular throughout the century – that the poor are in an entirely different category from their social superiors (even, as David Hume suggested, of a different physical make-up) and furthermore, they are lucky to be so. Both Adam Smith in his *Theory of Moral Sentiments* and the anonymous author of *The Economy of Human Life* offer this argument, since the beggar 'who suns himself by the side of the highway, possesses that security which kings are fighting for', while 'Debar'd from the dainties of the rich, [the poor man] escapeth also their diseases'.[14]

Such an attitude perhaps explains why the cottagers are offered no particular reward or thanks – of either a verbal or pecuniary nature. The reference to 'higher beings' rather implies that the gratitude should be all on the side of the hosts, not on that of their guests. The cottagers are also entirely amorphous and anonymous. By contrast, when the company subsequently leaves the island with the help of a local landowner, he is both named and given a worthy wife and family. Mr Mathews' assistance draws a rather different reaction from Lady Barton, inspiring her to remark that 'There is nothing affects my heart so much as benevolent actions' and to make at once 'all the acknowledgments that our joy would permit' (I, 21). 'Benevolence' in this sympathetic sense is clearly a quality that can only be aspired to by people of a certain rank; the whole episode gives the reader to understand that these primitive cottagers are not worthy of benevolence in either sense, that is, to bestow it or to receive it. Even the incident referred to above, in which Lady Barton shows benevolence to a tenant, in no way contradicts this since, as she herself subsequently makes clear, the relative positions of lord and tenant are affected by the particular property relationship which exists between them: 'it is [the tenants'] industry and labour which supports our affluence, and they certainly have a right to a certain share in our enjoyments, in proportion to their rank and situation' (I, 135). The social situation of the cottagers, on the other hand, since they have no hold on their exalted visitors through dependency, renders them completely outside the sentimental exchange as it is portrayed in *Lady Barton*.

In terms of class position, then, Lady Barton and the cottagers could not be further apart. But when gender is added to the problem, the heroine's relationship to them changes radically. The consequence of the cottagers' lowly position is anonymity and amorphousness: they have no individual identities according to any evaluation by rank. But it is not rank *per se* which identifies people; property, hailed by John Millar in his *Origin of the Distinction of Ranks* (1771) as 'the great source of distinction among individuals', is what counts.[15] As a married woman, Lady Barton can be described in terms of property no more easily than the cottagers: neither she nor they can be distinguished in this way – or, by implication, in any other way. Louisa's access to property, indeed, is the issue which undermines her apparent freedom from 'the common concerns of life'.

Left an independent woman of means at the age of 16, Louisa's marriage inevitably rescinds that economic independence, which she herself has already voluntarily given up, Clarissa-like, by determining never to marry without her brother Sir George's consent. This consequence of her marriage, crucially, only becomes an issue in the novel at the moment when she wishes to play the role of Lady Bountiful denied her by Sir William. Having rescued Olivia from Colonel Walter's house and determined to help her, it becomes clear that she is in no position to take independent action.

The role of benefactor has to be rapidly transferred to the unmarried (and therefore economically independent[16]) Fanny, who tells her that, having 'no person to whom I am accountable for [her] conduct', she stands 'clearer from difficulty in this affair' than Louisa (II, 43). It now appears that the very act of marrying endangers a woman's moral economy – in doing so she inevitably gives up her ability to dispense charity on personal impulse and, this being part of her virtuous femininity, both virtue and femininity are unavoidably tainted. Once more we return to the inescapable position in which the woman is 'always already fallen'. Of course, not only marriage imposes such controls – fathers and brothers can also do so, as Clarissa demonstrates. Harriet Guest writes that '[Clarissa's] estate ... poses the question of the extent to which women can be appropriately described in terms of bourgeois individualism'.[17] If what gives 'distinction', to use Millar's word, to the bourgeois individual is property, women can hardly be described in these terms at all. The sentimental novel has been seen as celebrating 'a christian, sentimental individualism'.[18] Clearly when the protagonist is a woman, the celebration of individualism of any kind is fraught with difficulty, not to say out of the question.

Harley's position 'above economy' is also intimately related to his rank, but in his case this rank is necessarily below that of aristocracy, although above that of trade. This is because the construction of society offered by *The Man of Feeling* finds aristocracy and trade inextricably linked. Great men in the novel are generally inaccessible and unsympathetic, and it is significant that Mackenzie's villainous representative of an unfeeling society in *The Man of the World* is an aristocrat who is also a sharp businessman.[19] Harley and Annesly are placed in opposition to both aristocratic power and commercial imperatives. This indicates no disapproval of aristocracy on principle, but rather the perception that elements of the commercial ethos have polluted aristocratic influence. Ben Silton, 'the baronet's brother' and man of feeling, is one of a dying breed; the baronet from whom Harley fails to gain his lease is part of an aristocracy which is now content to be complicit with the unscrupulous commercial morality of the age. Thus the only class position left for the man of feeling to occupy is one which eschews both title and commerce. Similarly, if more comically, John Homespun in *The Mirror* and *The Lounger* stands as an example of the honest country gentleman in a state of siege between the 'great ones' on one side and the upstart Mushrooms on the other.[20]

Defining Harley in this oppositional and perhaps vulnerable situation points up further aspects of his feminisation. In eschewing title and commerce, he implicitly turns his back on a masculine economy of ambition and competition and on the public, masculine economic sphere of material exchange. His class position is vital in his claim to be above economy, and also demonstrates how *The Man of Feeling* is able to fit unproblematically into an analysis which sees the 'high bourgeois ethic' of 'a christian, sentimental individualism ... threatened by the selfish materialism of a low bourgeois commercial culture'.[21] Yet there is a contradiction here which once again exhibits the flexible nature of Harley's feminisation. For while he is ostensibly uninvolved in the masculine economic world, he can still, unlike Lady Barton, be described in terms of bourgeois individualism because he has the necessary distinctive attribute of owning property. Paradoxically, this factor both demonstrates the disingenuous nature of the 'above economy' fantasy and enables it to be entered into with more success. Once again Harley has the striking ability to reject a masculine moral economy but to accept only selected features of a feminine one. His property enables him to retain, for all his lack of manly courage and self-control, the crucial ingredient of the masculine position within the sentimental exchange as described in Chapter 4 – as benefactor, he is never pressed into the feminine position of dependency suffered by the recipient. This discrepancy between the feminised protagonist of *The Man of Feeling* and the female protagonist of *Lady Barton* represents, in effect, a fictional demonstration of the double standard.

The complicated ways in which gender and class interact have not gone unremarked by critics of the eighteenth-century novel, and the extent of the complication is illustrated by the apparently divergent conclusions on the subject reached by Nancy Armstrong and Janet Todd. Writing of *Pamela* in *Desire and Domestic Fiction*, Armstrong asserts that

> critics tend to read Pamela's sexual encounters as psychological rather than political events. Thus they can pass off the ideological conflict shaping the text as the difference between a man and a woman rather than between a person of station and a person of low rank. Writing apparently gained certain authority as it transformed political differences into those rooted in gender.[22]

On the other hand, dealing with the question of the role aristocracy plays in the female novel, Todd concludes that it

> is not linked with social power and privilege. Instead it is a mingling of élitism, sensibility and impotence. Its purpose is to oppose insensitivity and power and to rebuke the middle class... . If gender is translated into class terms the confrontation of female impotence and male economic power becomes a less disturbing one for women: that between the economically powerful, insensitive middle class and an impotent but refined aristocracy.[23]

Armstrong sees class differences transformed into those of gender; Todd sees gender differences transformed into those of class. These transformations each have a different impetus, however. It is the presumably male 'critics' who wish to hide political difference behind gender difference in *Pamela*, whereas it is women writers who translate gender conflict into that of class in the female novel. Accordingly, Armstrong appears to find 'political differences' the more disturbing, where for Todd those differences are less disturbing for women than the differences in power between men and women. In each case, the less disturbing element is seen as being written over the more disturbing one in an attempt to nullify its effects. However, this attempt can never be wholly successful, since translation works both ways: where class has become gender it can be read back again as class, and vice versa – the crucial point being that for both Armstrong and Todd both elements are always present, even if one artificially masks the other. Their views are not, therefore, so much opposed as coming at the same problem from different directions. The value of the insight given by both into the need for the critic to read for class and gender simultaneously has, I hope, been demonstrated by the discussion of *The Man of Feeling* and *Lady Barton* above; I now want to address the broader ways in which the translation of such conflicts works in these novels.

While the possibility of Lady Barton being 'above economy' is ostensibly shored up by her superior class position, this position itself seems to be constructed oddly by comparison with other novels in this study. The 'economically powerful, insensitive middle class', to use the phrase provided by Todd's analysis, is easily identified in a novel such as *Julia Mandeville*; but *Lady Barton* features no Westbrook to fill this role. There is undoubtedly a class gap between Louisa Barton and the unfortunate women whose stories she hears and reads – and this gap appears to provide a reason why the economic concerns which loom so large for them need not affect her – but it is the gap between aristocracy and a middle class from the 'old professions' of church and army, not an economically powerful middle class based in trade. Indeed, unlike any novel examined so far in this study apart from *Tom Jones*, *Lady Barton* appears to ignore trade almost completely. Earning money is never the source of pride as it is in *The Countess of Dellwyn* or *Ophelia*. Olivia, Maria and Mrs N—— are all relieved just in time from what is clearly perceived as the disastrous necessity of 'labouring for their bread'. Where in *Amelia* the heroine's offers to work with her hands are couched in terms of determined optimism, offering a possibility of independence, here the associations are all unreservedly gloomy, foreseeing only 'a merciless world' where, 'in some obscure corner', one is reduced to 'a state of servitude' (II, 6; III, 72, 214). The only other possible connection with 'trade' the novel offers is in the figure of Margarita, the Italian prostitute who cheats Lord Hume and is, we learn, under the control of a pimp. Neither the least hint of business as enabling (as with Mrs Bilson and Caroline Traverse) nor even denunciations of trade as ignoble and corrupting (as in *Julia Mandeville*) are to be found. If the methodology outlined above works, however, we might expect to find these absences within a paradigmatic class conflict present as written into a conflict rooted in gender. This would mean that, to modify further the models provided by Armstrong and Todd, a novel by a woman writer translates class, or 'political', differences into those of gender. Whether this should be seen as a strategy which avoids or addresses the more 'disturbing' issue will only become apparent after further consideration.

Jane Spencer has commented that the 'lives' and 'histories' of minor characters found in many eighteenth-century novels 'were important as contrasts to the main story and as repositories for all the problematic feminine weaknesses purged from the picture of the ideal heroine'.[24] In the case of *Lady Barton*, the interpolated narratives both echo and diverge from the main story, providing not so much 'repositories' as dynamic testing grounds for the dilemmas surrounding the heroine. The stories are used by Louisa and Fanny both as an escape from their own problems and as a source of comparison and consolation. The suppression of Louisa's feminine moral economy by an unsympathetic husband becomes the economic oppression of powerless women by powerful men in the interpolated narratives, in a movement which helps to underline the gender conflict of the main story by rendering it in versions stripped of subtlety. Colonel Walter leaves Olivia pregnant and almost destitute; Mr W—— keeps Maria confined in a deserted castle and deprives his daughter, Mrs N——, of her rightful inheritance by his refusal to acknowledge his perfectly legal marriage to her mother. This rather depressing litany of conventionally ill-treated women carries with it, however, a more positive aspect which becomes central to the argument of the novel. For the solidarity implied by Louisa's and Fanny's sympathetic retelling of and reaction to these stories is the basis for an attempt to change the terms of the conflict, replacing female impotence with collective action.

The attempt to appropriate power in this way derives from the paradigm of female friendship so germane to many sentimental novels. Janet Todd describes it thus:

> As constructed in women's fiction of the last half of the century, this friendship is deeply sentimental; the most emotional tableaux and postures emerge from reunions and separations of female friends, and familial fellowship is frequently reduced, as in *Clarissa*, simply to a couple of persecuted and defensive female friends clinging together against a hostile world.[25]

Sentimental friendship in this style is clearly a key element in *Lady Barton*; apart from the sisters themselves there are Louisa's bosom companions Lucy and Harriet, along with Olivia and Sir George's lost love Delia whom Olivia providentially finds shut away in a French convent. What is significant about such friendship in the novel is that it moves in precisely the opposite direction from that in *Clarissa*: far from being reduced to 'a couple of persecuted and defensive female friends', it constantly expands. Leaving her sister behind, Louisa meets Lucy *en route* for Ireland and comes to know Harriet after her arrival. Her rescuing of Olivia, in which Lucy and Harriet are her allies, then leads directly to the discovery of the persecuted Delia. Even Louisa's maid Benson, who unlike many servants in such novels is never sentimentalised as an individual,[26] is allowed to become part of what is essentially a female network: Olivia's journey to England and to the protection of Fanny is accomplished through the help of a 'particular friend' of Lucy's and Benson's niece (II, 63).

This practical female solidarity finds its rationale in ideas going right back to the turn of the century, in the works of the early feminist writer Mary Astell, as well as in later works such as Sarah Scott's *Millenium Hall* (1762).[27] Lady Barton's indebtedness to such ideas is evident when she registers doubts about the desirability of Olivia and her child finding refuge in a convent, and yet cannot see any other alternative. What England needs, she tells Fanny, are Protestant asylums for women, where the distressed can retreat

> not from the world, but from the misfortunes, or the slander of it – for female orphans, young widows, or still more unhappy objects, forsaken, or ill treated wives, to betake themselves to, in such distress. For in all these circumstances, women who live alone, have need of something more than either prudence or a fair character, to guard them from rudeness or censure. (II, 56)

There are obvious connections between this proposition and the 'asylum' set up by the ladies of Millenium Hall for indigent gentlewomen. What makes Louisa's proposal particularly interesting, however, is the way in which it diverges from the model of female community to be found in Scott's novel. In this, both the original community and the asylum instituted by its members are retired from the world. The narrator does not give the real name of Millenium Hall, 'fearing to offend that modesty which has induced them to conceal their virtues in retirement', while Mrs Maynard tells Lamont that the women of the asylum 'are pretty well secured' from 'levity of conduct', 'by being exposed to few temptations in this retired place'.[28] This accords quite comfortably with the commonly held view that a position retired from 'the world' was the natural one for women.[29] In this sense, the female community conforms to, rather than challenges, received ideas about women's place. Harriet Guest, however, has demonstrated how this bourgeois ideal of retirement for women is complicated by a competing need for 'virtuous display': women must be visibly feminine, since ambiguity of gender difference signals a degenerate society.[30] This imperative seems to be operating in Lady Barton's version of the asylum, since once the unfortunate women have arrived there, they are to have 'all the pleasures and advantages of living still in the world', while gaining the protection of the 'respectable matronage' in charge and the mutual aid of having 'their conduct reciprocally vouched by one another' (II, 56–7). Seen as the necessary display of virtuous femininity, such presence in the world can be justified. But such an argument also allows the women Louisa Barton wishes to protect to gain 'pleasures and advantages' from the world. Where the idea of virtuous display seems to imply a one-way process in which the world is gratified by the confirmation of approved femininity in its women, the women of this asylum are apparently to enjoy a two-way traffic, gaining from the world at the same time as displaying to it.

The community of Millenium Hall seems to exhibit the movement of retreat which implies 'not a criticism of a period or structure of society, but of what can be abstracted as "the world"', and which John Mullan describes as 'a common property of novels of this period',[31] whereas Lady Barton's asylum is explicitly not a retreat from the world, but rather a way to enable women to take part in it more freely. If the development of female collective action in the novel is seen also in relation to the impossibility of describing women in terms of any kind of individualism, it becomes apparent how vital an alternative it could be. Rescuing women from the amorphous, indistinct and undistinguished mass, it restores to them the possibility of agency – an agency, what is more, within the world, not limited to the confines of a retired community. Furthermore if women, contrary to the dictates of an ideology of bourgeois individualism, can be distinguished from the amorphous mass, the possibility presents itself that the anonymous cottagers could also emerge as distinct agents.

In *The Man of Feeling*, 'the world' appears to encompass all that is unfeeling, self-interested, mercenary and deceitful – everything that Harley is not. He tells the grief-stricken Atkins that

[t]he world is ever tyrannical; it warps our sorrows to edge them with keener affliction: let us not be slaves to the names it affixes to motive or to action. I know an ingenuous mind cannot help feeling when they sting: but there are considerations by which it may be overcome; its fantastic ideas vanish as they rise; they teach us – to look beyond it. (p. 73)

As his death approaches, he has no regrets at leaving what he has called 'this world of semblance', in which he 'never much delighted'. If this view of 'the world' pervades the novel, it is nevertheless ruptured at certain moments. When the seducer Winbrooke explains to Miss Atkins that '"The world ... is a tyrant;

they are slaves who obey it: let us be happy without the pale of the world"' (p. 61), the proximity of the arguments of the sentimentalist and the libertine seems to implicate Harley in an unholy alliance with a morality seemingly quite opposed to his own. Similarly, Harley's ability to ignore the dictates of prudence links him with an economic morality equally at odds with his own views. Old Edwards believed that he managed his farm 'with prudence; I paid my rent regularly as it became due, and had always as much behind as gave bread to me and my children' (p. 87). Forced to take on a bigger area of land on the expiry of his lease, however, Edwards' management breaks down; and as a result of the land-lord's new policies, initiated by his new 'London-attorney' steward, Edwards and his family become destitute. From then on his story follows the inevitable sequence of bad to worse until Edwards, returning an old man from the army service he undertook to save his son, finds that his son and daughter-in-law have died and only his two grandchildren remain. The new commercial morality repre-sented by the London attorney values prudence as little, then, as the sentimentalist. If for the latter it becomes a mean, self-interested attribute, for the former it is simply an irrelevance in a world where profit, not prudence, counts. And in the ultimate but inevitable paradox of sentimentalism, it is all too often the cruel new morality which creates objects worthy of benevolence.

'The world' as unsympathetic and unyielding is certainly present in *Lady Barton* – for example, Louisa laments 'the rigid world' in her dilemmas over Lucan (II, 111) – but the development of female collective action and the determination not to see an asylum as a rejection of the world leads to a contrary movement of challenge. By contrast, *The Man of Feeling* finds in the world an object both of conflict and collusion. This collusive factor makes John Mullan's conclusion that the sentimental novel by 1771 had moved far from 'any politics of criticism or analysis' seem an attractive one.[32] Of Mackenzie's novels he writes, 'in their pages, the representatives of sentiment are hounded by villains and libertines who simply threaten all social virtues. Moral choice is not an issue; the novel of sentiment has actually purified itself of any vestiges of debate.'[33] The validity of this argument is endangered, however, by the way in which Mullan moves from talking specifically of Mackenzie's novels to generalising about 'the novel of sentiment'. He situates Mackenzie's work very carefully – and usefully – within its Scottish Enlightenment context, but in doing this he limits the extent to which he can apply his conclusions to the sentimental novel in general without considerable modification which takes into account the different contexts from which other examples emerge. *Lady Barton*, with its female Anglo-Irish author, cannot be assumed to follow the same pattern. The issue of moral choice, far from being irrelevant, is a crucial one here.

In *A Series of Genuine Letters*, when Frances tells Henry that custom has put courage and chastity on the same footing for men and women, she goes on to say, 'How inequitable a law that is, may be proved from this one consideration: That you have but seldom any occasion of exerting your imaginary point of honour; while poor weak women may have, every day, an enemy to combat, either within, or without; and sometimes, hard fate! may be attacked by both at once.'[34] The applicability of this observation to Lady Barton's situation is obvious: attacked from without by Colonel Walter and from within by her attraction to Lord Lucan, she suffers the worst fate which can befall a woman. In her effectual state of siege, moral choice becomes a daily activity. Some of these choices uncomfortably compromise her integrity, as when Colonel Walter writes to Lucy urging her to draw Louisa's attention to the hopeless passion Lord Lucan has patently, Walter claims, conceived for her. Challenged by Louisa, the colonel passes the letter off as a joke, and the heroine finds herself reluctantly, but 'in prudence, obliged to acquiesce with this insincere submission' (I, 92). Other choices involve embracing lesser evils in an attempt to avoid greater, as when Louisa confesses her love to Lucan as a preface to 'banishing him for ever from her sight' (II, 110–11). In each of the choices she makes, her sister and 'the rigid world' are her absent monitors; Fanny does not always approve of her conduct and loses no time in telling her why. If, as I have already argued, the dynamic of the novel forgives or exempts Louisa when Fanny will not do so, this renders the decision-making Louisa has to undertake no less crucial: she cannot finally escape the requirements of the feminine moral economy. For a woman, as Frances's comment makes clear, life can become a moral minefield in which any one step may lead to destruction.

For Mullan, the existence of moral choice as an issue in a novel clearly makes it more likely to deal with its material in a critical or analytical way than one which has no such aspect. In provisionally accepting this criterion, we see that *Lady Barton* evidently has this critical potential, since moral choice is continually an issue in the novel. This stems from the particular relation a woman necessarily has to the fantasy position 'above economy'. Where the feminised man escapes both his prescribed masculine moral economy and whichever aspects of the feminine moral economy that appear irrelevant or inconvenient, the woman has no such flexibility. And this differing position, rooted in gender but referring analogically to class, can help to explain the differing relations of *The Man of Feeling* and *Lady Barton* to 'any politics of criticism or analysis'. In opposing the bourgeois individualism which requires a property qualification for any distinction between people, with a collective response designed to restore the possibility of positive action to the undistinguished female, *Lady Barton* links gender and class to challenge the contemporary organisation of society, where *The Man of Feeling* tacitly accepts the status quo as the paradoxical condition of both Harley's existence as man of feeling and his necessary sentimental demise.

The similar decline of Lady Barton cannot be ignored, however. Her gradual progress towards death writes her firmly back into a virtuous feminine moral economy by confirming Adam Smith's proposition that a 'woman of gallantry laughs even at the well-founded surmises which are circulated concerning her conduct. The worst founded surmise of the same kind is a mortal stab to an innocent virgin.'[35] Dying, succumbing to the 'mortal stab' suffered by her innocence, becomes the only way in which Louisa Barton can finally prove her virtuous femininity. The act of death itself becomes a form of virtuous display which leads ironically to total invisibility. But this reaffirmation goes against key conclusions offered by the novel, where Harley's decline fulfils those of *The Man of Feeling*. If the end of *Lady Barton* reneges on earlier insights, it cannot efface them. Jane Spencer writes that Griffith's 'sentimental idealization of feminine purity prevents her from carrying her feminist arguments very far'.[36] In the body of the novel, however, what constitutes feminine purity becomes a subject for debate: the focusing on gender conflict becomes a strategy which addresses first the issue most immediately vital to women and then inevitably goes on to address issues of class politics – a strategy of engagement, rather than of avoidance.

The sentimental fantasy of a protagonist 'above economy' cannot then be seen as necessarily confirming the inapplicability of sentimental novels to any practical dilemma. When the protagonist is

female, her gender makes such a fiction not simply disingenuous –
it is already so just as much for Harley as it is for Louisa Barton –
but untenable; it leads to an analysis that must address social and
political organisation because it exposes the way in which women
are excluded from this organisation. Clearly, rather than having
reached 'a terminal formula', the sentimental novel certainly had
plenty more to offer the woman writer. But neither was the male
writer compelled to go the way of Mackenzie: in the final section of
this chapter a brief discussion will show how self-conscious
exploitation of gaps Mackenzie attempted to ignore allowed Sterne
in *A Sentimental Journey* the scope for critical analysis eschewed by
The Man of Feeling, and helped to indicate directions the genre
would take in the decade that followed.

> I had a strong desire to see where they had laid him – when,
> upon pulling out his little horn box, as I sat by his grave, and
> plucking up a nettle or two at the head of it, which had no busi-
> ness to grow there, they all struck together so forcibly upon my
> affections, that I burst into a flood of tears – but I am weak as a
> woman; and I beg the world not to smile, but pity me.[37]

The scene at Father Lorenzo's grave confirms perhaps more explicitly than any other in the novel, the feminisation of the protagonist
of *A Sentimental Journey*. Like Harley, Yorick rejects a masculine
economy of courage and selects only those aspects of a feminine
moral economy that suit: the sensitive body and the impulse
towards benevolence are accepted, while prudence is considered
only to be discarded. As Yorick sits feeling the Grisset's pulse, he
thinks of his friend Eugenius and muses:

> How wouldst thou have laugh'd and moralized on – Trust me,
> my dear Eugenius, I should have said, 'there are worse occupa-
> tions in this world *than feeling a woman's pulse.*' – But a Grisset's!
> thou wouldst have said – and in an open shop! Yorick –
>   So much the better: for when my views are direct, Eugenius, I
> care not if all the world saw me feel it. (p. 53)

'The world' can think what it likes; Yorick is innocent and will not
be deterred by the ideas of others – a luxury, of course, the contemporary woman could never afford.[38]

But while *A Sentimental Journey* has this much in common with *The Man of Feeling*, it does not follow that it too adopts a strategy of avoidance, rather than engagement, when it comes to critical analysis. Crucial differences in approach demonstrate that, while the use of the figure of the feminised man *can* allow the disingenuous glossing over of contradictions inherent in his, and sentimentalism's, positions, this is not inevitable.

In *Sterne's Comedy* (1966) Arthur Cash argued that *A Sentimental Journey* cannot be read accurately unless read alongside Sterne's *Sermons*. For Cash, the *Sermons* explain the *Journey*, allowing the reader to see any apparent capriciousness in the latter as consistent and reasonable when understood in the light of the former. Thus, the moral and social values the *Sermons* seek to propagate are also imparted by the *Journey*.[39] Such a reading of the *Journey* is clearly at odds with the views of more recent critics, and indeed John Mullan explicitly differentiates the *Sermons* and the *Journey* in his analysis of the novel:

> the self-induced throb which, in the *Sentimental Journey*, is the sign and pleasure of benevolence cannot easily be identified with any set of practical precepts or social obligations. Sterne's latitudinarian pronouncements as a preacher are not an immediate guide to the mingled self-attention and benevolent impulse that distinguish Yorick. In fact, Sterne encounters problems in his *Sermons* because, for didactic purposes, he has to attempt to project benevolence as a general human faculty. In the *Sentimental Journey* he avoids the difficulty of this by making it a minority experience.[40]

Here, what distinguishes the *Sermons* from the *Journey* is precisely the extent of their applicability to broader concerns: where the *Sermons* have 'didactic' purpose, the *Journey* is marked by the self-regarding irrelevance that is to prove, it is argued, the downfall of the genre.

Mullan concentrates on the way in which emphasis on Yorick's body ensures the construction of the sentimental experience as irreducibly personal and visceral; the reader of the *Sentimental Journey*, he contends, is 'made to realize that feeling is whimsical, quixotic, and simply unusual. It is not the currency of the world.'[41] As that last phrase suggests most tellingly, the conclusion that Yorick is also 'above œconomy' in the terms described earlier seems an attractive one. Yorick travels, Yorick gives, Yorick experiences exquisite feelings – all with a fine disregard for practical considerations such as where the money to pay for all these activities comes from. To quote Robert Markley once again, 'Like most eighteenth-century sentimental narratives, *A Sentimental Journey* suppresses questions about how one acquires the wealth to be able to afford one charitable act after another.'[42]

Yet a closer look at the *Journey* (to say nothing of 'most eighteenth-century sentimental narratives') suggests that this rather attractive argument does not necessarily hold good. For a start, given the number of sentimental encounters Yorick experiences, he succeeds in committing himself financially remarkably infrequently. On only three occasions does he give money charitably, and on one of these occasions he is actually *buying* something, even if something he does not strictly need, rather than simply bestowing largesse. Furthermore, the question of resources and their limitations is precisely highlighted at various points in the text, not least in the scene when, on leaving Montriul, Yorick engages in 'the first publick act of my charity in France': 'A well-a-way! said I. I have but eight sous in the world, shewing them in my hand, and there are eight poor men and eight poor women for 'em' (p. 36). What follows shows Yorick deciding which of the sixteen beggars shall receive, and which shall not. The scene becomes a kind of parody of the 'inspection' and 'enquiries' required by the Bilsons of *The Countess of Dellwyn* before they allow their benevolence to be exercised. At the end, Yorick confesses, 'I could afford nothing for the rest'; this, alongside the conventionally disingenuous claim that he has 'but eight sous in the world', suggests that far from throwing his money around in the fond belief that it will last for ever, Yorick is working within a budget of some kind.

The limitation, rather than the inexhaustibility, of resources is drawn to the reader's attention once again in Paris. On Sunday morning, La Fleur appears 'so gallantly array'd, I scare knew him':

I had covenanted at Montriul to give him a new hat with a silver button and loop, and four Louis d'ors *pour s'adoniser*, when we got to Paris; and the poor fellow, to do him justice, had done wonders with it.

He had bought a bright, clean, good scarlet coat and a pair of breeches of the same – They were not a crown worse, he said, for the wearing – I wish'd him hang'd for telling me – they look'd so fresh, *that tho' I knew the thing could not be done, yet I would rather have imposed upon my fancy with thinking I had bought them new for the fellow*, than that they had come out of the *Rue de friperie*. (p. 99; my emphasis)

Here Yorick can be seen as directly alluding to the fantasy of being 'above economy': he would have liked to have been able to maintain that fantasy, but La Fleur's comment makes abundantly clear the extent to which Yorick's economy is, by contrast, a fixed and limiting reality.

A Sentimental Journey, then, seems to work with a self-conscious awareness of the split between sentimental fantasy on the one hand and practical limitations on the other. This seems entirely consonant with the presentation of Yorick, whose ideals and actual behaviour are constantly being set beside one another in ironic contrast. For example, as has often been noticed, no sooner has he uttered the words, 'was I a King of France ... what a moment for an orphan to have begg'd his father's pormanteau of me!' (p. 4) than he sees the monk and is instantly 'predetermined not to give him a single sous' (p. 5). The irony serves, as does that of Sarah Fielding in *David Simple*, to draw attention to the gap between the ideals of sentimentalism and the ability of human beings to fulfil those ideals; but where David Simple is thwarted principally by a hostile external world, Yorick is repeatedly thwarted by his own wayward nature. The limitations on the sentimental traveller, it seems, are both practical (the source of money is finite) and emotional (the heart cannot always be relied upon to live up to sentimental expectations).

A Sentimental Journey, however, does more than demonstrate the practical limitations on sensibility; it also demonstrates the practical *value* of sensibility, going in the process some way towards refuting Mullan's claim that 'It is not the currency of the world'. For sensibility in *A Sentimental Journey* stimulates commerce as much as it stimulates charity. If Yorick gives eight sous to the poor of Montriul and a crown to the *fille de chambre*, he buys the cake from the Chevalier (p. 79), two pairs of gloves that don't really fit him from the beautiful Grisset (p. 56) and a pair of ruffles from the Grisset sent up by the *maître d'hôtel*, despite his determination to spurn her blandishments in order to take his revenge (p. 97). His purchases are purely the result of his sensibility and, like the sympathetic purchases made of Mrs Bilson by her aristocratic customers, suggest that sensibility is a commercially useful quality. More than that, there is a sense in which the financial transactions in certain cases become a replacement for the sexual transactions Yorick's sensibility might otherwise lead him into. Yorick's purchase of two pairs of gloves that will be useless to him is not an indication of his inability to deal with the commercial world – as was, for example, Moses' acquisition of the 'groce of green spectacles' in *The Vicar of Wakefield* – since he knows exactly what he is doing, and the gloves become the payment for a sexual encounter that never gets further than the look in beautiful Grisset's eyes. (The link between economically adept women and sexually experienced women is, of course, entirely maintained in this episode.)[43] Commerce in this case saves Yorick's sexual virtue, just as it is his previous gift of a crown that guarantees the safety of the *fille de chambre* in their later encounter:

> It was a small tribute, I told her, which I could not avoid paying to virtue, and would not be mistaken in the person I had been rendering it to for the world – but I see innocence, my dear, in your face – and foul befal the man who ever lays a snare in its way! (p. 66)

Thus *A Sentimental Journey* begins to develop a link between commerce and sensibility, a link partly forged around matters of morality. Neither the comedy of the *Journey* nor the manifold ambiguities of Sterne's writing allow this link to be in any sense an uncomplicated one, but the very presence of such a development suggests that the strategy of Sterne's fiction differs greatly from that of *The Man of Feeling*. It suggests too that the potential of sentimental fiction had far from run out for writers of either gender. Indeed, it is arguable that some of its most interesting possibilities were yet to find expression, as the next chapter will show.

6

'The first soft system': Commerce, Sensibility and Femininity in *Barham Downs* and *Anna: or Memoirs of a Welch Heiress*

> The minds of men are contracted, and rendered incapable of elevation. Education is despised, or at least neglected, and the heroic spirit is extinguished. To remedy these defects would be an object worthy of serious attention.[1]

So thought Adam Smith in considering the disadvantages of 'a commercial spirit'. Both Robert Bage's *Barham Downs* (1784) and Agnes Maria Bennett's *Anna: or Memoirs of a Welch Heiress* (1785) are concerned to 'remedy these defects'. In the process, each novel relies on the convergence of discourses rarely seen, thus far, as explicitly compatible: on an openly intimate and beneficial relationship, that is, between commerce on the one hand and sensibility and femininity on the other. Examining the lines of thought that enabled such a relationship to develop reveals its crucial connection with a particular tradition of eighteenth-century social theory.

As already noted in the previous chapter, in *A Series of Genuine Letters Between Henry and Frances*, Frances claims that it is the 'charms, virtue and decorum' of women 'which inspire mens [sic] hearts, refine their minds, and polish their manners'.[2] In doing so, Frances allied herself with an argument developed during the eighteenth century which linked women with culture, civilisation and social progress. As Sylvana Tomaselli has written, according to this tradition, women 'not only benefited from culture. They were its agents. They brought it about, kindled it and nurtured its advancement.'[3] Thinkers from Montesquieu and Diderot to John Millar and

William Alexander found a necessary and dialectical relationship between the improvement of society and the improvement of women's position within it. The identification of virtuous womanhood with socially and morally benign influence can of course be a double-edged weapon, as discussion of *Lady Barton* showed; in this chapter it is the terms in which this identification is couched that I want to focus upon. In *A Father's Legacy to His Daughters* (1774), John Gregory asserted that women were 'designed to soften our hearts and polish our manners',[4] while Hannah More, in her popular *Essays on Various Subjects* (1777), also claimed that the 'rough angles and asperities of male manners are imperceptibly filed, and gradually worn smooth, by the polishing of female conversation, and the refining of female taste ...'[5] Gregory and More retain the vocabulary employed by Frances, with its emphasis on a finishing process by which the raw materials of masculinity are given their final form and lustre through contact with an already refined femininity. Sensibility, a distinctively feminine attribute, is described by More, in her days of enthusiasm for the quality, as operating on the mind in a similar way:

> To melt the rich materials from the mine,
> To bid the mass of intellect refine,
> To bend the firm, to animate the cold,
> And heav'n's own image stamp on nature's gold;
> To give immortal MIND its finest tone,
> Oh, SENSIBILITY! is all thy own.[6]

This vocabulary is also precisely that employed by William Robertson in his *View of the Progress of Society in Europe* (1769), with one vital difference. Robertson is referring to the benign influence not of woman nor of sensibility but of commerce, which, he says, tends to 'wear off those prejudices which maintain distinctions and animosity between nations. It softens and polishes the manners of men.'[7] Thus commerce assumes a distinctly feminine character: it provides the finishing gloss necessary to civilise 'the manners of men'.

Such a view of the benign influence of commercial activity was not entirely new when thus expressed by Robertson at the end of the 1760s. Albert O. Hirschman traces its development from seventeenth-century France, and finds its most important expression in Montesquieu's *De l'esprit des lois*, first published in 1748 and rapidly translated into English, and from which Robertson could have taken almost verbatim the phrase 'softens and polishes' as describing commerce.[8] Of more immediate interest, Henry Brooke's *The Fool of Quality* (1765–70), a sentimental novel of much influence and popularity, also gave voice to such an attitude and warrants a brief examination at this point.

Very early in the narrative, a character later shown to possess one of the novel's two principal feeling hearts expatiates on the benefits of trade, telling an aristocrat (who is subsequently revealed to be his estranged brother) that

> [t]he merchant, above all, is extensive, considerable, and respectable, by his occupation. It is he who furnishes every comfort, convenience, and elegance of life; who carries off every redundance, who fills up every want; who ties country to country and clime to clime, and brings the remotest regions to neighbourhood and converse; who makes man to be literally the lord of the creation, and gives him an interest in whatever is done upon earth; who furnishes to each the product of all lands, and the labours of all nations; and thus knits into one family, and weaves into one web, the affinity and brotherhood of all mankind.[9]

Gone is the explicit contempt for trade embodied, for example, in the character of the rapacious and selfishly materialistic Westbrook in *Lady Julia Mandeville*; instead in this passage *The Fool of Quality* provides an apparently unequivocal and rhapsodic affirmation of commerce as a pacific, civilising activity. Yet there are problems. Finding that *The Fool of Quality* identifies 'sentimental virtue with a rising trading class', John Mullan points out that even so, 'the merchant, his wealth successfully accumulated, has to retire from the world to enjoy and communicate the full benefits of feeling'.[10] It is not simply the merchant's retirement which qualifies the affirmation of commerce, however.

Harry Clinton, second son to an earl, is apprenticed to a trader and as a result is believed by his elder brother to have lost 'all title to gentility' (p. 24). The two lose touch; Harry becomes a partner in a successful business and marries his partner's daughter, Matty. They have children, and for some years the family prosper. In the conventional manner of the sentimental novel, however, when disaster strikes it does so with a vengeance. The children die of smallpox; Matty miscarries and also dies. Her father laments that he has 'been hungering after the goods of this world' and having 'acquired all that it could give me', his soul 'like a sick stomach, disgorges the whole' (p. 208). He too dies, leaving his vast fortune to Harry:

> I now found myself in possession of near a million of money, which, however, in my disposition of mind at the time, appeared no worthier than so much lumber in a waste room. And I know not how it was, that, through the subsequent course of my life, although I was by no means of an economical turn, though I never sued for a debt, nor gave a denial to the wants of those who asked, nor turned away from him that desired to borrow of me, yet uncoveted wealth came pouring in upon me. (p. 212)

Wealth earned through trade undergoes a transmutation at this point in the narrative and becomes one with the wealth bestowed upon Allworthy in *Tom Jones* (and finally upon the hero himself, of course) as a result of birth and virtue. As the developments in the novel make clear, it also becomes part of a providential design to make Clinton the instrument of divine charity. Deliberately eschewing mercantile 'economy', he nevertheless finds himself permanently swamped by wealth which he gives away in thousands to the needy. Robert Markley identifies a key sentimental impasse when he writes, 'the more you give, the more virtuous you become, although your actions leave you with less, and therefore limit your capacity to keep on demonstrating your virtue'.[11] In this respect, *The Fool of Quality* becomes the ultimate sentimental fantasy: there are no limits, and Clinton's wealth assumes mythical proportions. His nephew Harry, whom he abducts from his father the earl in order to give him an appropriate sentimental education, tells his father on his return that he has already 'squandered away above £50,000' of his uncle's money in charitable acts (p. 346), while Clinton himself laments to a debtor attempting to repay him, 'My wealth already overflows; it is my only trouble, my only encumbrance' (p. 370).

Commerce recedes in importance for the central characters as the novel progresses: where Clinton's first wife was the daughter of a tradesman, his second wife is a French aristocrat; where the children of the first marriage die, one daughter from his second marriage survives to become the wife of a North African emperor and to provide a daughter with a suitably aristocratic pedigree to marry

Clinton's nephew. Despite Clinton's commercial experience, his family's noble blood is not mixed with a drop of plebeian blood, and such first-hand experience of trade is not seen as at all necessary for the exemplary education in sentiment and nobility Clinton provides for his nephew. In such ways – ways that will be seen to contrast with methods employed in the two novels principally under examination in this chapter – *The Fool of Quality* undercuts its own enthusiasm for commerce. Nevertheless, the palpable presence of such enthusiasm provides further evidence of changing alignments in discourses of commerce and sensibility, changes which were to become increasingly important as the century progressed.

Montesquieu's *De l'esprit*, which Hirschman finds so important in the development of ideas linking the advance of commerce with that of civilisation, is also one of the works which Sylvana Tomaselli identifies as contributing to the development of the idea that 'women were the barometers on which every aspect of society, its morals, its laws, its customs, its government, was registered': by the 1780s, she argues, it was an idea that 'had gained much ground since the publication of Montesquieu's *De l'esprit des lois* in the middle of the century'.[12] Three discourses, then, can be seen developing: one helping to bring about what Hirschman describes as 'the emergence of money-making as an honored occupation',[13] another binding woman and social progress firmly together, and a third similarly linking sensibility and the development of culture: the related and at times identical terms in which they are expressed demonstrate the existence of a vital and dynamic relationship between the three. Commerce becomes feminine and sensible, femininity and sensibility appear in this light to be commercially desirable qualities, and all three acquire central importance in the progress of civilised society.

The articulation of this relationship in Bage's *Barham Downs* and Bennett's *Anna* comes at a significant historical moment for the sentimental novel. Written in the 1780s, *Barham Downs* and *Anna* appeared at a time when sentimental works, while still enormously popular, were increasingly coming under attack.[14] This is particularly apparent in the text of *Barham Downs*, which incorporates and defuses such an attack through the opinions of both Sir George Osmond and the lawyer William Wyman, self-confessed sceptics on the subject of sensibility whose 'conversions' (particularly that of the former) constitute a major victory for the sentimental way of thinking. *Anna*, meanwhile, distinguishes between those who adopt sentimental postures simply as a fashionable accessory and those of real sensibility. The determination to define and defend a 'right sensibility' against its imitators and detractors, so much a feature of 1790s writing, was already gathering momentum. With this determination, I would argue, came a new willingness to attach sensibility to commercial values, in a move represented as beneficial to both. This development is one which disrupts earlier configurations while still depending upon them for its own defining terms. For of course, earlier versions of commerce as lacking sensibility, of feminisation as undesirable effeminacy, or of sensibility as wanting all practicality do not conveniently disappear as the century moves into its penultimate decade. However, the advent of the more recently elaborated 'softening' discourses, as I hope to show, materially changes the parameters of discussion.

Henry Osmond, the hero of Robert Bage's second epistolary novel *Barham Downs* (1784), is the younger son of a younger son of 'a family of wealth and title'.[15] His father however, like Clinton in *The Fool of Quality*, did not take up either of the usual professions allotted to younger sons – church or army – but instead became a merchant. Even when he went on to inherit the title somewhat later in life, as Henry tells his principal friend and correspondent Wyman, he retained the belief that 'it is to the exalted character of a merchant, mankind owes its opulence, its refinement, its liberality of sentiment, and all the blessings derived from these rich sources' (I, 3).[16] This wholehearted confidence in the desirability of commercial activity for the improvement of society in general, while firmly associated here with an individual entitled to call himself a gentleman, is yet at one remove from the character of the hero himself. As the younger son of a man so convinced, Henry is naturally pressed into the same career, being 'placed in an eminent house' at 18 and commencing merchant on his own account at 23 (I, 3); but he fails to achieve the success of his father, and after some years in business finally goes bankrupt. The reasons for this bankruptcy, and the terms in which it is related, are however such that the confidence of the father is not necessarily undermined by the experience of the son.

Initially, Henry represents himself to William as temperamentally unsuited to the role of the man of business, offering as proof his tendency to relieve himself 'from the fatigues of business by a few pages of Virgil or Horace...'[17] His taste for poetry marks him out as a man of feeling, but it is not this classical predilection which is cited as being responsible for the growing problems he experiences;

it is rather the 'failure of remittances from abroad' and 'other contingents' (I, 4). Having struggled for two years, he gives in: 'On the day of my surrender, many of my creditors shed tears ... . I was solicited to suffer my statute to be superseded, and two very worthy merchants offered me loans to any amount I chose. I was deaf to every overture of this kind' (I, 37). Henry manages to pay some of his debts, upon which his 'humane creditors insisted on closing the statute, and leaving me the remainder, if I could get it' (I, 37). This is clearly a financial collapse very different from those experienced, for example, by Mrs Bilson's profligate husband or the Booths. Henry is in no danger of imprisonment, nor is he hounded by heartless officers of the court. His creditors are 'humane' men of sensibility, who are moved to tears by his plight. This feminised reaction from men of business stands in obvious contrast to the rapacity of representatives of commercial values such as the 'London-attorney' who turns old Edwards out of his home in *The Man of Feeling*. Henry combines the roles of gentleman and businessman and in a reversal of expected sentimental allegiances, the sentimental community so often based around the family fails to materialise, while instead the commercial community steps in to provide the humanity and tearfulness Henry's situation demands.[18] His avaricious older brother Sir George refuses to rescue him from his difficulties, while the phrase 'other contingents' is revealed as a reference to Henry's generosity in advancing £2000 to his faithless first-love, Lucy Strode (who proceeds to marry Sir George), and £5000 for his sister's dowry (which Sir George had refused to pay). Such generosity no longer seems inappropriate for a man of business, if a definition of such a man can now include the characteristic signs of sensibility manifested by his creditors. This is supported by the way in which Henry's generosity, like that of David Simple, is carefully distinguished from profusion, a quality exemplified in the novel by the dishonourable nobleman Lord Winterbottom, who is also Henry's rival for the affections of Annabella Whitaker, daughter of the local Justice.

A positive compatibility between commerce, sensibility and femininity is also developed in Agnes Maria Bennett's *Anna* (1785), in which the genealogy of the heroine offers an interesting comparison to that of Henry Osmond. Like Henry's, her father is the son of a family of wealth and title who engages successfully in trade. He is however the eldest son, and when he falls in love with the daughter of 'a tradesman who dealt in butter and oats'[19] his noble father, the

Earl of Trevanion, is so outraged that he locks up his heir, who is then rescued by his future brother-in-law and escapes to be married and enter commerce in Jamaica. Anna's exemplary sensibility, then, which renders her heart 'naturally soft and tremblingly alive to sympathy and compassion' (II, 36), is produced by a mixture of aristocratic and commercial blood. Orphaned early in life and left by a series of accidents alone in London at the age of four, Anna is more or less providentially looked after by a number of people as an individual entirely without connections of any kind, and ends up working to support herself. Anna's parentage is unknown almost until the end of volume three, and this allows assumptions about what qualities are appropriate to which stations in life to be effectively questioned. At one stage Anna works as an assistant in the dressmaking business of Peggy Dalton, the daughter of the couple who first took care of Anna, and is visited by Mrs Wellers, a woman held in high esteem locally. Anna's arrival in the village has caused much gossip owing to her beauty and superior appearance, and Mrs Wellers visits out of curiosity: 'having no apprehensions of giving offence, where the offer of her services would so fully compensate for any transient mortification. The journeywoman of a mantuamaker could not be thought to carry much sensibility about her ...' (II, 211). The irony here is threefold. There is the obvious point that Anna is in fact so much more than 'the journeywoman of a mantuamaker' and therefore her possession of sensibility need, at least in retrospect, be no surprise. But there are the further ironies that Mrs Wellers herself is the wife of a merchant 'who had retired from trade with a decent competency' (II, 183), while Anna is both the granddaughter of 'a tradesman who dealt in butter and oats' and, for the time being at least, a mantuamaker's assistant. The secret of Anna's identity works both ways: it both confirms and denies the truth of the assumption that 'the journeywoman of a mantuamaker could not be thought to carry much sensibility about her ...'[20]

If Anna's position allows for some doubt in the compatibility of commerce and sensibility, it is that of Mrs Wellers herself which illustrates the union most unproblematically and, indeed, most schematically. Mrs Wellers becomes a crucial figure in the novel's inner circle of feeling hearts; her son, by contrast, is a man of business, 'a plain, honest, moral man' who is known for the integrity of his dealings and his 'rigid probity', but who is untouched by 'the softness and humanity, the warmth of friendship, and the entire love of virtue which softened [his mother's] whole soul' (II, 261–2). Here commerce does not appear amenable to softening; but nevertheless at the end of the novel the money concerns of all the main characters are entrusted to Mr Wellers: 'a circumstance however of equal advantage to both parties; since the large sums constantly in his hands, could not be more profitable to him, as a speculative man, than his strict probity and exact honesty, as well as invariable regularity, was to them' (IV, 271). The divide between Mrs Wellers and her son thus becomes the schematic representation of a mutually beneficial relationship between commerce and sensibility, a relationship which also demonstrates the tendency to 'think of exchange as advantageous to both parties' which Louis Dumont identifies as characteristic of societies turning away from a traditional 'disparagement of trade and money' and towards 'economics'.[21]

When Anna's ancestry is finally revealed, her mixed lineage is an issue of great importance. Mr Mordant, her newly-found maternal uncle, tells her, as he gives her her due inheritance,

'although not a Trevanion, I am a proud Briton; Lady Cecilia Edwin [Anna's paternal aunt] cannot be more anxious to preserve the honour of her noble blood, more tenacious of its dignity, or value it higher, than I do the title of a British Merchant. Inflexible integrity, industry without parsimony, hospitality without extravagance, a noble confidence in the spirit of commerce, and above all, rectitude of heart and probity in dealings, are the marks which always should, and in general do, distinguish our respectable body.

'You, Lady Ann, are nobly descended on your father's side; your mother's will not disgrace you; you must not affront a merchant by interrupting him in an act of common honesty; the money is your just right; I am too rich and too proud to accept the property of another; the uprightness of my dealings have [sic] rendered them prosperous ...' (IV, 50)

This key passage takes the kind of supreme moderation previously attainable only by such characters as Lord and Lady Belmont in *Julia Mandeville* and appropriates it instead for an apparently substantial commercial community: 'our respectable body'. It also makes clear the provenance of Anna's distinguishing qualities of independence, economic ability and hard work, none of which is shared by her wholly aristocratic cousins Hugh and Cecilia Edwin, who, like Lord Winterbottom in *Barham Downs*, are notable rather for dissipation, profusion and debauchery. Pure-bred aristocrats are also degenerate aristocrats; as Cecilia Edwin writes to her mother towards the end of the novel, 'the truth is, our blood has from generation to generation, by flowing in the same regular channel, at last wearied itself by its own sameness...' (IV, 259–60). The figure of Anna herself, in her ancestry, sex and personal experience of work, unites commerce, sensibility, femininity and nobility, and in the process revitalises the 'wearied' aristocratic blood of the Edwins with the qualities of an energetic but softened commercial character.

Anna's situation, then, displays a tension between representing a commercial position and an aristocratic inheritance. Similarly, Henry Osmond's position is contradictory. He is apparently a representative of 'the middling sort' in his commercial background and his opposition to Lord Winterbottom, and of the aristocracy in being of a family superior to Winterbottom's, 'bating my Lord's hasty slip into the peerage' (I, 244). This, I want to suggest, is because at the same moment as commerce was coming to be seen as softer, more amenable to sensibility and femininity, it was also wrestling with notions of effeminacy and honour. While appropriating the civilising and refining qualities of femininity, commercial discourses were also adopting a more masculine vocabulary of nobility and heroism, in order to combat the long-held association – clearly articulated in the quotation from Adam Smith with which this chapter began – between commerce and narrow-minded self-interest, an association which implied lack of public spirit and cowardliness.

Barham Downs sets Lord Winterbottom up as the very figure of aristocratic villainy; in doing so, however, the novel grafts onto this figure defects which are more readily recognisable as distinctive features of the commercial character than that of the aristocrat. Winterbottom's profusion, debauchery and dissipation are standard upper-class vices, but his cowardice and mean-mindedness belong to the merchant tainted by the undesirable elements of the commercial spirit as deplored by Smith. Conversely, Henry Osmond is allowed to have been 'an honourable and worthy merchant' (I, 244) while also going on to display the physical courage and daring associated with nobility. Following his bankruptcy, Henry moves to the country and changes his name to Davis, in a determination to embrace retirement. This determination is strongly opposed by both Wyman and Sir Ambrose Archer, a neighbour at Barham Downs with whom Henry becomes friendly. Where his involvement in commerce and his sensibility are represented as benignly feminising qualities, his retreat from public life is seen by his friends as unmanly – effeminate rather than feminised. When Annabella Whitaker disappears from her father's house, Henry's first impulse is simply to draw further into himself and mourn her loss. Sir Ambrose urges him to pull himself together as becomes a man:

> To sigh in secret ... to give up the reins of your imagination to sentiment and sensibility; to be a woman, when you are called upon to shew the active spirit of a man. You ought to appear in public, to counteract the malevolence of busy tongues, which will be ready enough to suggest that Miss Whitaker and you are gone together ... (I, 190–1)

This passage indicates the importance of recognising the degree and kind of sensibility that is desirable. Following this exhortation from Sir Ambrose, Henry does not cease to be a man of feeling, but he does throw off his assumed name in favour of his ancestral one, and exchange his plain dress for clothing more appropriate for a gentleman; he then challenges Lord Winterbottom to a duel. The process of providing commerce with an acceptable masculine face, then, includes an attempt to strengthen or, perhaps, in some way 'masculinise' sensibility.

On receiving Henry's challenge, Winterbottom hastily retreats to London on pressing affairs of state, and Henry finds himself reluctantly forced into a fight with Winterbottom's sycophantic companion Captain Wycherley, whom he seriously wounds. This event rehabilitates Henry in the eyes of Sir Ambrose and Wyman. Sir Ambrose writes approvingly, 'Never in my life did I see such manly sense united with such mild manners' (I, 204). This reliance on the sword to assert masculinity contrasts graphically with the scene in *The Man of Feeling*, discussed in the previous chapter, in which Harley rejects the code of masculine honour in favour of a feminine declaration of sympathy.[22] It also contrasts with the explicitly anti-duelling stance adopted in the latter half of the novel;[23] and given this, it is significant that in his letter refusing to fight Henry, Lord Winterbottom claims that to do so would be below him: 'You cannot call yourself a gentleman, when you reflect upon your past-gone occupation' (I, 199). Henry's re-emergence on the public scene as a man of courage is necessary in order to validate trade, his 'past-gone occupation', as an activity not inevitably extinguishing a proper 'heroic spirit' and certainly as compatible with calling oneself a gentleman. This point is further emphasised through the portrayal of the other principal aristocratic figure in the novel, Corrane. A younger son like Henry, he chooses the more conventionally 'heroic' occupation of soldier, but proves through his heartless treatment of Kitty Ross his utter lack of the honourable qualities possessed by the hero.

However, this process of bolstering the commercial spirit with qualities usually assigned to nobility is undoubtedly compromised in various ways in *Barham Downs*. Henry, however worthy and honourable a merchant he might have been, nevertheless retreats from commerce and is saved from the necessity of ever engaging in it again by a present of £60,000 from his reconciled and repentant brother Sir George. He is also, we are to believe, more genuinely aristocratic and from an older family than Winterbottom, who while he represents upper-class villainy is in his 'hasty slip into the peerage' not so far removed from the Mushrooms whose existence Harley's aunt so deplored in *The Man of Feeling*. Like Mackenzie's novel, Bage's work seems to be making a distinction between a venal aristocracy which colludes with unacceptable values and an aristocratic ideal represented by the late Ben Silton, 'the baronet's brother'[24] or the well-born Henry Osmond. This apparent similarity, however, in fact demonstrates how far *Barham Downs* does go in an affirmation of the commercial spirit. For in *The Man of Feeling* the unacceptable values of the new aristocracy are those of trade, whereas in *Barham Downs* they are directly opposed to any commercial code; it is the ideal aristocracy which has links with trade, albeit in a recent past rather than the present. And while a revitalisation of the aristocratic ethos has already taken place when the novel opens, it has nevertheless been effected through an infusion of the commercial spirit into the present generation via practical experience. The young Harry in *The Fool of Quality*, by contrast, is not required to serve any such apprenticeship in trade.

Anna, in a movement not unlike that in *Barham Downs*, associates commerce and sensibility in order to soften the former and then, mindful of the 'defects' deplored by Adam Smith, goes on to strengthen both. Clearly Mr Mordant's 'noble confidence in the spirit of commerce' is part of such a movement. His fortune, acquired honourably in the West Indies (the issue of slavery is conveniently ignored) is set in opposition to the ill-gotten gains of Colonel Gorget, whose cruelty and greediness in India result in quite undeserved glory and riches: 'His fame as a commander reached the country he had disgraced, and his coffers filled beyond his hopes' (I, 89). This contrast between the fortune acquired by trade and that acquired through military exploits recalls William Robertson's conviction that commerce is an antidote to 'animosity between nations' and supports Hirschman's consequent supposition that the 'image of the trader as a *doux*, peaceful, inoffensive fellow may have drawn some strength from comparing him with the looting armies and murderous pirates of the time.'[25] In both *Barham Downs* and *Anna* any conventional link between the heroic spirit and a military occupation is explicitly denied. Instead the novels present the heroic spirit as an entirely appropriate feature of the trading life.

What makes *Anna* particularly interesting, however, is that the principal vehicle employed to achieve the strengthening of commerce and sensibility is the heroine herself. While endowed with sensibilities every bit as acute as those of a Julia Mandeville or a Lady Barton, Anna is also allowed tougher and more active qualities such as righteous indignation and pride which combine with the softer elements. While her pride is an appropriate quality to have inherited from her aristocratic forebears, Mr Mordant's 'British Merchant' speech makes it clear that Anna's plebeian antecedents would also claim a share in its formation. Its utility in the defence of female honour becomes obvious in the course of the novel, as on the occasion when she is accused by the Daltons of receiving visits from a married man: 'her heart, which had been softened by her sensibility, now became stout in her conscious integrity'. This leads to the presentation of a female figure whose masculine 'calm determined voice' 'demanded to know who it was that dare accuse her', while simultaneously 'her whole frame evinced her inward disorder' in the prescribed manner of the painfully sensitive feminine body (II, 216).

This transmutation of the sensible heroine into an hermaphroditic figure can be seen again in the way the narrative deals with the question of how Anna is to support herself. In the novels examined so far in this study, the women who have actually worked (that is, Mrs Bilson and Caroline Traverse) have been characters marginal to what is ostensibly the main line of the plot, rather than the heroines themselves.[26] Amelia's offers 'to work with her hands', while highly significant, are not taken up and in any case share with the labours of Mrs Bilson and Caroline Traverse the sanction of working for the sake of the family. However unprecedented their action, and however much satisfaction they may get from their activities – and satisfaction is an evident element for them both – the ideal of the self-sacrificing wife willing to do anything for her husband and children provides a certain justification for their unconventional behaviour. Anna, on the other hand, as both heroine and single woman, is in a rather different position. Her orphaned state provides plenty of opportunities for the narrative to bewail her forlorn situation: 'she was wholly without acquaintance, destitute of friends, and had very little money: not a creature in the created space of nature could she apply to for protection or assistance ...' (III, 21). At such moments, Anna's fate seems to be wholly beyond her control; if she is forced to work to earn her bread it is a contingency thrust upon her, inescapable rather than willed. Yet this construction of the heroine as the passive victim of circumstance is opposed by an alternative version in which her achievement of paid labour is the product of her own desire for independence and is the result of choice, not necessity. In this version the vocabulary employed to describe her motivation is again that of pride, integrity and self-esteem, a masculine vocabulary which owes much to the terms of Mr Mordant's eulogy and nothing at all to a feminine discourse of melting sensibility.

This contradiction comes about by virtue of the narrative's readiness to accommodate two versions of the heroine's position. One of Anna's most stable homes is with the Mansels in Wales, where she lives from the age of 15. They refer to her as their niece, and she adopts their name. Mrs Mansel, who before her marriage was Anna's governess at the home of the Melmoths, is now the heroine's 'more than mother' (II, 51); the relationship between the orphan and both Mrs Mansel and her husband, the local rector, is represented as an ideal sentimental attachment. Despite this representation we are told even at this stage that Anna 'had a great share of pride, which often rendered the sense of her dependant situation on the charity of strangers very grievous to her' (II, 9–10). The description of the Mansels as 'strangers' to Anna is allowable in so far as they are not blood-relations; but to refer to them in this way and to find her need for their charity 'grievous' represents a marked departure from the notion of a sentimental obligation which is equally pleasurable on both sides and within which such feelings of irksome dependence must be both inappropriate and unnecessary.

A little later, the narrative tells us of Anna's conviction that 'to live always on the bounty of her friends was insupportable' (II, 45); the promotion of the Mansels from strangers to friends only throws into sharper relief the rejection of the kind of sentimental bond accepted wholeheartedly by the friends in *David Simple*. Whereas the earlier novels examined in this study identify the weakness of the sentimental obligation as being the ease with which it can be counterfeited or abused by the unfeeling and the unscrupulous, *Anna* seems to find such an obligation unsatisfactory in itself, even when both parties fulfil all the requirements necessary for the sentimental benefactor and recipient. Indeed, the very depth of Anna's sentimental attachment to the Mansels makes the obligation harder, not easier, to bear. Gratitude, far from being an integral part of the bond, becomes impossible to express adequately precisely because of the existence of financial obligation. As Anna tells the Mansels on giving them the first payment she has received for her embroidery, 'it would enable her ... to look at them without confusion, if she might but hope she should ever be able to shew them the gratitude of her heart, independent of her obligations' (II, 11). Anna's inclination towards independence can be traced back to the pride of both the aristocrat and the self-made man, but it is significant that the means for that independence are given her by a woman, and one who has known dependence herself. It is Mrs Mansel who realises how precarious Anna's position with the Melmoths really is, and who accordingly 'blended her domestic needle-work with ornamental' specifically for the purpose of making her 'an useful member of society', as 'the greatest service she could do the young creature she entirely loved' (I, 66–7).

On Mrs Mansel's death, Mr Mansel's sister comes to the rectory to act as housekeeper; her unfriendly behaviour towards Anna precipitates her leaving to attempt earning her own living. The unfriendliness, however, comes in the form of an opinion echoing Anna's own thoughts, if in a less palatable guise, for Mrs Jane Mansel 'hated to see those who are able, and having nothing of their own, unwilling to work, loitering about as if their whole business in the world was to be maintained at other people's expence' (II, 77). But Mrs Jane is not only unfriendly; she is also 'so

extremely ignorant and low bred, it was impossible to associate'
with her (II, 77). Here Anna's innate sense of breeding comes into
play. We already know that she is 'blessed with a person and
manner that stamped the gentlewoman on her appearance' (I, 170).
In the manner of so many literary orphans, Anna never needs to be
told her class position, in spite of her ignorance of her family background. Leaving Mr Mansel's protection is infinitely preferable to
living familiarly with someone so evidently her inferior.

Mr Mansel's last words to Anna as she leaves are '"Remember
you have a home, and I am your father"' (II, 81). This reminder, as
the earlier quotation illustrates, is precisely what the narrative of
the novel wishes to forget at certain moments. For when it is
brought to mind, as it is at irregular intervals, it reminds us that
Anna's destitute situation is willed, that her arrival on the labour
market is ultimately the result of choice, rather than necessity. It
has entailed a decision not to take up the offers of a haven she has
had not only from her 'father' Mr Mansel but also from Mrs
Wellers' friend, the elderly and eccentric Mr Bently. And the decision results in great satisfaction to the heroine, as the narrative
makes clear. As she completes her first piece of work in London,
the embroidering of a waistcoat, we are told that 'No princess could
be happier than Anna Mansel while so laudably employed', and
when she is promised constant employment as a result of the high
quality of her work, 'Her heart bounded with joy' and she immediately settles 'a price for her board and lodging, as beneficial' to her
landlady Mrs Clark 'as convenient to herself' (III, 195). Once again
the benign reciprocity of exchange is invoked.

The strengthening of sensibility in its relation to commerce thus
seems to involve the most comprehensive reassessment we have
yet seen of the desirability of sentimental ties and obligations when
these are (as they almost invariably are) grounded in financial considerations; and in the process, rather than promoting a narrow and
mean-spirited turn of mind, commerce becomes both the ally of
and an encouragement to laudable independence. The indirect way
in which this is approached in *Anna*, with the narrative claiming at
times that independence is an unpalatable necessity for the friend-
less orphan and implying at others that it is the result of her own
proud spirit, can be seen as a consequence of enshrining that independence in the figure of a woman. Writing of the late eighteenth
century, Janet Todd has commented that 'independence in a
woman was almost always viewed as a sad necessity, the result of

the failure of the man to provide for her, or of the woman to procure a husband'.[27] Anna's independence is obviously temporary, but the parts of the narrative which see it as willed, and as affording her joyfulness and satisfaction, nevertheless provide a challenge to such a view.

The identification between commerce and independence, and thus between commerce and qualities related to independence such as pride and integrity, not only goes some way towards 'remedying the defects' identified by Adam Smith, it also hints at a further benefit to be gained from the development of a commercial spirit, and one which has particular relevance to women. This benefit is the reduction of arbitrary and authoritarian power – an issue with which both *Barham Downs* and *Anna* are very much concerned.[28] Associated with a corrupt aristocracy, tyranny is presented as an evil which the newly civilised and strengthened spirit of commerce is ideally placed to combat.

In *Lady Barton* the woman who needed to work for her living was seen as having sunk to 'a state of servitude' – so much a victim of the 'sad necessity' of Todd's assessment that thoughts of beneficial independence simply do not occur.[29] In *Anna*, by contrast, 'servitude' of various kinds is precisely what the heroine avoids by working. On considering her options while still at Mr Mansel's, Anna concludes, 'Servitude must be her last resource; she heard there were means in the metropolis by which women of good education might earn a decent subsistence, with a tolerable appearance ...' (II, 79). Anna's antipathy to 'servitude' but desire to 'earn a decent subsistence' can be usefully considered in comparison with one of Richard Price's fundamental assertions in his *Observations on the Nature of Civil Liberty* (1776): 'In general, to be free, is to be guided by one's own will; and to be guided by the will of another is the characteristic of *Servitude*.'[30] Anna's wish to avoid servitude is the wish to avoid being 'guided by the will of another' and the submission to tyrannical power this implies; the progress of the narrative demonstrates that, at least up to a point, working, far from being equivalent to servitude, enables her to fulfil that wish.

Anna's initial faith in what the metropolis may be able to provide is not entirely justified; her predicament is essentially no different from that of the unfortunate 'Females, Fashionably Educated, and Left without a Fortune', described by Mary Wollstonecraft in *Thoughts on the Education of Daughters* (1787) and for whom 'Few are the modes of earning a subsistence ...'.[31] Anna's

first position as companion to Lady Edwin is not the humiliating experience described by Wollstonecraft; it is the ill-nature of
Madame Frajan and the jealousy of Cecilia (an upstart and a
degenerate, respectively), rather than the caprice of her employer,
which lead to her dismissal. Nevertheless, while living at
Grosvenor Square she still finds occasion to wish that she had fixed
'on a trade, whereby she might subsist, with some little claim to
independence' (II, 118). Her realisation that her skill in ornamental
embroidery offers 'a mode by which she might perhaps procure
the means of subsistence, more flattering to her pride than going to
service' (III, 182) is then followed by the joyful achievement of this
aim. It is, significantly, ornamental embroidery rather than more
functional needlework that provides Anna with the 'means of subsistence' she desires. In the same way as Mrs Bilson, Anna, a model
of frugality and minimal consumption herself, produces goods for
the luxury market.

If Mrs Bilson's position was 'essentially contradictory',[32]
however, Anna's position needs to be viewed differently, situated
as it is within a discourse attempting to reconcile commerce with
sensibility and femininity while avoiding effeminacy and cowardliness. For Anna's occupation pinpoints the cause of one of the chief
'defects' identified by Adam Smith. If in a commercial society
'among the bulk of the people military courage diminishes', this is
because 'By having their minds constantly employed on the arts of
luxury, they grow effeminate and dastardly'.[33] Clearly *Anna*,
through such figures as the heroine herself and the diligent
Wilkinson, puts forward the view that production need not be
morally pernicious and can indeed have a positive moral value. But
it is in its treatment of consumption that the novel departs
most markedly from earlier examples. In a way not dissimilar to
Julia Mandeville, *Anna* offers two models of consumption. On the
one hand there is the undesirable model, embodied in the
Fondville/Westbrook alliance in *Julia Mandeville* and in Cecilia
Edwin and Mrs Edwin in *Anna*.[34] On the other, there is the
approved model of 'moderate magnificence' exemplified by Lord
Belmont and Anna herself once she inherits her rightful fortune.
One point crucially distinguishes *Anna* from the earlier novel.
Where *Julia Mandeville* associates ostentatious consumption with
those who have made their money in trade, *Anna* associates it
directly and almost exclusively with the aristocracy. The heroine's
ability to adhere correctly to tasteful splendour[35] stems from her

connections – both familial and personal – with trade and from her experience of hard work and frugal living.

It is not just the 'servitude' implied in 'going to service' that Anna avoids by gaining a more independent form of employment, however. Perhaps more crucially, it enables her to avoid the tyranny of men: the degree to which she is harassed by their designs on her depends, quite explicitly, on her economic position. Colonel Gorget is a wealthy nabob who first meets Anna when she is only 14 and living with his acquaintances, the Melmoths. His plans to bring about her ruin fail at this stage, although he does attempt to rape the horrified Anna, and succeeds in having her thrown out of a household in which she has lived happily for six or seven years. When a few years later Gorget, now Lord Sutton, finds Anna living in Layton with the Daltons and contributing to her keep by helping Peggy, he decides that, to gain his desires, it 'was necessary to subdue her pride as well as virtue; to do this she must become dependent on him – his friendship must be indispensably necessary to her subsistence' (II, 180). Sutton's professions of friendship to the Daltons, and more decisively the generous material donations he bestows upon them, effectively secure their wholehearted support for whatever he wishes to suggest. His decision to offer Anna marriage seems irresistible to them, and her continued resistance to the proposal enrages Dalton, who hopes for all kinds of advantage from such a prestigious connection. He finally threatens to demand by law everything she owes him for her maintenance and upbringing. Sutton is of course very willing to extricate her from this predicament and only Anna's hasty flight from Dalton's house to anonymity in London saves her, the narrator assures us, from becoming 'in all probability ... the property of the man she most hated on earth' (III, 38).

The attempt to use economic pressure to enforce Anna's compliance with male desire is repeated in London by Lady Edwin's son Hugh, who discovers by chance her place of refuge. He first offers her the opportunity to become his mistress and, when she rejects that, wants her 'to suffer him to visit her as a friend, and to supply her with any money she might have occasion for' (III, 188). Such persecution becomes irrelevant once she has succeeded in finding work: 'Mr. Edwin called in vain at her door; his letters were returned unread, and every offered favour declined with resolution and consistency' (III, 195). The focus of the conventional plot of rape or seduction is displaced from the heroine's body onto her work; Edwin is just as convinced as Sutton that rendering Anna economically helpless is the key to gaining her sexual favours. Thus when his servant Bates finds an opportunity to steal the gown upon which Anna is currently working, he takes it with alacrity, 'having often heard his master curse the embroidery, as the means of her being enabled to support herself independent of him' (III, 216). In this version of the power dynamics between women and men, an economically independent woman is one over whom men cannot tyrannise. *Anna* draws up the condition of women's helplessness on unequivocally economic lines, recognising that here the economically independent woman is also defending her prescribed moral economy; the persecution from which economic strength can deliver her is quite clearly one in which sexual demands and financial 'economic' pressure cannot be divided.

Such issues are inseparable from the role women play in relation to property; the extent to which they themselves are viewed as property is a major indication of the extent of their freedom. In *Barham Downs*, Annabella apparently disappears from her father's house. Her sister Peggy admits that she knows her whereabouts, but will not reveal them because it 'would be a breach of trust'. Justice Whitaker replies,

'Suppose I had lost a horse, and the thief had trusted you with the place where it was concealed; you would not tell me because it would be a breach of trust?'
   'My sister is not a horse, Papa; nor has she been stolen.'
   'But is not she my property, Miss? Answer me that.'
   'She is your *daughter*, Sir.' (I, 252)

It is the property invested *in* Annabella which Lord Winterbottom desires, while the Justice can only see her *as* property. Yet oddly by comparison with the situation in *Anna*, Annabella's sexuality is something to which Lord Winterbottom, for such a libertinous villain, is gloriously, almost comically, indifferent. Following the rescue of Annabella from Winterbottom's retreat near Milan, Sir Ambrose writes to Wyman that she has 'escaped without dishonour' (II, 184); and later it is discovered that 'a half rusty stilletto [*sic*]' has been hidden by Annabella in a drawer with a view to self-defence had Winterbottom ever come to her room in the night (II, 216). The noble lord's sexual energies, however, are fully engaged by his Italian opera-singer mistress on the one hand and the wife of his hanger-on and accomplice, the clergyman Delane, on the other. When Delane agrees to the stratagem of making Annabella believe herself married, he also exacts a promise from Winterbottom 'that nothing should be attempted against Miss Whitaker's honour':

'It is true, my Lord yielded this point easily, and I am convinced had no desire of breaking this part of the convention; for what betwixt my damned wife (may heaven forgive me for swearing) and Signora Mantorina with whom he sleeps every night – I believe I need not be more explicit.' (II, 238)

Thus, while in *Anna* the pursuit of the heroine unites the sexual and the economic in the case of both Sutton and Edwin, in *Barham Downs* the two kinds of pursuit are at least putatively separated. Corrane's pursuit of Kitty Ross is principally in search of sexual gain, while Winterbottom's determination to marry the heiress Annabella stems from financial exigency. Clearly each kind of pursuit implies the other – Kitty's lowly economic position is the condition of Corrane's seduction, while Annabella feels, and is meant to feel, sexually threatened whether or not Winterbottom has any intention of putting this threat into practice. Nevertheless, the way in which they are separated points to a double standard of Bage's text brought about, ironically, by the very radical stance which might be supposed to challenge such anomalies. For while there is unusual sympathy and rehabilitation for Kitty after her 'fall', Annabella's sexual purity is still a fundamental element in her status as heroine – so much so that one of the first considerations of the men on rescuing Annabella, quite as important as her poor physical health and state of mental confusion, is to establish whether that purity has been tainted. Sir Ambrose takes Mrs Delane aside in order to enquire, '"Has Lord Winterbottom ... ever presumed upon the privilege of a husband?"' (II, 213). This solicitude effectively creates a new kind of double standard: Kitty's ideal purity is tainted, but as a minor character she is allowed to retain her status as virtuous woman, whereas in Annabella's case the requirements of a heroine seem to demand that the connection between virtue and the sexual act is still operative.

Kitty's story, with its radical implications, should by no means be wholly undermined, however, and it clearly belongs to the set of approaches and narrative developments within Bage's work that prompted Chris Jones to suggest that 'Bage could be called one of the major feminists of the period'.[36] Kitty comes to Wyman as a client and ends up as his wife. Wyman tells her story to Henry in letters dispersed through the novel, which effectively divide the tale into three sections, the first two 'parts' of the story ending at conventional moments of crisis in the sentimental narrative. At the end of the first section Kitty, the daughter of a surgeon-apothecary, has just fallen victim to the advances of the nobleman Corrane. The second section ends with her abduction from her place of refuge by Corrane's servants. The standard distresses of the sentimental heroine are, however, significantly altered in Kitty's story in that she falls, as an unsympathetic hearer of the story puts it, 'at the first attack' (I, 74): 'Kitty, unable to resist the flood of tumultuous sensations, gave herself up to be plundered without resistance' (I, 73). The use of the word 'plundered' – goods carried off *by force* – alongside the somewhat contradictory 'flood of tumultuous sensations' and 'without resistance' indicates the way in which, in Kitty's story, female sexuality is understood at once traditionally, as property, and radically, as having its own autonomous pleasure.

Wyman's telling of Kitty's story is quite definite about the immediate cause of her fall, and Annabella's understanding of and reaction to this cause convinces Henry of her worth: '"She sunk under the full force of her own strong sensibilities"', Annabella concludes, and asks, '"Can any other possible compulsion be half as powerful?"' (I, 74). In this respect *Barham Downs* demonstrates the radical affiliations of Bage's work very clearly. Not only is the fallen woman an object of compassion, she is also rehabilitated with a good deal more speed and less penance than, for example, the woebegone figure of Adelina in Charlotte Smith's *Emmeline*, published four years later – although as already shown it is significant that Bage has not made the final leap from dealing with the fallen woman in a subplot to promoting her to the status of heroine, a development waiting for the nineties and Mary Wollstonecraft. The gender of the author cannot be ignored here: no one was likely to cast aspersions on Bage's personal sexual morality as a result of his portrayal of Kitty, even if one contemporary reviewer was anxious about the moral position of *Barham Downs* and the tendency of its author towards 'a levity of sentiment, which hath a strong cast of irreligion and infidelity'.[37]

If the immediate cause of Kitty's fall thus validates female sexual arousal, the process of rehabilitation provides equally radical conclusions for the socially benign influence of both commerce and those who engage in it. As a middle-class girl 'plundered' by an aristocrat, Kitty's story takes its place beside many others of the period. Her much more uncommon chance for rehabilitation, however, arises from her meeting with Isaac Arnold. Arnold is a man of business and a dissenter, a Quaker apothecary, grown rich 'by my own industry; and still richer by the death of an only brother', a chemist (I, 309). It is his sensibility to Kitty's distress which provides her with a home after she has miscarried, and his care which ensures her rescue after the abduction. When Corrane's brother, Lord Cronnot, arrives to dissuade Arnold from pursuing charges against Corrane, they have the following conversation:

> 'Would it not raise the indignation of any man breathing to hear a fellow talk of hanging the son of an Earl for a little freedom with an insignificant girl?'
> 'Wouldst thou have talked in this strain, if my brother had taken the like freedoms with thy sister?'
> 'Curse your comparisons! you are taking every opportunity of putting yourself upon a level with me.'
> 'I am wronging myself then.' (II, 79)

Here again it is the aristocrat whose mind is 'contracted', who labours under prejudice and is confined to narrow modes of thinking; but the potential these ingredients have for tyrannising over the female sex is dissipated by the benign influence of a man whose affiliations are with the commercial world.

Thus the relationship between commerce and the reduction of arbitrary, authoritarian power is also represented in *Barham Downs* as having peculiar significance for women, and a similar pattern can of course be observed in the main plot of the novel. Annabella, courted and then abducted by the morally and financially bankrupt Lord Winterbottom for the substantial dowry he hopes to gain with her, is then rescued from the sway of such arbitrary power by Henry, whose duel with Wycherley has already vindicated trade as an occupation befitting a man of courage. Gary Kelly has seen figures such as Isaac Arnold and particularly Henry Osmond as examples of 'the characters whom Bage depicted as the natural enemies of his depraved aristocrats, the merchants and wealthy farmers, or at least their less work-soiled and more handsome sons.'[38] This representation of the situation needs some development and qualification, however. The provenance of the principal 'depraved aristocrats' in *Barham Downs* and *Anna*, for example, makes an interesting comparison. Winterbottom and Sutton share the position of 'mushroom' aristocrat, recently elevated to the peerage but with no noble family background to justify such an ascent. In contrast, Corrane and Hugh Edwin come from ancient families and display the arrogance of birth untempered by any idea that plebeians may have wants and needs too. It is thus new *and* old aristocrats who attempt to oppress in direct and indirect ways the representatives of 'the middling sort' in both novels. Yet these representatives themselves combine, in the key examples of Henry Osmond and Anna, aristocratic credibility and the wholehearted adoption of a softened commercial ethos, thus demonstrating the necessity of the latter in the production of individuals beneficial to society, while still clinging on to an increasingly undermined notion of aristocratic superiority. Tyrannical actions by a degenerate and corrupt nobility are opposed by an alternative which continues to replicate many of the nobility's characteristic qualities.

Furthermore, when identifying the 'natural enemies' of 'depraved aristocrats', the women in both *Barham Downs* and *Anna* are as germane to the process as characters such as Henry or Mr Mordant. Both novels explore the possibility that it is in women that the inheritors of an ideal of British 'liberty' can be found. Given the feminising of commerce, and the view that the development of commerce is an infallible antidote to the progress of tyranny, this argument needs further consideration. Tomaselli's comment that women became a social 'barometer' can be usefully recalled here. She quotes Montesquieu: 'Everything is closely related: the despotism of the prince is naturally conjoined to the servitude of women; just as the liberty of women is tied to the spirit of the monarch.'[39] As the principal victims of the tyranny exercised by 'depraved aristocrats', women become the figures who articulate most clearly the terms of a possible opposition. Indeed, as one passage in *Anna* would have it, this articulation is an inevitable function of the female mind and body, since it is 'the gentle sex, whose nature shrinks from tyranny, and whose eyes involuntarily turn from the perpetrators of unfeeling barbarity!' (I, 73). The similarity between this formulation and the descriptions given by conduct writers such as Fordyce and Wilkes of the way in which chaste women naturally 'shrink' from sexual advances, confirms the extent to which tyranny for women meant sexual dominance.[40] Such assertions also provide explanations for why Annabella, even before she knows any details of Winterbottom's corrupt and sordid life, is wholly averse to his proposals. In addition, they provide a context for the views and role of Annabella's sister Peggy.

Deceived by the plausibility of Lord Winterbottom, and seduced by the prospect of having a countess as a daughter and a title for himself, Justice Whitaker becomes, in his violent insistence that Annabella marry Winterbottom, both an extension of aristocratic tyranny and an example of the unreasonable exercise of paternal authority. Annabella, while horrified at the thought of marriage to Winterbottom, also prefigures Miss Campinet in *Hermsprong* (1796) in her determination to adhere to a strict notion of filial duty. It thus falls to Peggy to take up the significance of her father's demands, if in a playful manner. She leads him to ask, '"What! are you ripe to dispute a father's authority?"', and replies,

> 'No, indeed Sir; none they can show a good title to. But I am told there are people in the world at this day, who make a doubt whether a father can lawfully put his daughter to death.'
> 'What then, impudence?'
> 'Why, it is death you know Sir, to marry a young lady to a man she hates ...' (I, 115)

It is significant that this active resistance is transferred from the figure of the heroine to that of her sister; the active measures the heroine takes at key points in the narrative of *Anna* provide a clear contrast to the essentially passive behaviour of Annabella in *Barham Downs*, in which, as Gary Kelly writes, 'eventually the conspiracy of arranged marriage, that cardinal iniquity of women's romantic fiction ever since *Clarissa*, is overthrown, not by rebellion, but by stoic endurance and virtuous candour, the traditional recourse recommended to women.'[41] Transferring the resistance to Annabella's arranged marriage from Annabella herself to Peggy constitutes a kind of displacement similar to the way in which Kitty's virtue is allowed a wider latitude: it tempers but cannot entirely efface the impact of the resistance. Peggy's continual sparring with her father, then, can still be read as a gesture of support for assertions such as Richard Price's, that 'The tendency of every government is to despotism ... . Opposition, therefore, and resistance, are often necessary.'[42] Making a connection of this kind involves an acknowledgment of the close relation between the private and the public announced in the words of Montesquieu above; and such an acknowledgment is brought to bear directly on the action of *Barham Downs*. Attending a masquerade in London, Annabella sees Folly and Harlequin enact a charade in which Folly gives the following advice: 'My son, DECEIVE – and GOVERN. It is the maxim of the day. Courts adopt it, and men believe' (II, 4). Knowing as we do that Lord Winterbottom's 'integrity – has been at court' (I, 8–9), the parallel between a corrupt policy imposed on a nation and the stratagems used to deceive Annabella is not hard to make. It is not merely a static parallel, however. If the dialectical relation between the position of women and the state of society is taken into account, each becomes in some sense a product of the other: while women are subject to such tyranny, the nation will suffer authoritarian government, and vice versa.

The existence of such a relation is also clear in *Anna*. 'Deceive and govern' is essentially the maxim operating within the Daltons' marriage, in which Dalton, in order to maintain his influence over his wife, 'had, indeed, been as particularly careful to guard every sentiment of his own which would lessen her confidence in his religious practice from her as from the rest of the world, which, from her disposition was easy enough to effect ...' (II, 206–7). Acknowledgment of the close relations between state policy and women's liberty is provided overtly in the text through the use of a standard political vocabulary specifically associated with questions of government and the position of the individual: 'passive obedience and non-resistance he had long taught her ...' (II, 206). The implication that such quintessentially Tory principles lie behind the unpalatable methods of one of the novel's chief villains further justifies seeing Anna's active resistance to tyranny as a politically liberal, even radical, development in the text. Such a conclusion must be made with reservations, however, and this is clearly illustrated by the novel's treatment of Anna's first significant personal encounter with a potential tyrant.

Madame Frajan, who replaces Mrs Barlow (on her marriage to Mr Mansel) as the governess at Melmoth Lodge, is 'Ignorant, haughty, and ill-bred; commanding, with an air of insolent pride, those, who not being used to such manners, scorned to obey' (I, 123). Anna's antipathy to Frajan arises from at least two sources. As with her dislike of Mrs Jane Mansel later on, it is based partly on an immediate recognition of Frajan's innate inferiority in class terms; it is also fuelled by an automatic distaste for all things

French and an association of French nationality with lack of hygiene, immoral conduct and vulgarity. Such class consciousness and xenophobia are not restricted to any one strand of eighteenth-century political thinking, but here they serve to demonstrate that a rhetoric of resistance ('scorned to obey') is not always attached in the novel to a politically radical agenda. The additional association of France and tyrannical government becomes in this instance simply a vehicle for an implied comparison between an unfortunate, enslaved other and a 'free' Britain.

An ideal of British liberty, then, can function in two ways. It can serve as a myth which promotes the patriotic association of Britain and freedom in all circumstances – the kind of myth ripe for exploitation when convenient by political groupings of any persuasion. As Janet Todd writes, the English of the mid-eighteenth century 'thought of themselves as peculiarly free from despotism ... peculiarly just in their laws ... and peculiarly egalitarian' whatever the evidence to the contrary. And while this clearly effective idealisation of British liberty was 'especially a Whig phenomenon', by mid-century the acceptance of both parties of 1688 as a watershed for British freedom makes it difficult to draw distinctions.[43] However, such an ideal of liberty can also serve as a myth which raises – at least in theory – the political status of women. In this usage of the ideal, women become the bearers of a broadly liberal version of liberty, their condition being (to refer once more to Tomaselli's vocabulary) the barometer which measures its health throughout society in general and in government in particular. Both *Barham Downs* and *Anna* draw on this model, despite their differing political affiliations – a difference which bears examination, as it points up the dangers of assuming necessary and uncomplicated correlations between political radicalism and radical conclusions on the status and role of women on the one hand, and political conservatism and conservative conclusions about women on the other.

Criticism of Bage has always seen him as a radical author. Gary Kelly's *The English Jacobin Novel* (1976) identifies him as one of the earliest of a group of 'jacobin' novelists whose common features included opposition to tyranny in any form, a belief that all distinctions between men not based on moral qualities or virtue were irrelevant, and a conviction that 'reason should decide the issue in human affairs and human government, not power based on money, age, rank, sex, or physical strength'.[44] More recently, Chris Jones in *Radical Sensibility* (1993) has discussed Bage's novels (although not

Barham Downs) in terms of their use of sensibility, concluding that
'Bage never loses contact with the benevolence of sensibility or its
basis in a "naive" response of personal feeling, despite his attacks
on conservative and degenerate sensibility.'[45] The difficulty of
pigeonholing all beliefs as specifically 'radical' or 'conservative' is,
however, acknowledged by Jones and usefully drawn attention to
by Peter Faulkner, who comments:

> the question as to which attitude is the radical one cannot be
> answered unequivocally. Many radicals were optimistic about
> the effects of commerce in creating a more flexible kind of
> society, while at the same time their ideal community (as can be
> seen in Rousseau) was often small and uncompetitive … [Bage's]
> indecisiveness is within a range of radical ideas.[46]

It is obviously therefore important (and indeed useful) to recognise
'a range of radical ideas' rather than formulating any hard-and-fast
rules to determine what constitute radical beliefs. As already seen,
Bage's novels undoubtedly do provide opportunities for the expression of views within such a range: a further striking example in the
context of this study can be found in the support *Barham Downs*
gives to the radical appropriation of 'economy'. The recommenda-
tions of economy found in earlier novels carried contextual connections with the advice to be found in conduct literature. Links
between the private (and usually feminine) sphere of this form of
economy and the public domain clearly existed, but principally by
analogy. In *Barham Downs*, on the other hand, economy is firmly tied
to 'national œconomy' and thus to the later meaning of the word,
'managing the resources of a nation to increase its material prosperity'; the advocates of economy are now middle-class radicals setting
themselves up against a luxurious, aristocratic government. The
terms are familiar, but the alignment has changed, as will be seen.

In Volume I of *Barham Downs* Lord Winterbottom is in favour at
court, a wholehearted and, of course, wholly villainous supporter
of the current administration (explicitly identified as that of Lord
North, which ran from 1770 to 1782 [I, 85]). When asked by Justice
Whitaker whether ministers should not pay more attention to
economy, Winterbottom replies:

> National œconomy, my dear Sir, is a very childish term. How can
> it have escaped the penetration of a man of your sagacity, that

the more the government spend, the greater circulation is produced; and the greater the circulation, the wealthier and happier,
the body of the people. (I, 82–3)

Crudely as this theory is expressed, it is essentially a simplified
version of the theory of circulation, as put forward by Adam Smith
in *The Wealth of Nations*. Capital, Smith explains, can be either fixed
or circulating, but every fixed capital 'is both originally derived
from, and requires to be continually supported by a circulating
capital'.[47] The difference between Winterbottom and Smith is, of
course, that while believing that wealth creation depended on circulation, Smith was no advocate of the growth of the public debt,
which is the key point at issue here.[48] There were indeed writers
who supported Winterbottom's argument; the French writers
on economics, J. F. Melon and Isaac de Pinto, for example,
both maintained that the public debt supported 'circulation' and
thus advanced a country's prosperity.[49] It may seem inconsistent,
moreover, that writers favourable towards commerce such as
Bage should find an extension of such movable wealth into the
public domain unacceptable. However, as Hirschman shows, their
objections were political:

> It turns out in fact that their criticism stemmed from the same
> basic concern over the excesses of state power that had led them
> to a *positive* assessment of the increase in other types of movable
> wealth, such as bills of exchange. The latter types were welcomed
> by Montesquieu and others because they were expected to con-
> strain the government's willingness to engage in *grands coups
> d'autorité*. But this ability, and governmental power in general,
> could only be enhanced if the treasury became able to finance its
> operations by going into debt on a large scale.[50]

Thus opposition to the public debt becomes an integral part of
Richard Price's necessary opposition to tyranny, and consequently
part of the radical programme. It is quite consistent, then, for the
Government speaker in the mock parliamentary debate on the
whereabouts of Folly, which takes place at the masquerade, to find
her 'dealing out her high-flown principles of liberty from the press;
or in taverns or coffee houses. You will find her distributing plans
of œconomy, and teaching a nation the arts of a miser. In short, you
will find her any where – but here' (II, 11). The advocacy of

economy has become identified with the extra-parliamentary activities of the radicals. In his *Observations on the Nature of Civil Liberty*, Richard Price included a significant appendix, 'Containing a State of the National Debt' and urgently recommended 'putting the national debt into *a fixed* course of payment ... subjecting to new regulations, the administration of the finances; and establishing measures for exterminating corruption and restoring the constitution.'[51] Lack of economy (meaning both frugality and prudent management) in national affairs endangers 'the constitution' and thus liberty. Economy, then, has moved from representing private restraint to symbolising, and comprising the key condition of, national freedom.

The satirical framework within which most of the overt political comment in *Barham Downs* is placed prompts consideration of how far such a framework adds to or detracts from the power of the critique. Certainly bathos is a feature of the polemical passages in *Barham Downs* and such a strategy in Bage's work has been seen as reinforcing 'the idea that the romantic plot rather than the political subtext is the primary purpose of the work'.[52] Sir Ambrose Archer attends a meeting, 'called an association, the object of which is ... to call upon Parliament with a loud voice to redress our grievances'. He communicates these grievances with characteristic humour – 'our representatives endanger their healths – by too long sitting' – and concludes that the 'result of all our wit, and all our argument, was petition, and then – we went to dinner' (I, 274–5). Clearly such bathos underlines the difficulty of effecting reform and can also seem to suggest a certain futility in the attempt to do so, but it need not result in the total eclipse of the political by the romantic. The extent to which his contemporaries recognised Bage's work as actively supporting the radical viewpoint needs to be remembered. As Peter Faulkner points out, contemporaries certainly regarded *Hermsprong* primarily 'as a political work'.[53] It is not the general political radicalism of Bage's work that I wish to query, but rather the extent to which his female characters benefit from it.

The general political tendencies in *Anna* are perhaps at first sight less easy to identify. The active promotion of commerce and the 'Tory' affiliations of the villain Dalton are compatible with a radical outlook, while the novel's final drawing of the heroine back into a neo-feudal Wales can be seen in the same light as the conflict between the commercial ethos and the small ideal community in *Barham Downs*. The public life of Lord Sutton, too, bears similarities to that of Lord Winterbottom. We learn how, having ruthlessly acquired his vast fortune in India, Sutton 'had purchased a borough, and bought off his petitioning opponent; he had taken his seat in the senate, and made a speech there, which called forth the civility and attention of the minister ...' (I, 97). While Sutton is clearly at one with the administration, Sir William Edwin, a far more upright figure in every way, is in opposition: 'Though no person living (the prime minister for the time being excepted,) ever found an enemy in Sir William Edwin, he was a constant railer at taxes; not because he paid them, but because his friends did; the country party was sure of *him*' (I, 234, emphasis in original). The identification of Sir William, who is an exemplary and benevolent landlord, with country ideology, and the morally bankrupt Sutton with the court interest, seems to have remarkable radical potential for a novel prefaced by a fulsome dedication to Queen Charlotte, until it becomes clear that *Anna* makes a subtle but definite distinction between the court and its servants.[54] In *Barham Downs*, the court is wholly corrupt: it both corrupts those who go there and draws to it corrupt individuals. In *Anna*, by contrast, the court is the seat of virtue – 'the brightest in the known world' (IV, 57); but it is being invaded by undesirable elements.

The accession of Colonel Gorget to the peerage provides a case in point. The narrator concedes that her reader may find it hard to believe that such a villain should be 'graced with the favour of a virtuous Prince', but explains that this anomaly came about 'some how or other by dint of his interest with Lady Waldron' (II, 137–8). Lady Waldron has already been encountered in Volume I, an aristocrat of dubious virtue who recommends the villainous Madame Frajan 'as the most proper person in the world' to become the Melmoths' governess. She is part of the degenerate aristocracy to be replaced by the revitalised line represented by Anna. At the close of the novel, Anna's husband Charles Herbert (now Lord Trevanion) 'by degrees, divested Sir William Edwin of his prejudices, and changed his opposition to the minister, into a patriotic zeal for the good of his country, and the honour of his prince, which he at length convinced him were synonymous terms' (IV, 272). Thus the oppositional stance given some credence earlier in the novel is subsumed into an orthodox 'patriotic zeal', and Lord Trevanion, 'a watchful and independent guardian of the privileges and benefits of the nation at large' (IV, 272), becomes a late example of the omniscient great man, able to see and judge all correctly from his unique vantage point. His benign influence ensures that an ancient landed interest, reinforced by commercial contact, will prevail over both degenerate aristocracy and undesirable upstarts.

In some ways then, *Anna* bears a striking resemblance to that exemplary conservative novel published nearly 30 years later, *Mansfield Park*. The revitalising of Mansfield with the youth of Portsmouth, early schooled in 'hardship and discipline',[55] parallels the revitalising of degenerate aristocratic blood with a hardworking commercial variety which takes place in *Anna*; the errors of Sir Thomas are close to those of Sir William, the ill-judged education of their children in each case being the key to their subsequent disappointment. Even the views of the 'enthusiast' Bently look forward to the influence of Evangelicalism on the later text.[56] Where the novels part company is in their treatment of commercial values. The Crawfords, with Mary's 'true London maxim that everything is to be got with money', represent a rejection of commercial attitudes, as 'speculative, acquisitive, calculating, and irreverent', in Tony Tanner's words.[57] This is a far cry from *Anna*'s careful bringing together of 'speculative' and right feeling individuals. It is this difference between Austen's work and Bennett's which demonstrates how *Anna*'s political position is complicated; for while in many ways the novel can be seen as taking part in a specifically conservative tradition of women's writing, the attitude to commerce and the use made of it to support a model of women as bearers of liberty and monitors of social and moral health point in a different direction. For if women are to act as society's barometer they must be visible. Once more there appears to be a possible tension between an ideal of retirement as the natural position for women and a need for female display to serve a specific function.[58] The way in which *Anna*'s approach to this problem differs from that of *Barham Downs* brings into focus their divergent conclusions about the position of women.

The reconciliation of display with virtue in *Anna* reveals, as might be expected, a pivotal role for commerce, which in turn is intimately connected with ideals of femininity and liberty. When Anna leaves the Daltons to escape a forced marriage with Lord Sutton, Bently makes many efforts to find her. He is supported in this by Dr Collet and Mrs Wellers, until Hugh Edwin's appearance at the Daltons' house to collect Anna's clothes seems to confirm that she is now being kept by him. They accordingly conclude that 'they had been too sanguine in the acquittal of Anna, who, however blameless hitherto, had, at last, entirely forfeited all claim to esteem' (III, 190). The condition attached to any aid is unblemished virtue; once virtue has been tarnished, all possibility of help is withdrawn, whatever the details of the situation. Bently withholds judgement a little longer, but when he sees Anna at the window of a house which Edwin's manservant is known to visit frequently,

> he had almost given her up, when the woman of the shop, addressing her husband, remarked how industrious that poor sick young woman was. 'She is now,' added she, 'poring between the lights, – no wonder she looks so ill; – poor thing, I am sure she does not eat the bread of idleness.'
>
> This caught his attention – and seeing a bill for a two pair of stairs front room to be lett [sic] to a single man, he immediately took it, and mounting to his new lodging, had then watched our heroine, till he was convinced her own labour supported her, as he overlooked her whenever he pleased. (III, 257–8)

Thus the display of commercial activity is the means by which Anna's virtuous femininity and freedom from undesirable masculine influence is confirmed. Commerce provides her with liberty in enabling her to support herself independently; and it is that very independence which protects her virtue, a connection of some importance which sanctions the 'willed' aspect of Anna's independence discussed earlier.[59] However, the display, paradoxically, is private; Anna fulfils the crucial condition without knowing that she is doing so. In contrast, the public display to which Anna is subjected at her trial is, in keeping with her femininity, almost overwhelmingly distressing and the arrival of the father-figures of Bently and Mr Mordant is necessary to save her from being thrown into jail. The narrative recognises the importance of display, but simultaneously continues to associate the heroine with the requisite feminine shrinking from such an ordeal.

The necessity of the careful negotiations by which display, via commerce, is rendered compatible with virtue in the case of the heroine is demonstrated by the way in which display is also strongly linked to the morally degenerate characters of Mrs Edwin and Cecilia Edwin. In their case, display becomes purely, to use Harriet Guest's phrase, 'worthless conspicuousness', indicating their complete lack of moral rectitude.[60] As 'a woman of fashion', 'the admiration of the multitude' is of paramount importance to

Mrs Edwin, leading her to insist on continuing with her social engagements when decency requires giving them up as a sign of respect on the death of Mr Herbert (III, 152–3). The subsequent appearance of Mrs Edwin and her sister-in-law at the opera results in their receiving such condolence from friends that they are made to feel, 'in pretty plain terms, the indecency of their appearing in public while the affair was so recent'. Public display, however, is still open to them, should they choose it; it is from 'private and select parties, and in places where women, whose presence carried propriety with it' that they find themselves excluded (III, 164). Along with this unfeminine desire for public exposure goes an implicit rejection of the woman's essential role, that of 'softening and polishing' the manners of men. Having ostentatiously embraced sensibility for its dramatic potential as teenagers, Cecilia and Mrs Edwin fail to maintain its values:

> they both set out determined to be heroines of the sentimental passions; but fine cloaths, fine company, and fine jewels, with the very fine speeches of a few as fine beaus, totally overthrew the first soft system, and introduced an inordinate love of dress, pleasure, and admiration; sensibility was banished and the finer feelings were no more. (II, 119–20)

Married to the libertinous Hugh Edwin, and 'not in the possession of her husband's affections', Mrs Edwin 'despised the ridiculous advice of her mother-in-law, and scorned to court, where her vanity told her she ought to be courted' (III, 107). This failure, not only to reform her wayward husband, but even to make any attempt to do so, confirms Mrs Edwin's fallen status. Hugh Edwin, like Sir William in *Lady Barton*, could also be seen as culpable in failing to draw out his wife's virtuous femininity, but the behaviour of Mrs Edwin, who takes quite literally Lady Barton's oddly incongruous statement, 'dissipation must now be my resource',[61] deprives her of any sympathy. Her dismal end as an alcoholic married to a miserly husband provides suitable punishment.

Display in *Anna* thus exhibits the kind of duality which might be expected, given the competing demands of an ideal of feminine retirement on the one hand, and the role of women as monitors of social and moral health on the other. In *Barham Downs*, however, slightly different imperatives are at work. In some respects, the divide seems clear: Annabella's virtuous preference for 'domestic stillness' and the pleasures of the needle, reading and familial relationships (I, 110) is contrasted with the addiction to the fashionable life possessed by Lady Osmond and Lady Connollan. Once again, women who embrace this life relinquish their 'softening' role: Lucy rejects Henry because his financial generosity bodes ill for her spending power once married, and Henry tells her, 'The woman who wants sensibility, Lucy, wants a woman's principal excellence' (I, 31). As a corollary, Lucy's domestic skills are also found wanting. As Lady Osmond, she neglects the management of Sir George's household and, when challenged, tells him that she superintends his household 'as ladies of quality generally do' (I, 94). Her elopement with Lord Connollan is only one of a series of affairs which naturally follow from this dereliction of feminine duty. The vocabulary employed reveals where the different women stand in relation to display. While in London, Annabella is pressed to attend a masquerade; although reluctant, she agrees, but 'no persuasion could induce me to render myself conspicuous by dress' (II, 1). Lady Osmond, on the other hand, outfaces her shame when accidentally confronted with her husband while accompanied by her second lover, O'Donnel. In Henry's words, 'It is impossible to have made a finer retreat. The true quality manner was conspicuous through the whole of it' (II, 41). For Annabella, 'conspicuousness' is to be avoided at all costs; for Lady Osmond, it is an inevitable consequence of her position.

However, Annabella has another duty to fulfil, that of virtuous display. Not only does she appear unwilling to take this on, but in addition the narrative makes it virtually impossible for her to do so. Once abducted by Lord Winterbottom, and living in the same house as him, she tells him he has given her two choices: 'To live secluded and lose the world's esteem; or to marry your Lordship, and lose my own.' She has decided to 'embrace the first as the lesser evil' (II, 162). The decision which she is forced to take would seem necessarily to deprive her of the womanly roles of registering society's health and improving men's morals: if she is not visibly virtuous these cannot function. Yet shortly after this, when she has been rescued from Lord Winterbottom, her illness affects Sir George 'with a flood of new and softening sensations' (II, 189), while Henry asks her to marry him regardless of what the world thinks of her prolonged residence with a known libertine. Clearly this outcome is consistent with a standard sentimental rejection of 'what can be abstracted as "the world"';[62] it can also – given the happy result of the rejection in this case – be seen more positively as an attempt to release women from enslavement to appearance, a more modest way in which Annabella, as heroine, can benefit from some of the relaxation in severity enjoyed by Kitty Ross. But, ironically, in giving the female individual more latitude in behaviour, women as a whole in society lose ground. Rejection of 'the world's' values reinscribes women more firmly than ever within the private sphere, without influence beyond the small sentimental circle such as the one which centres on Barham Downs at the close of the novel. In rejecting the world's scruples over feminine sexual purity Henry does not injure himself; he has already proven his ability to fulfil the world's requirements for the masculine moral economy. As a man, he can enjoy continuity between his position as an individual and his public persona; Annabella, on the contrary, is forced to choose one or the other, she cannot have both. If this is a 'realistic' conclusion, it is also a gloomy one.

Thus the lack of neat correlation between political radicalism or conservatism and corresponding conclusions about the status and role of women becomes clear. For in *Anna* the seemingly conservative acceptance of the 'worldly' convention that a woman must display her virtue, because it is done via commerce, also gives the heroine a role in the public world of beneficial exchange. While her active participation in this world is admittedly temporary, she retains the symbolic function of such a role even when her days of productive labour are over. Janet Todd has written that in *A Vindication of the Rights of Woman* (1792), Mary Wollstonecraft

> made an unusual attempt to associate the new self-reliant woman she envisaged with the entrepreneurial self-made man of the middle class, the man who owed nothing to the privilege of birth and who made wealth rather than consumed it. But this idealisation of the thrusting mercantile personality was untypical of women, whose utopias tended to follow the model of the conservative communal *Millenium Hall* rather than the individualistic *Wealth of Nations*.[63]

In the light of this study, however, this association is one which might be expected given the entrepreneurial spirit of Mrs Bilson and the economic abilities of Ophelia, Amelia, Anne Wilmot and Tabitha Bramble. The positive presentation of the association in *Anna* – albeit with obvious modification on such issues as 'the privilege of birth' – thus provides further justification for seeing a specific line of writing mainly by women which makes connections of precisely this 'unusual' kind between women and commerce, women and economic dexterity. In *Barham Downs*, the radical process of civilising (feminising) and simultaneously strengthening (masculinising) commerce is done wholly through the male representative, but in *Anna* the association of this process is almost entirely with the female line – through the heroine herself, and her mother's family. Whatever the political affiliations of the novels in other respects, *Anna* is finally more optimistic than *Barham Downs* about the possibility of women influencing and taking part in public affairs.

While *Anna* differs from *Barham Downs* in this respect, however, both novels studied in this chapter demonstrate the extent to which the sentimental novel in the 1780s was still able to provide new material and new connections. If sensibility was shifting its allegiances and modifying its features, this indicates its ability to adapt and endure rather than its imminent demise. Whatever the iconic significance of *The Man of Feeling* as the critics' archetypal sentimental novel, on the evidence of *Barham Downs* its publication did not prevent male novelists from using the genre in ways which allow for social and political criticism. And while *Anna* does not – indeed cannot – avoid the dangers of accepting a model which ultimately relies on the efficacy of benign feminine influence as the basis of women's access to power, in its brief portrayal of the virtuous heroine as an independent producer, it allows the sentimental novel to broaden significantly the parameters of what is possible for women. Yet by the end of the century sentimentalism's course was largely run, and it is therefore on the effects of 1789 and the decade that followed that attention must now be focused.

7

'The mild lustre of modest independence': Economies of Obligation in Novels of the 1790s

'"I am determined not to live in a state of dependence,"' declares the unprotected Miss Forbes in Helen Maria Williams's novel *Julia* (1790). In doing so, she raises a brief but unfulfilled hope that she will follow Anna's example and earn her own subsistence, thus embodying what Mary Wollstonecraft saw as 'the true definition of independence'.[1] But Miss Forbes finds it very difficult to provide herself with '"a proper situation"' (II, 192); hounded out of the house of her now dead benefactress by unsympathetic treatment, she discovers that living in lodgings leaves her a prey to persecution from the unprincipled (and married) Mr Seymour, and so in her desperation accepts an offer of marriage from Captain Meynell. It is as Mrs Meynell that Julia meets her, displaying 'sweetness of temper, exemplary resignation, and uniform submission to [her husband's] will', despite his 'sordid meanness, vulgarity, and ill-humour' (II, 201–2). Such expressions of the desire for independence, followed by the failure to translate this desire into reality, come to be a feature of novels by radical women in the 1790s. The difficulty of defining (and finding) 'a proper situation', given the varied implications of that phrase – work suitable to the seeker's station in life, consistent with propriety and commensurate with her abilities – becomes a key problem for those writers attempting to free their female characters from feminine dependency and endow them instead with a masculine independence.

Julia, of course, was actually in the process of composition during the months which saw the first events of the French Revolution; the fall of the Bastille breaks into the novel in the form of a poem supposedly written by a former inmate of the prison (I, 268).[2] If radical novelists in the 1790s encountered even more problems than were faced by earlier writers, in the endeavour to solve the dilemmas surrounding dependence and independence for women, this is symptomatic of the changes in the political atmosphere caused by the Revolution and the subsequent progress towards war with France in 1793. Words which have been of central importance in unravelling the workings of sentimentalism and contemporary economic analysis are, in the 1790s, still more fraught with contested meanings as a result of the overt politicisation of all forms of writing (even, of course, those writings penned by women protesting the utter unsuitability of the female mind for political analysis).[3] Both *Anna* and *Barham Downs* have already shown the ways in which the sentimental novel could be used to comment on forms of government and political organisation; the analogical use they make of private for public (and vice versa) becomes in the following decade the mechanism by which writers of all persuasions find indications of national importance in the stories of private individuals, or implications for the organisation of all private lives in the actions and destinies of governments. In novels of the nineties, the sentimental heroine becomes the figure for the vulnerable nation, the rake the carrier of the pernicious ideals which will bring about her downfall.[4]

Obligation, dependence and independence become terms of particular significance in the revolutionary decade because of their contemporary association with forms of government. Obligation and dependence, on the one hand, belonged to a conservative, Burkean ideal in which 'our state, our hearths, our sepulchres, and our altars' are cherished 'with the warmth of all their combined and mutually reflected charities',[5] a view essentially supported by Hannah More, in her *Strictures on the Modern System of Female Education* (1799), when she writes:

> Now it is pretty clear, in spite of modern theories, that the very frame and being of societies, whether great or small, public or private, is jointed and glued together by dependence. Those attachments which arise from, and are compacted by, a sense of mutual wants, mutual affection, mutual benefit, and mutual obligation, are the cement which secure the union of the family as well as of the state.[6]

On the other hand, independence was crucial to the ideal of social organisation (or lack of it) put forward by the radical William

Godwin in his *Enquiry Concerning Political Justice* (1793), in which it is stated that 'the most desirable state of mankind is that which maintains general security, with the smallest incroachment [*sic*] upon individual independence.'[7] Thus the lines of the debate seem drawn up: certainly use of the words 'dependence' and 'independence' became a significant part of the apparatus by which writers identified themselves – and others – as politically conservative or radical.

The by now common currency of the terms 'conservative' and 'radical' in describing political allegiances of the 1790s tends, however, to give an oversimplified view of the situation. While the Revolution and subsequent war with France certainly contributed to a sharp polarisation in political opinion, the temptation to view the unique pressures of the period as producing a simple binary opposition between radical and conservative must be resisted. As other critics have pointed out,[8] this view overlooks assumptions and aims shared by commentators on both sides of the debate: the need for improvement in women's education, for example, asserted so forcefully by both Wollstonecraft and More. This point has been made most fully with regard to sensibility by Chris Jones in his book on the 1790s. In arguing that 'the ideological complexion of eighteenth-century sensibility is far from consistent', he goes on to suggest that Wollstonecraft, 'as well as most of her critics, has difficulty distinguishing clearly between the conservative and radical senses of sentimental terminology' so that different trends are often found 'uneasily cohabiting within the same text'.[9] I would endorse this view entirely, and argue further that examination of the significance of the concepts of dependence and independence, and their relationship with both sentimental and economic discourses, reveals the extent to which the labels 'radical' and 'conservative', while by no means redundant, yet require considerable qualification if the ideological tendency of individual writers is to be at all accurately assessed. In the discussion that follows, I shall continue to use the terms 'radical' and 'conservative' to describe writers and their views, along those dividing lines which have indeed been conventional since the 1790s themselves;[10] but I shall also attempt to demonstrate ways in which these divisions have failed to pick up other configurations of opinion, configurations which may find the 'radical' writer side by side with the 'conservative'.

If mutual dependence became a hallmark of conservative ideology in the 1790s, it was also, as my previous chapters have made clear, the ideal of the sentimental community well before it became a popular theme with conservative writers. Mutuality was seen as the desirable – indeed, natural and inevitable – state of society by both kinds of writer, notwithstanding the fact that the purveyor of 'sentimental' vocabulary became one of the first objects of attack for conservative polemicists as the decade wore on.[11] The 'mutual obligation' so commended by More arguably also sums up the sentimental philosophy and recalls the position of the Bilsons with Lady Dently in Sarah Fielding's *Countess of Dellwyn*: 'This Family, equally happy in obliging and receiving obligations ...'.[12] If this is the ideal state of affairs, however, the sentimental novel, as has been seen, more often than not deals with much less agreeable arrangements. In these, dependence is exposed as not necessarily mutual at all but frequently distinctly one-sided, involving humiliating submission and total reliance on the whims of a more powerful individual. This is one of the analyses that reveals the existence of radical potential in sentimentalism: rather than the confidence evinced by Burke and More, that mutuality works in all societies, 'whether great or small, public or private', the fear of the sentimental novel has been that a model of society as mutually dependent breaks down at the very moment when it attempts the transfer from private to public, from a small group of like-minded friends to that notoriously hostile body, 'the world'. Thus dependence as mutuality, whether purveyed by writers more usually labelled 'sentimental' or 'conservative', can become a convenient cloak for its less palatable forms (an operation, as subsequent discussion will show, particularly in force with regard to contemporary attitudes towards the poor). The revelation of dependence as humiliating submission, however, characterises a particular tradition of the sentimental novel, the two possible sentimental conclusions about dependence (the optimistic and the pessimistic or, perhaps, the conservative and the radical) being conveniently exemplified in the two parts of *David Simple*, as discussed in Chapter 2.

Dependence provides a link between sentimental ideals and the beliefs of those conservative writers who were (ostensibly at least) attacking them. Attacking sentimental postures was not an activity limited to conservatives, of course; in her study of sensibility Janet Todd describes how

[t]he radicals, on their side, were just as eager as the conservatives to align sensibility with their opponents, and they attacked as sentimental the reactionary nostalgia and emotional callous-

ness they saw promoted in the *Anti-Jacobin*. Clearly neither side wished to be left in possession of a now unfashionable sensibility, but neither side wanted to abandon entirely the power of emotive, sentimental language.[13]

It was not only the attraction of the power afforded by 'emotive, sentimental language' which ensured that the modes of 'a now unfashionable sensibility' were still very much in use, however. Referring to Todd, Nicola Watson suggests that 'radicals were interested in conserving some part of the revolutionary potential of sensibility'.[14] Conservatives were also concerned to retain sensibility, suitably modified, as a vital component in their construction of femininity. Indeed, even while radicals questioned the definition of female virtue, the conservative emphasis on sensibility as the quality which defined and validated the virtuous woman was one that they were frequently unable to escape. The contest over sentimentalism in the 1790s consists not simply in which group can heap the most opprobrium on an outmoded and politically suspect movement, but also in which group can successfully appropriate the elements of sensibility most useful to its purposes. Novels of the decade demonstrate that, while the terms 'sentiment' and 'sentimental' come in for a great deal of criticism, 'sensibility' escapes relatively unscathed. Criticism of 'affected sensibility', with its obvious implication that 'unaffected sensibility' exists and is to be preferred, leaves open the way for novelists from Wollstonecraft to Jane West to allow their heroines 'sensibility', albeit hedged round by appropriate provisos.[15] Sensibility is thus involved in a tug-of-war which regularly pulls individuals from one camp into the other. Significantly, this is an effect which can also be seen to result from the treatment of commerce.

The rhetoric of mutuality in which the enthusiasm for dependence is often expressed is also common to the discourse of economic analysis in the period, a point which has already been the subject of some discussion in Chapter 4. The radical Thomas Paine thus has views on commerce which incongruously echo the terminology of his ideological opponents in his stress on 'the mutual dependence and reciprocal interest which man has upon man'.[16] In this guise commerce allies itself with dependence, but there is, as *Anna* has shown, an important version of commerce which wishes to strengthen the feminine character of a commercial model based on dependence and thus sees itself as intimately related to a masculine independence – the version mediated through the figure of the 'British Merchant' and exemplified in the character of Mr Mordant. Again we have an incongruous agreement of terminology, this time between the Godwinian and commercial affirmations of independence. Godwin's attitude to trade was unenthusiastic to say the least, but which view of commerce – his condemnation, or Paine's promotion of it – is to be seen as the 'radical' point of view on the subject is by no means obvious. Partaking, depending on the context, of both dependence and independence, commerce thus provides a crucial illustration of the inadequacy of the categories radical and conservative, and it is frequently in their attitude towards commerce that writers reveal the complexity of their political allegiances.

Paine's views on commerce, for example, are clearly indebted to the development, discussed in the previous chapter, of a discourse which represented commerce as feminine, as a softening and civilising influence on human society. In his *Rights of Man*, commerce is pacific, facilitating 'the unceasing circulation of interest, which, passing through its million channels, invigorates the whole mass of civilised man'.[17] His fellow radical Godwin, however, did not go along with this opinion. While his ideas on many subjects may have struck his contemporaries as dangerously innovative, Godwin's attitude to trade is perfectly familiar, drawing as it does on a long tradition which saw commercial activity as fostering narrow self-interest and deadening the finer faculties.[18] Given the polarity of Paine's and Godwin's views, identifying a definitively 'radical' attitude towards commerce is clearly no simple matter. It is certainly a mistake to suppose, for example, as Kelly does in a note to *The Wrongs of Woman*,[19] that Mary Wollstonecraft unreservedly shared Godwin's point of view on this subject. The spectrum of radical opinions offered her far more choice and, as I hope to show, wholesale condemnation of commerce was never as simple for a woman writer as it was for her male counterparts, whatever her political sympathies.

If the change in political atmosphere caused by the French Revolution loaded words such as 'dependence' and 'independence' with added significance in the decade that followed, specific political views aired from 1790 onwards also threatened to undermine the very basis of sentimentalism. The advent of theories of rights so changed the dynamic of the benevolent action as entirely to alter its nature. Mary Wollstonecraft sounded the keynote of this development in her *Vindication of the Rights of Men* (1790):

> If the poor are in distress, [the rich and weak] will make some
> *benevolent* exertions to assist them; they will confer obligations,
> but not do justice. Benevolence is a very amiable, specious
> quality; yet the aversion which men feel to accept a right as a
> favour, should be rather extolled as a vestige of native dignity,
> than stigmatized as the odious offspring of ingratitude. (empha-
> sis in original)[20]

Clearly in this version of assistance for the poor, the obligation is all
on the side of the donor; the recipient has a right to expect such aid,
and thus the donor has a duty to provide it.[21] Wollstonecraft does
not at one sweep do away with all the distinctions which had previously applied in the distribution of charity. She implicitly retains,
for example, the distinction between the deserving and undeserving in her view that it is only the 'industrious' poor whose misery
demands assistance as a 'birthright'. Yet the vicious are not thereby
denied aid – their fellow-men 'ought to forgive, because they
expect to be forgiven'.[22] Ironically, however, Wollstonecraft's
radical departure from orthodox notions that the poor must be
grateful for whatever their superiors see fit to bestow upon them
impels her towards a rhetoric of social organisation which has clear
affinities with that used by the sentimental and conservative
models she is challenging: 'charity is not a condescending distribution of alms, but an intercourse of good offices and mutual benefits,
founded on respect for justice and humanity.'[23] Mutuality, as in the
Burkean model of society favoured by Hannah More (or, of course
Paine's version of commerce), is still the desirable end; but its foundation 'on respect for justice and humanity' differentiates
Wollstonecraft's ideal from that of her conservative opponents
because it implies the belief that equality is achievable in this life. In
Burke's view, absolute equality was not only unattainable but also
undesirable; inequality was part of the natural order of things and
established in 'the order of civil life … as much for the benefit of
those whom it must leave in an humble state, as those whom it is
able to exalt to a condition more splendid, but not more happy.'[24]
    In a sense Wollstonecraft's recognition of the unjust nature of
benevolence had been foreseen by the sentimental novel itself
which, as I have already pointed out, frequently sets up an ideal of
mutual obligation only to demonstrate in the narrative that follows
the numerous ways in which this ideal fails to materialise. But
while sentimentalism could thus be sufficiently self-reflexive to

identify its own shortcomings, it was also ultimately inclined to greet such evidence against its own ideals with expressions of resignation in the face of a higher authority, or simply to overlook it entirely in the process of providing an orthodox 'happy ending', rather than making overt demands for those ideals to be altered or given up. This tendency does not neutralise the power of the contradictions and gaps uncovered in the course of sentimental novels, but it can successfully contain them. Theories of rights provided the language with which to make these demands, but the way in which such language was used, or left unused, in novels by writers of apparently radical tendencies in the 1790s demonstrates the power that traditional sentimental models still retained.

Thomas Holcroft's *Anna St. Ives* (1792), for example, attempts to bring new discourses of perfectibility, rationality and equality into the sentimental arena. And benevolence is one of the areas on which these new discourses are brought most significantly to bear. As with Wollstonecraft, the former dynamics of obligation are challenged: Anna writes to Louisa Clifton that her brother Coke

> seems oppressed, as it were, with a sense of obligation to Frank; which the latter endeavours to convince him is wrong. Reciprocal duties, he says, always must exist among mankind; but as for obligations, further than those, there are none. A grateful man is either a weak or a proud one, and ingratitude cannot exist; unless by ingratitude injustice be meant.[25]

'Obligation', in the oppressive sense in which Coke Clifton is supposed to feel it here, is bound up with society's unequal distribution of wealth. Ideally, all should be 'equally obliged to labour for the wants of nature, and for nothing more', bringing to an end 'the present wretched system, of each providing for himself instead of the whole for the whole' (p. 209). In such a situation, benevolence in the sense of provision for those who have nothing by those who have much ceases to have meaning and becomes instead 'that spirit of universal benevolence which shall render [mankind] all equals' (p. 172).

Anna St. Ives, however, deals with the problem of the existence and relevance of a utopian theory in an imperfect world – the problem with which *David Simple* had to deal and which, arguably, all sentimental novels address. In a letter, Coke reports Frank Henley's opinion 'that what the world calls nature is habit' (p. 96);

the novel itself goes on to demonstrate that recognition of this is not enough on its own to challenge the strength of such habit. If the views expressed by Anna, Louisa and Frank seem to imply the demise or radical alteration of sentimental values, Frank's virtue is still revealed and confirmed in sentimental style through traditional acts of benevolence; and while he may reject the notion of 'obligation' in theory, in the current state of society his benevolent actions confer obligations in practice and thus render him powerful. Indeed his very unwillingness to recognise this contributes to the maintenance of his power. Sir Arthur, Anna tells Louisa, explains to Frank that 'we were all his debtors; very deeply; and he should be happy to find any mode of discharging the obligation' (p. 251). In protesting that he wants nothing, Frank effectively keeps the balance of power in his favour. 'Obligation', then, is more easily argued away in theory than in practice. Even if they attempt to overcome the feeling, and explicitly regard it as misguided, characters in *Anna St. Ives* still interpret benevolent actions as putting the burden of obligation onto the recipient, and as conferring the advantages of the situation on the donor.

In spite of this reliance on the traditional sentimental model, however, the novel retains its essential optimism. Coke is not given up even after events have proved him capable of the most vicious acts, including kidnapping and murder. The kind of irony seen in earlier sentimental novels seems not to be working in the same way here; Anna and Frank retain both physical and mental strength throughout their ordeals and are not reduced to figures of oppression in the same way as the Vicar of Wakefield or David Simple. *Anna St. Ives* tests new theories against old situations and, while it does not find them infallible, neither does it ultimately reject or lose faith in them. Its publication date of 1792 might provide external reasons for this: supporting principles associated with the French Revolution was not yet as unpopular as it was to become. By the time Elizabeth Inchbald's *Nature and Art* was published in 1796, its political content had been toned down,[26] and its ending can be seen as showing the effects of the reaction to the Terror, as it effectively turns its back on the radical views developed in the early part of the novel.

Like many earlier novels, *Nature and Art* exposes the absurdity of supposedly civilised contemporary society through the introduction of the *ingénu*. Brought up in Africa, young Henry sees through uncorrupted and unsophisticated eyes; his thoughts and words correspond directly as, 'strongly impressed with every thing which appeared new to him, [he] expressed, without reserve, the sensations which those novelties excited'.[27] In this uncontaminated state, it is the duty to feel 'obligation' with which the poor are burdened that strikes him as 'the greatest hardship of all'. When asked to explain himself by Lord Bendham, whose benevolence to the poor extends to a 'gift' of a hundred pounds during the frost at Christmas, Henry replies that it seems to him to be a hardship '"that what the poor receive to keep them from perishing should pass under the name of *gifts* and *bounty*. Health, strength, and the will to earn a moderate subsistence, ought to be every man's security from obligation"' (pp. 265–6) This point of view merely raises a smile from Lord Bendham; but given that young Henry, in a fashion characteristic of the novel in the 1790s, is already established as very much the centre of moral authority in the novel, 'obligation' is clearly presented as something it is desirable to avoid rather than a condition involving pleasurable sensations of any kind. When, at the close of the novel, young Henry and his father form 'an humble scheme for their remaining life' it is 'a scheme depending on their *own* exertions alone, on no light promises of pretended friends ...' (p. 372). Their plan is expressly designed to avoid the miseries of obligation to apparent 'benefactors', as experienced by David Simple. Independence is chosen in preference to the hazards of dependence. But this apparently radical allegiance to independence runs side by side with a tendency to idealise both self-sufficiency as 'cheerful labour' productive of golden age contentment (p. 373) and even poverty itself as vastly preferable to wealth, since the poor have nothing to lose and, not possessing any things of this world to which they can become mistakenly attached, need have no fear of dying (p. 374).

The independence recommended at the end of *Nature and Art* has much in common with that advocated by Malthus two years later in his *Essay on the Principle of Population* (1798), in which he severely criticised the Poor Laws as providing the poor with a disincentive to save and as encouraging men 'to marry with little or no prospect of being able to maintain a family in independence'.[28] Malthus appropriates a potentially radical rhetoric of independence to serve his purpose of demonstrating the futility of attempting to improve the condition of the poor through external benevolence. The process of social amelioration is not a political process but must rather be accomplished by means of the internalisation of certain values on the part of each individual. The Poor Laws – and indeed any other schemes designed to provide the poor with subsistence – stifle rather than encourage such a process of internal improvement:

> The love of independence is a sentiment that surely none would wish to be erased from the breast of man: though the parish law of England, it must be confessed, is a system of all others the most calculated gradually to weaken this sentiment ... . Hard as it may appear in individual instances, dependent poverty ought to be held disgraceful. Such a stimulus seems to be absolutely necessary to promote the happiness of the great mass of mankind; and every general attempt to weaken this stimulus, however benevolent its apparent intention, will always defeat its own purpose.[29]

Seen in this context, the final pages of *Nature and Art* clearly inculcate a distinctly reactionary morality, despite Inchbald's 'Jacobin' sympathies.[30] The suggestion that the poor have a 'right' to relief is transmuted into the assertion that such relief saps their ability to support themselves and is thus simply an encouragement to idleness. In the name of independence, all forms of assistance are withdrawn from the poor.

Where Inchbald's novel moves from espousing a radical discourse of rights to urging what is in effect the opposite of this, Jane West's *A Gossip's Story, and a Legendary Tale* (1796), published in the same year as *Nature and Art*, is written overtly from the standpoint of a 'conservative moralist'[31] determined from the outset to demonstrate the futility of such views. *A Gossip's Story* concerns itself with dependence and independence, and with the ways in which these relate to commerce and sensibility. As Marilyn Butler has pointed out, the novel 'has attracted notice for its obvious similarities with Jane Austen's *Sense and Sensibility*':[32] two sisters, Louisa and Marianne – of whom Marianne, the younger, is 'tremblingly alive to all the softer passions' (I, 19) – have to decide on the suitability of the various men who court them. The results demonstrate, in Butler's view,

> that objective evidence should be preferred to private intuition ... . And if feeling is an unreliable aid in choosing a husband, it is equally wayward as a general guide to conduct. Instead of the doctrine of the cultivation of the self, Mrs West recommends

humble, selfless service of others. Moreover, she urges a lowering of expectations, a scepticism about the rewards available in this life.[33]

I cannot entirely agree with this assessment, however. Written, as the preface informs the reader, with the intention of illustrating 'the Advantages of CONSISTENCY, FORTITUDE, and the DOMESTICK VIRTUES; and to expose to ridicule, CAPRICE, AFFECTED SENSIBILITY, and an IDLE CENSORIOUS HUMOUR',[34] *A Gossip's Story* signals its conservative allegiance while clearly allowing the possibility of 'true sensibility', reliable 'private intuition', to linger on – a possibility, in my opinion, then fully endorsed by the text. I would argue rather that *A Gossip's Story*, no less than *Sense and Sensibility*, wishes to retain many of the aspects of the 'feeling heart' under certain conditions[35] and that, in West's novel at least, this has a crucial relationship with the commercial life.

Louisa and Marianne's merchant father, Mr Dudley, seems to be a true heir to *Anna*'s Mr Mordant: 'Mr. Dudley possessed in an eminent degree the virtues of the head and the heart. Blessed with the early advantages of a liberal education, he united the character of the true Gentleman with the no less respectable name of the generous conscientious merchant' (I, 13–14). With its equal weighting of 'gentleman' and 'merchant', there is no hint here of the view that the latter occupation is more usually the pursuit of narrow-minded, self-serving individuals. Moreover, Mr Dudley's position as a merchant who has lost most of his accumulated wealth through misfortune makes him particularly well placed to provide a counter to Godwin's characterisation of the rich man who is so only '"From the accident of birth, or from a minute and sordid attention to the cares of gain."'[36] In answer to Louisa's arrogant (and ultimately rejected) suitor Sir William Milton, Mr Dudley replies,

'If by reminding me of the profession I once followed, you mean to throw any reflection on the general character of a British merchant, you rather expose your own want of information respecting the resources and wealth of this empire, than discredit me. I glory in having stimulated the industry of thousands; increased the natural strength of my country; and enlarged her revenue and reputation, as far as a private individual could. My fall has not been accelerated by vice, extravagance, or dishonesty ...' (I, 182)

Thus Mr Dudley argues that his career in commerce has been one devoted to the public good, not personal gain; his personal loss of fortune cannot undo the good his work has done for 'this empire', and indeed is no hardship to him except insofar as it affects Louisa's prospects, since Marianne is already safely provided for by a substantial inheritance from her grandmother.

The rhetoric employed around the figure of the 'British Merchant' in *A Gossip's Story* is clearly reminiscent of that used in *Anna*, and, like *Anna*, West's novel explicitly links commerce with an independence desirable because it is bound up with approved virtues such as fortitude and hard work. This independence in the novel exists side by side with the notion that society is and should be ordered on a Burkean model of dependence involving 'mutual wants, general imperfection, and universal kindred' (I, 49). Of himself and Louisa, Mr Dudley tells Lord Clermont, father to Marianne's future husband, '"Both of us, my lord, have independent spirits"' (II, 33). In Mr Dudley himself, independence goes quite plausibly with his character as an honest and industrious merchant: he writes to Louisa, again in terms strikingly similar to those of Mr Mordant, '"Integrity is no less the character of an English merchant than enterprise"' (II, 173). Louisa, however, is not given the opportunity to demonstrate her independence in so masculine a way as active participation in commerce; unlike Anna she does not display her honesty and enterprise in any remotely commercial venture. Instead, the inheritance of the mercantile 'independent spirit' bequeathed to her by her father is internalised as self-control. Self-control in the novel then effectively becomes an acceptably feminised version of independence. Where in *Anna* the female protagonist takes on independence in what is perceived to be its masculine form, *A Gossip's Story* appropriates independence for women by rendering it suitably internal, bringing its influence to bear not upon the external world but upon the potentially refractory female psyche.

The importance of internalisation is demonstrated by the way in which Marianne, emotionally dependent on the chimerical idealisations of love and marriage which she has imbibed through her voracious reading of 'memoirs and adventures' (I, 37), is nevertheless financially independent, having complete control of the fortune left to her by her grandmother. Marianne's emotional dependence is, of course, attributable to her sensibility or rather, crucially, to 'sensibility indulged till it became a weakness' and the related tendency to adhere to 'a romantick standard, to which nothing human ever attained' (I, 46–7). As is usual with her erring heroines, West insists that Marianne's 'heart was really excellent' (I, 106); it is the indulgence of sensibility, not the possession of it, that spells her downfall. The vindictive Lady Clermont terms her daughter-in-law's 'sensibility and refinement, affectation' (II, 147), but the narrator is careful never to question Marianne's sincerity, only her wisdom. The consequence of Marianne's emotional dependence is, however, to render her financial independence ineffective; the money goes where her overindulged sensibility leads her – that is, into an ultimately disastrous marriage, thus leaving her dependent on both counts.

Louisa, on the other hand, is presented as far from well-off financially, but emotionally self-sufficient. Explaining the situation to Sir William, Mr Dudley 'feared he could rate her value at little more than a mind, which would not be destitute of comforts, even in depressed circumstances' (I, 58). This financial deprivation, however, turns out to be relative. If Louisa does not have Marianne's splendid fortune, she does possess Seatondell, a small estate in Lancashire left to her by her grandfather. Residence at Seatondell allows Louisa to display the practical benefits of her freedom from emotional dependence on unattainable ideals. Although it is described as lacking rustic charm to compensate for its modest size and income, Louisa determines to make the best of the estate, encouraging her father in his plans for 'agricultural improvement' (II, 55) and engaging in much charitable work in the local community, despite the fact that the 'inhabitants of Seatondell certainly presented no very alluring qualities to a polished mind' (II, 59). Having proved her capacity for 'œconomy and management' (I, 190) and her ability to stay cheerful under trying circumstances, Louisa is finally rewarded with the love of Mr Pelham, originally a suitor to Marianne but the man for whom Louisa has cherished a suppressed regard throughout her stoical residence at Seatondell.

Yet this narrative of female self-control in which independence has become chiefly an internal principle rather than an external activity, and in which the suppression of private inclination is rewarded, is not unambiguous. Early on, the narrator explains that 'Louisa had so little sentiment, that she was more inclined to laugh at her sister's apprehensions, *than to pour balm into the wound*' (I, 53; emphasis in original). This lack of sentiment, however, is applicable only because Marianne's 'apprehensions' are foolish; given the appropriate occasion, Louisa is quite capable of providing material for a sentimental tableau. On being told of Sir William's proposal of marriage, for example, she 'sunk upon her knees, and clasping her father's hands, with eyes swimming in tears, and looks full of anxiety and consternation, exclaimed, "My dearest Sir, do not marry me to Sir William Milton"' (I, 60–1). Subsequently, Louisa takes an heroic decision to accept the proposal, telling Mr Dudley, '"You have convinced my reason, Sir"'; although her horrified realisation that she is falling in love with Mr Pelham, still courting Marianne at this stage, is given as a key ingredient in this supposedly rational decision. Sir William is then discovered to have kept a mistress while an army officer in the Indies, and to have left their children cruelly deprived of any support; Louisa's 'private intuition' on first meeting him is thus revealed as a much more reliable guide to character than the 'objective evidence' available at the time. Far from demonstrating the dangers of allowing feeling to guide judgement, this story validates such a way of proceeding – always providing, of course, that the sensibility involved is of a moderate, restrained variety and not overindulged as Marianne's has been. Describing 'those sentiments of pious sorrow' experienced by Louisa and Mr Pelham at the death of Mr Dudley, the narrator asserts that they 'were elevated and devout, and a feeling mind may easily conceive them' (II, 206); the appeal is to those with 'right feeling' as opposed to those with no, or false, sensibility. In the context of the novel it is Lady Clermont, not Marianne, who falls into the latter category. While clearly contrasted, Louisa and Marianne are separated not by kind or degree of feeling but by the degree of control they are able to exercise over it.

Louisa's internalisation of independence enables her to reconcile an idea of independence with specifically domestic qualities: its innovative tendencies are thus effectively contained. Her 'œconomy and management' are strictly confined to her estate and are described in exemplary conservative terms. *A Gossip's Story* allows women the possibility of a limited autonomy at the apparent price of vigilant self-control; the temporary (and often private) breakdown of that vigilance at key moments, however, enables Louisa to demonstrate her capacity for feeling, a capacity essential to render her attractive in the eyes of Mr Pelham. In many ways the novel provides a demonstration of Laetitia Matilda Hawkins' conservative proposal that 'the true and only source of happiness is in ourselves, that it has nothing to do with external circumstances, that by those who know the secret of possessing it, it is unalienable, and by those who seek it in the world unattainable ...'[37] Using a strategy clearly related to that employed by Malthus in his argument about poor relief, this perennial argument against social change is articulated in West's novel through an appropriation of independence, rather than an attack upon it. And where *Anna* challenged the gender specificity of dependence and independence by endowing the heroine with a supposedly 'masculine' independence, *A Gossip's Story* defuses the threat of independence by showing that in a woman the principles it supports are the internally directed ones of fortitude and self-control, not externally directed ones such as pride in economic self-sufficiency.

Other women writers were not contented with such a limited, internal autonomy, however. They wrestled with a desire for significant economic independence which had also, like West's position, to be worked out in the context of attitudes to and relationships between commerce and sensibility, dependence and independence. Furthermore, self-control, the product of the internalisation of independence used so shrewdly by West and Malthus, was also an issue with which radical women were concerned. Before turning to one of the key texts of the decade in these respects, Wollstonecraft's *Wrongs of Woman*, I want first to discuss Mary Hays's *Memoirs of Emma Courtney* (1796) and the novel written in part as a 'reply' to it, Charles Lloyd's *Edmund Oliver* (1798). Together, they usefully exemplify some of the particular problems that surface with even more urgency in Wollstonecraft's work.

The heroine of *Emma Courtney* is the product of an unhappy alliance between the aristocracy and commerce, in an interesting contrast to the successful union of aristocratic and commercial heirs in *Anna*. Her father is 'of a superior rank in life' and possesses accordingly the appropriate vices (he is 'dissipated, extravagant, and profligate'); her mother, daughter and 'sole heiress' to a rich trader, was prompted by all the wrong motives (that is, by vanity and self-love) to marry him and paid the price by dying in childbed twelve months later.[38] As a result, Emma is brought up by her uncle and aunt, Mr and Mrs Melmoth, an exemplary bourgeois couple who display both the industry and economy necessary for a successful commercial career and the sensibility and fondness for literary pursuits indicative of a liberal and civilised outlook on life. Despite this combination of qualities, however, the description of her uncle indicates that he is not, as Mr Dudley was, a straight-forward successor to Mr Mordant:

> My uncle's cheerful and social temper, with the fairness and lib-erality of his dealings, conciliated the favour of the merchants. His understanding was superior, and his manners more courte-ous, than the generality of persons in his line of life: his company was eagerly courted, and no vessel stood a chance of being freighted till his had its full cargo. (pp. 11–12)

It is noticeable that Mr Melmoth is specifically distinguished from 'the generality of persons in his line of life', even if it is that very distinction which ensures his commercial success. In the process, commerce as an activity *per se* retains some of the 'narrow' qualities its critics discovered in it, although at this point in the novel the qualities associated with a civilised existence can nevertheless combine harmoniously with a commercial life to render it both more socially acceptable and more profitable. Significantly, however, the confidence to be found in *Anna* and *Barham Downs*, and indeed *A Gossip's Story*, that the commercial 'line of life' in itself creates and promotes the development of a civilised society, is clearly lacking.

Disaster inevitably strikes to destroy this picture of prosperity. Mr Melmoth dies, his ventures suffer unprecedented losses and his wife dies a few years later. Emma's solid bourgeois commercial upbringing might suggest that supporting herself through her own labour as Anna did would now be the natural way forward. But Emma's position is complicated in various ways. Her aristocratic father is able to leave her a small fortune – or rather, a 'small pit-tance … insufficient to preserve me from dependence' (p. 31). The fortune *is* sufficient to preserve her from destitution, however (the crisis necessary to justify the heroine taking up independent employment), and confirms Emma's social position on the outskirts of gentility. Her status in the various houses she inhabits – the Mortons', Mrs Harley's, her cousin's – is not strictly that of a dependant. Indeed, she writes to Mr Morton 'to enquire on what terms I was to be received by his family. If merely as a visitor for a few weeks, till I had time to digest my plans, I should meet, with pleasure, a gentleman whose character I had been taught to respect; but I should not consider myself as subject to controul' (p. 32). Thus Emma is oddly situated: not rich enough to feel herself wholly independent, neither is she poor enough to be fully dependent (or indeed poor enough, as Anna was, to be conveniently driven to independence).

Awkwardly positioned as she is, two other factors jeopardise Emma's hopes of independence. One is her sensibility. Janet Todd has described *Emma Courtney* as 'an actual sentimental novel which purports to be a warning against sensibility',[39] a description which could equally apply to other novels written in the 1790s, but which succinctly points out the way in which sensibility in *Emma Courtney* is deplored for its weakening effect on self-control and yet retained as the absolute indicator of moral worth.[40] The advice of her dying aunt had been, '"Endeavour to contract your wants, and aspire only to a rational independence; by exercising your faculties, still the importunate suggestions of your sensibility"' (p. 27), while Emma's Godwinian mentor Mr Francis exclaims, 'Why will you thus take things in masses, and continually dwell in extremes? You deceive yourself; instead of cultivating your reason, you are fostering an excessive sensibility, a fastidious delicacy' (p. 48). If the definition of what constitutes a 'rational independence' is open to debate, it is nevertheless clear that Emma's keen sensibility is seen as responsible for much of her misery because it drives her to ask more of life and other people than it, or they, can offer, at least in the prevailing dispensation. Her father, Mrs Melmoth and Mr Francis all encourage Emma to suppress this excessive sensibility, the view they offer differing from that of the narrator of *A Gossip's Story* in the distinctively radical appeal to the rule of reason as the justification for their attitude. Emma appears to acquiesce in this judgement intellectually while finding it difficult to do so emotionally, a situation which frequently results in painful internal conflict: 'I struggled to subdue myself – I stifled the impetuous suggestions of my feelings, in exerting myself to fulfil the duties of humanity ...' (p. 151).

The phrase from *Julia* discussed at the beginning of the chapter encapsulates the second problem: the range of 'proper situations' for Emma Courtney is more limited than that available to Anna; it almost certainly does not include that of ornamental embroiderer, since Emma's overwrought sensibility requires her independence to be gained in a way compatible with her perception of her abilities. She deplores the dependent condition of women, asking 'Why was I not educated for commerce, for a profession, for labour?' (p. 32);[41] she makes it clear however that she does not wish simply for employment, but for appropriate employment, explaining that she is 'ever desirous of *active and useful employment*' (p. 35) and hinting in a conversation with Augustus 'at my wish *to exert my talents* in some way, that should procure me a less dependent situation' (p. 74; my emphases). When Emma eventually becomes destitute (on the failure, significantly enough, of her attempt to secure independence by purchasing an annuity), her melodramatic outburst – 'I will go to service – I will work for my bread – and, if I cannot procure a wretched sustenance – *I can but die!*' (p. 167) – recalls the pessimistic lamentations of women in *The History of Lady Barton* rather than the satisfaction gained by Bennett's Anna in working for her bread. The horror of servitude is one shared by both Anna and Emma,[42] but the definition of the term seems to have become broader for the later heroine. Whereas for Anna servitude meant specifically going into service – working for another, rather than for yourself – the above quotation seems to indicate that for Emma 'going to service' is not appreciably distinct from 'working for my bread'; for her, the important distinction lies between working for bread and exerting talents. The former is still essentially servitude; only the latter deserves the name of independence. This distinction is then further complicated by the situation of Augustus Harley, whose talents disincline him to earn a living at all. As a man, Augustus is free from 'the peculiar disadvantages of my sex' noted by Emma (p. 55); but, ironically, it is his situation which most clearly demonstrates the essential contradictions in Emma's notions of independence for women.

Augustus is an anomalous character, a man of feeling whose uncertain status as a first-generation gentleman is reminiscent of David Simple's situation. The son of a merchant, he receives an education 'for the law', but 'disgusted with its chicanery' he determines instead on what is essentially a gentleman's existence, his 'narrow income' receiving a convenient boost from a timely legacy. This legacy enables him to complete a gentlemanly grand tour, 'travelling on the continent for three years'; he then lives with his mother in the country and in London, dividing his time 'between liberal studies, and rational recreation' (pp. 52–3). This adoption of a leisured, cultured (and thus quasi-aristocratic) existence is an integral part of Augustus's attraction for Emma; yet the terms of the legacy (in order to qualify for it, Augustus must not marry) ensure that he is not independent, while the life he chooses to lead also feminises him, unfitting him for the manly task of earning a living. When the existence of Augustus's wife and family is revealed, Emma comments that 'His education and habits had unfitted him for those exertions which the support of an encreasing [sic] family necessarily required' (p. 152). The education 'for commerce' received by his brothers (p. 52) would clearly have been of more practical value; with such an education, however, it is doubtful whether Emma would ever have fallen in love with him. The mistake made by Emma's bourgeois mother in marrying a man of superior rank with aristocratic habits and vices is ironically replicated by Emma's infatuation with the gentlemanly but ineffectual and feminised Augustus. Emma's sentimental belief that genuine independence is to be gained through the exertion of one's particular talents is thus shown to be incompatible with the view that the various ways of earning a living offered by the world inevitably stifle, rather than enhance, those talents.

The impasse to which the novel's rhetoric of sensibility leads can however be viewed in a more positive light. If Emma's sensibility is the stumbling-block which prevents her achievement of a 'rational independence', it is arguably also the means by which more radical demands to do with women's employment are kept alive. From one angle, Emma's horror of 'working for her bread' in some menial capacity may be indicative of her unreasonable expectations and failure to embrace independence at any price; from another, it can express indignation that an individual capable of so much more should be reduced, by virtue of her sex, so low. The rational self-control urged by radical writers differs from that proposed by West in that it associates self-control in women with their capacity to become active citizens in the public sphere rather than models of domestic decorum. Nevertheless, the repressive possibilities of self-control cannot be entirely avoided and reasonable contraction of wants is, perhaps, not so far from acquiescence in the current order of things. In this context, to retain sensibility, as Emma does, is to retain at least some sense of how great the gap is between the aspirations of the individual and the opportunities afforded by the structures of the society within which she must live.

Herein lies one aspect of sensibility's 'revolutionary potential', a potential *Emma Courtney* acknowledges but neglects to explore fully as a result of the novel's progressive tendency to find sensibility incompatible not only with menial labour but with practical occupations of all kinds, including, of course, commerce. At the end of the novel this is illustrated by the problems Emma faces in

educating her own daughter and Augustus's son; she tells
Augustus the younger:

> It now became necessary that your educations should take a
> somewhat different direction; I wished to fit you for a commer-
> cial line of life; but the ardor you discovered for science and liter-
> ature occasioned me some perplexity, as I feared it might unfit
> you for application to trade, in the pursuit of which so many
> talents are swallowed up, and powers wasted. (p. 193)

Thus Emma herself becomes an inevitable accomplice in perpetuat-
ing the sexual division of labour, foreseeing the pinnacle of happiness for herself and her daughter only in the wished-for marriage
between the latter and young Augustus. The early death of young
Emma is perhaps an appropriate end for one whose only options –
dependence, destitution, marriage – have already been tried and
found pitifully wanting by her mother. Furthermore, Emma's lin-
gering faith in 'a commercial line of life' as the most acceptable way
of earning a living (she rejects the law, the church and the universi-
ties as morally degenerate) is coupled here with a Godwinian conviction that trade is incompatible with the finer 'talents' and
'powers' which naturally accompany sensibility. The harmonious
combination achieved by her uncle seems forgotten; instead we are
left with the contradictory conclusions that, on the one hand, sensibility is the necessary prerequisite for the possession of 'talents'
which could be exerted for the benefit of society (as Emma wished
to do), while on the other hand, practical exertion apparently
destroys such desirable abilities. And so *Emma Courtney*, despite
certain promising signs, ultimately drives a wedge between sensibility and commerce, and indeed all practical occupations. In the
process, the novel is finally unable to envisage a state of independence for women (or for the feminised man) which could successfully fulfil the needs of sensibility.

Charles Lloyd's *Edmund Oliver* (1798) is, as I have already indicated, at least in some respects an overt answer to views expressed
in *Emma Courtney*: footnotes direct the reader to corresponding passages in Hays's novel at two points of particular significance in the
text to ensure that the moral is not missed.[43] The misguided
Gertrude is to be understood as Emma Courtney's heir, giving
voice to a creed which her subsequent history (desertion, the birth
of an illegitimate child, suicide) demonstrates to be both ethically

and practically disastrous. This direct reference seems very conveniently to place *Edmund Oliver* and *Emma Courtney* in opposite camps, Lloyd's novel providing a conservative critique of Hays's. Marilyn Butler refers to Edmund as among the 'anti-jacobin protagonists' and, while she acknowledges both the 'jacobin' tone of the novel's attitude to militarism and Lloyd's association with revolutionary ideas, she asserts that 'As a whole the action of the book has a very different tendency.'[44] Attitudes in the novel towards dependence, independence and commerce, however, both reinstate *Edmund Oliver* as a text which retains some revolutionary ideals and demonstrate its closeness to *Emma Courtney*.

Early in the novel Edmund confesses to his friend and chief correspondent Charles Maurice that he has often indulged a daydream in which he has imagined himself

> master of some forty acres, which I cultivated with my own hands. I have planted myself in a green woody vale, too picturesque to let my feelings slumber, and yet too confined to excite restlessness of thought or desire: quietness and entire seclusion formed the character of my retreat. I have moreover fancied myself a father and a husband – my children have followed the plough, and *have acquired* independence from a negation of wants – their souls have been pure ... (I, 69; my emphasis)

Such a fantasy of economic self-sufficiency is of course a familiar feature in other eighteenth-century novels; its role in both *Ophelia* (1760) and *Lady Julia Mandeville* (1763), for example, has been discussed earlier in this study. Its occurrence in *Edmund Oliver*, however, is marked by the association of such self-sufficiency with a particular brand of independence, an independence which results 'from a negation of wants'. This independence is defined, as the novel progresses, by its hostility to commerce and its affinity with a more equitable distribution of property. It is an independence 'of that unchangeable nature, which arises from physical robustness, and firmness of mind, rather than from vast possessions' (II, 53); and, as the vocabulary indicates, it is primarily a masculine independence. Women's access to it is only possible through their role as helpmeet, since this role provides all the stimulus and fulfilment necessary for the feminine character; as Edmund's sister Ellen explains on her marriage, 'all my desires are gratified – all the feelings of nature have their proper object – I look up to Henry as to a superior being ...' (II, 281). This robust independence is also to be distinguished from narrow concern with 'the accumulation of a *personal* independence' which leads to the inevitable 'duty relative to their situations in the mechanic and merchant, to stifle intellect and repel the delicious exuberances of genius' (II, 54–5; my emphasis). Far from conferring genuine independence, commerce is seen as fostering a debilitating version of dependence in its creation of 'artificial wants' (I, 178).

This distinctly Godwinian position with regard to commerce is also compatible with the view finally endorsed by *Emma Courtney*, and a further echo of Hays's novel is produced in the trajectory of Edmund's financial position, at least until he recovers his inheritance at the very end of the novel. The son of a merchant (who, characteristically for a narrow-minded adherent of commerce, is 'jealous, reserved, unforgiving, and severe' [I, 5]), Edmund is at first apparently assured of a secure economic future. He lives expensively at university, but is then cut out of his father's will in favour of two unworthy but artful cousins. Even when this will is later proved to be a forgery, Edmund refuses to undertake the unpalatable task of reclaiming his rightful fortune. After a period travelling in Europe with Charles, Edmund returns to London where his obsession with his childhood sweetheart Gertrude once more dominates his thoughts and actions. Like Emma Courtney, although by a different route, the emotionally overwrought Edmund is brought to the very brink of destitution. He enlists as a soldier but is soon rescued by Charles, who then proposes that, since Edmund is voluntarily destitute, he should take a share of his fortune. Charles argues:

> Human wants are few, and I deem it criminal, indeed an actual robbery, to devote more to myself or family than would fall to our share, were property equalized ... accept of a situation in which your powers become your own – a situation in which you may use them for the improvement and instruction of millions – a situation which relieves you from the debilitating pressure of every physical and moral inconvenience ... (II, 52, 56)

Edmund, after an internal struggle, exclaims '"I yield – I yield – I could call myself thy debtor, but I will not"' (II, 57).

This sequence involves a complex mix of discourses both radical and sentimental. Edmund is offered independence at the price of one enormous obligation. In keeping with contemporary radical theory, however, that obligation is supposedly negated because Charles's offer is not in fact one of unprecedented benevolence but, by his own logic, one of simple justice. The emotionally charged atmosphere in which the offer and its acceptance take place, affirms, in contrast, its status as a sentimental drama; and the 'little society of love and virtue' which Edmund, Charles and their wives and friends form at the end of the novel is difficult to distinguish from the 'Union of Hearts' offered by *David Simple* 50 years earlier. Significantly, however, the offer which Charles made so earnestly and Edmund accepted with such dramatic intensity is never put into practice. Edmund's fortune is restored to him via his brother, who had no scruples about exposing the fraud perpetrated by their cousins. Edmund tells Charles, '"Had not this independence *in the course of things fallen to my lot*, I should have availed myself of your offer"' (II, 234; my emphasis), thus attributing to fate what has been the result of human agency and in the process restoring material wealth almost to the providential status it enjoyed in *Tom Jones*.

Edmund Oliver retains the ideal of property in common: in the community of friends with which the novel closes they 'have banished the words *mine* and *thine*' (II, 292). This undeniably radical method of social and financial organisation is to be achieved, however, via the kind of individual, internal reform advocated by conservative propagandists as the very reverse of revolution (I, 185). The redefinition of independence as a 'negation of wants' leads both to the condemnation of commerce and the retention of dependence as it exists in the model of an ideal sentimental community. While advocacy of commerce in a novel is by no means any guarantee that radical alternatives to dependence will be seriously considered, opposition to commerce does seem to result in the reinforcement of ideals attached to gentlemanly or even golden age ideologies, a reinforcement which produces essentially conservative novels, despite such features as *Emma Courtney*'s attempt to construct independence for women or *Edmund Oliver*'s belief in the redistribution of property.

The possibility that a radical woman writer will ultimately produce a novel with conventional conclusions, despite manifest attempts to break free from such constraints, also seems to hover around Mary Wollstonecraft's second and posthumously published novel *The Wrongs of Woman: or, Maria* (1798). Maria's lover,

Darnford, describes his experiences in America and remarks of the American people that

> [t]he resolution, that led them, in pursuit of independence, to embark on rivers like seas, to search for unknown shores, and to sleep under the hovering mists of endless forests, whose baleful damps agued their limbs, was now turned into commercial speculations, till the national character exhibited a phenomenon in the history of the human mind – a head enthusiastically enter-prising, with cold selfishness of heart.[45]

It is this passage which leads Kelly to note that Wollstonecraft believed, in common with Godwin, 'that commerce blunted the finer sensibilities'.[46] Indeed Darnford's speech, along with his later comment 'I detested commerce' (p. 102), and the portrayal of Maria's husband George Venables ('commerce and gross relax-ations were shutting his [faculties and taste] against any possibility of improvement …' [p. 137]) clearly do give voice to this point of view, the view which comes to dominate *Emma Courtney* and is all-pervasive in *Edmund Oliver*. Allowing these elements in *The Wrongs of Woman* to override all others, however, means both that qualify-ing factors within them are easily ignored and that alternative atti-tudes expressed elsewhere in the novel are simply overlooked.

For Darnford's opinions, it must be recognised, cannot be taken as a reliable source for those of the work as a whole. His views on women indicate libertine tendencies, and this aspect of his charac-ter is confirmed in at least one of the possible conclusions to the novel: 'Divorced by her husband – Her lover unfaithful – Pregnancy – Miscarriage – Suicide' (p. 183).[47] In addition, the undesirable effects of commerce on the heart which Darnford claims to have seen in the Americans, are not exactly demonstrated in the narrative of the moral degeneration of George Venables, despite the apparent tendency of the above quotation. In taking over his father's successful business, George lacks the experience 'to conduct their affairs on the same prudential plan' and indeed 'despised his [father's] narrow plans and cautious speculation' (p. 127). Here, that narrowness so often identified as one of the failings of commerce is unquestionably a virtue, adherence to which may have helped to preserve Maria's future husband from his downward course. Having 'acquired habits of libertinism' in London, George carefully conceals these 'from his father and his commercial connections': 'The mask he wore, was so complete a covering of his real visage, that the praise his father lavished on his conduct, and, poor mistaken man! on his principles, contrasted with his brother's, rendered the notice he took of me peculiarly flattering' (p. 127). The implied probity of the 'commercial connections' in comparison with George's libertinism (which clearly carries class significance as well, the commercial middle classes favourably compared with the practices of a dissolute aristocracy) and the sentimental apostrophe, 'poor mistaken man!', indicate that, if commerce is not a great aid to good taste, it is nevertheless the 'gross relaxations' which are chiefly responsible for George's moral decline. This is confirmed when Mr S—— reveals to Maria that as a result of dubious financial transactions George's '"character in the commercial world was gone. He was considered ... on 'Change as a swindler."' Lest the value of the 'character' conferred by 'the commercial world' be in any doubt, it is at this moment that Maria feels her 'first maternal pang' (p. 150).

The attitudes to commerce expressed in the pages of *The Wrongs of Woman* encompass both the contemptuous and the approving; and unlike *Emma Courtney*, there is no evident development away from the latter and towards the former as the novel progresses. The unfinished state of Wollstonecraft's novel could be a reason for this, but I would argue that both internal and external evidence point to more interesting conclusions. At the end of the previous chapter I put forward the view that Janet Todd's inclination to see Wollstonecraft's 'attempt to associate the new self-reliant woman she envisaged with the entrepreneurial self-made man of the middle class' as 'unusual' did not take account of the way in which novels by women make recurrent connections between women and commerce, and between women and economic dexterity. Todd however goes on to conclude further that this association 'was untypical of Wollstonecraft herself who quickly came to see that, in a world where financial or economic considerations dominated or even coexisted in equality with moral ones, women and the poor would surely become commodities.'[48] This is equally surely to simplify the problems Wollstonecraft's writings had to accommodate. Her *Rights of Woman* is centrally concerned with dependence and independence: 'slavish dependency' (emotional and material) being the condition in which women have lived and are living, and independence being the state of grace to which Wollstonecraft would like to bring them. The emotional dependence on chimerical pleasures which their inadequate (or indeed totally misdirected) education has given women cannot be challenged except by material independence: in the words of the *Vindication*, 'It is vain to expect virtue from women till they are, in some degree, independent of men.'[49] Such independence can only be gained through recognition of 'financial or economic considerations'; indeed it is difficult to imagine how Todd believes these could be circumvented: Wollstonecraft certainly did not try to do so, and in the *Vindication* she prompted her reader to consider '[h]ow many women thus waste life away the prey of discontent, who might have practised as physicians, regulated a farm, managed a shop, and stood erect, supported by their own industry, instead of hanging their heads surcharged with the dew of sensibility, that consumes the beauty to which it first gave lustre...'[50] Far from being an unusual and temporary reflection, this concern goes on to become one of the major issues explored in *The Wrongs of Woman*. As the above passage indicates, inescapably related to the problem of women's independence was the dilemma surrounding their sensibility. Sensibility, which in the *Rights of Woman* is so roundly criticised as the quality that enslaves women by affording them a delusory and morally bankrupt power,[51] resurfaces in Wollstonecraft's subsequent novel as an essential attribute for her heroine, just as it was for the protagonist of her first novel *Mary, A Fiction* (1788).[52]

Introduced as 'one, true to the touch of sympathy' (p. 85) Maria, like Emma Courtney before her, has constantly to struggle to establish control over a susceptibility which is nonetheless a valuable and valued indicator of her moral fibre. The independence which becomes so desirable a goal, not only for Maria but for the other women in the novel whose stories we hear – Jemima, Peggy, Maria's sisters – also threatens to deprive them of their sensibility. It is the characteristic of sensibility (as the experience of David Simple demonstrated early on in this study) to deprive its possessor of the power to act. Primrose's inability to save his daughter from drowning demonstrated his dependence on Sir William; the collective paralysis in the face of difficulty (either physical or mental) from which women as a sex were supposed to suffer as a result of their finely strung nerves and delicately tuned feelings similarly demonstrated their dependence upon men. The exertion (a favourite word with Wollstonecraft, indicating self-control in its positive aspect) necessary to break this dependence thus also destroyed their distinctively feminine access to exquisite sensation.

In *The Wrongs of Woman* this impasse is also involved with the need to establish woman's equal ability to use and respond to reason. In the *Vindication*, Wollstonecraft concludes 'that reason is absolutely necessary to enable a woman to perform any duty properly, and I must again repeat, that sensibility is not reason'.[53] This stark dichotomy is not reproduced in the novel, however; speaking of Jemima's early and apparently instinctive wish to alleviate Maria's sufferings, the narrator explains,

> [t]hough she failed immediately to rouse a lively sense of injustice in the mind of her guard, because it had been sophisticated into misanthropy, she touched her heart... . A sense of right seems to result from the simplest act of reason, and to preside over the faculties of the mind, like the master sense of feeling, to rectify the rest; but (for the comparison may be carried still farther) how often is the exquisite sensibility of both weakened or destroyed by the vulgar occupations, and ignoble pleasures of life? (pp. 88–9)

Here, the 'sense of right' that responds to reason and 'the master sense of feeling' seem to be related qualities, and the healthy mind can have an 'exquisite sensibility' to both. Sensibility is not reason but, it seems, sensibility is necessary in order to be able to appreciate reason. Similarly, the supposed tension between sensibility and self-control is challenged by *The Wrongs of Woman*, which finds 'True sensibility' and 'Genuine fortitude' to be mutually reinforcing rather than mutually exclusive (pp. 163–4). If, then, 'the vulgar occupations, and ignoble pleasures of life' destroy sensibility, they also, as an unavoidable consequence, destroy the efficacy of any appeal to reason and the ability to exercise self-control. The destructive results of such 'vulgar occupations, and ignoble pleasures' point forward to the later condemnation of the undesirable effects on George Venables of 'commerce, and gross relaxations'. Yet, just as other aspects of his story reveal at least an ambivalence towards trade and at best a positive affirmation of its social and moral value, so Jemima's narrative demonstrates that Maria's fears about 'vulgar occupations' may not be entirely justified, thus enabling the possibility of a version of female independence which can accommodate sensibility, the version which *Emma Courtney* was unable to envisage. Given that in the *Vindication* Wollstonecraft had seen sensibility as instrumental in the enslavement of women, this may seem an unlikely direction for the novel to take; but it is a direction that demonstrates the interest radicals had in retaining, to repeat Nicola Watson's phrase, 'the revolutionary potential of sensibility'.[54]

On first being imprisoned, Maria soon runs out of books to read and turns to writing to pass the time and 'escape from sorrow'. This occupation rapidly leads to the determination to relate 'the events of her past life' in the hope that this will 'instruct her daughter, and shield her from the misery, the tyranny, her mother knew not how to avoid' (p. 90). In her narrative Maria's relation of her sisters' experiences has particular force. They are accomplished women for whom Maria can only with difficulty find places as governesses, an occupation which anyway affords only a bare subsistence and is 'a dependence next to menial'. However, further on in the same paragraph, Maria's outrage that women with talents, to use Emma Courtney's word, should be reduced to such expediency is partially transferred from Maria herself to her youngest sister; in her sister, outrage at the unsuitability of the work available to talented women becomes genteel unwillingness to perform tasks inappropriate for her station in life – and as such, it becomes the object of Maria's censure:

> She had abilities sufficient to have shone in any profession, had there been any professions for women, though she shrunk at the name of milliner or mantuamaker as degrading to a gentle-woman. I would not term this feeling false pride to any one but you, my child, whom I fondly hope to see ... possessed of that energy of character which gives dignity to any station; and with that clear, firm spirit that will enable you to choose a situation for yourself, or submit to be classed with the lowest, if it be the only one in which you can be the mistress of your own actions. (p. 141)

Maria's sister's attitude in *The Wrongs of Woman* is censured for its class-consciousness, while in *Emma Courtney* Emma's distaste stems rather from a kind of (arguably justifiable) intellectual pride; practically speaking, however, their views result in the same unwillingness to consider independence when not in an acceptable guise. Maria's affirmation of the value of any kind of work, if it offers independence, implies a confidence in the value of independence *per se* lacking in *Emma Courtney*, and also points to the way in which the conclusions of Wollstonecraft's work alter through time: in *Thoughts on the Education of Daughters* (1787) the lack of 'respectability' of trades is lamented; in the *Vindication* the way in which milliners and mantuamakers are 'reckoned the next class' to prostitutes is described, but any attempt by women to earn their own living is nevertheless 'a most laudable one'.[55] In *The Wrongs of Woman*, the barrier of respectability is actually breached: better a milliner or a mantuamaker than a dependant, whatever your class position.

Retrospectively, then, Maria's exhortation to cling to independence beyond all other considerations can also be seen to have been at work in Jemima's narrative. Jemima's tale of abuse and degradation can give no 'mild lustre', as my chapter title has it, to independence;[56] her options as 'a slave, a bastard, a common property' (p. 112) amount only to a choice of evils; but even so, degrees of dependence and independence figure significantly in her description of her various modes of subsisting. During her miserable existence as a street prostitute and pickpocket, she tells Maria and Darnford,

> 'Detesting my nightly occupation, though valuing, if I may so use the word, my independence, which only consisted in choosing the street in which I should wander, or the roof, when I had money, in which I should hide my head, I was some time before I could prevail on myself to accept of a place in a house of ill fame, to which a girl, with whom I had accidentally conversed in the street, had recommended me.' (p. 112)

Her move from the street to the 'house of ill fame' is described as a move back 'into servitude' (p. 113); driven to this measure by persecution from the watchmen, Jemima makes the move reluctantly, despite the horrors of her life as it is. Her 'independence' on the streets is both a parody of the real thing and yet, in one sense, a viable version of it, for even in this wretched guise independence is worth having, and hard to give up.

When, towards the end of her narrative, Jemima describes how 'The offer of forty pounds a year, and to quit a workhouse, was not to be despised, though the condition of shutting my eyes and hardening my heart was annexed to it' (p. 119), the issue of independence and sensibility is brought to the fore in the apparent necessity of officially forfeiting the latter in order to gain the former. Yet ultimately Jemima does not fulfil – indeed cannot be forced to fulfil – the 'conditions' attached to her employment: the discovery that Maria's four-month-old baby 'had been torn from her, even while she was discharging the tenderest maternal office' awakes 'the woman ... in a bosom long estranged from feminine emotions' (p. 88) and the reciprocal kindness her treatment evokes from

Maria 'overcomes' her (p. 119), confirming Maria's final conclusion that 'Jemima's humanity had rather been benumbed than killed ...' (p. 120). Despite her knowledge of aspects of life hitherto portrayed as utterly hostile to virtuous sensibility, Jemima is allowed to retain a feeling heart. In its defiance – through, of course, Maria's story as well as Jemima's – of the dogma which attached virtuous sensibility to a chaste domestic life, and in its related linking of sensibility with independence rather than dependence, *The Wrongs of Woman* succeeds at least in part in discovering some of sensibility's 'revolutionary potential'.

The Wrongs of Woman demonstrates more clearly than *Emma Courtney*, and ultimately more positively, that the radical woman writer cannot afford to reject commerce because she cannot afford to reject any means by which an independent subsistence may be earned. Neither novel, however, can offer such an optimistic attitude towards the relation between women and economic activity as that implicit in the stories of Mrs Bilson or Ophelia, Anne Wilmot or Anna. Indeed, conclusions reached by novels of the 1790s end this study on what is perhaps a pessimistic note. Two reasons for this change need consideration: the effect of an increasingly vociferous conservative reaction to 'Jacobin' views as the century came to its close,[57] and the simultaneous subjection of the practical problems associated with women and work to greater scrutiny, as already shown, by writers from both sides of the political divide. These two factors can be illustrated together in a brief discussion of Priscilla Wakefield's important text, *Reflections on the Present Condition of the Female Sex* (1798) and two novels which attempt to realise fictionally the kind of measures it proposes: Hays's *The Victim of Prejudice* (1799) and Fanny Burney's *The Wanderer; or, Female Difficulties* (1814).[58]

Wakefield's work is pervaded by a set of contradictions of particular significance for the late 1790s. She was certainly determined to appropriate commerce in the course of her search for 'useful occupations' for women and asks,

> Can it be accounted for, on any other ground than that of prejudice, in a country like England, where commerce forms one of the principal sinews of the national strength, where the character of the merchant is honourable, and no obstacle to a favourable reception in the highest circles, that degradation should attend the female who engages in the concerns of commerce, and that she, whose good sense and resolution enable her to support

herself, is banished from that line of company, of which she had perhaps previously formed a distinguished ornament?[59]

Here 'the merchant' is clearly of the same kind as Mr Mordant and Mr Dudley, and it is the overt adoption of his role achieved by Anna, rather than the internalisation of it accepted by Louisa, that is urged for women. However, Wakefield's radical proposal that women be allowed to support themselves independently in a whole variety of occupations ranging from engraving and ornamental gardening (pp. 102–5) to 'light turnery' and farming (p. 126) is developed alongside explicit adherence to key conservative values in terms of both gender and class.

For example, 'Domestic privacy' is vital for young women and almost as important for the 'grave matron'; the virtues are gendered and women's gentleness, sympathy and benevolence are the natural result of 'The delicacy of their frame, and the dependence on the other sex in which nature has placed them ...' (p. 8). The prohibition of women from roles in public life is consistent with 'reason and decorum', while educating women will enable them to see more clearly the wisdom inherent in the dominant position of men (p. 77). Her advocation of female solidarity, moreover, is framed in terms guaranteed to reinforce rather than erase class divisions: the opinion that 'the female nobility' have a duty 'to countenance, in an especial manner, the industry of their own sex ...' (p. 78) allows for a radical reorganisation in women's favour lower down the social scale (trades Wakefield sees as having been unfairly appropriated by men would, under such pressure from above, fall once more into female hands) while retaining intact the absolute difference between female nobility and the women whose businesses they are being encouraged to patronise with their custom. Essentially Wakefield is asking for a significant shift in the relationship between gender and labour which will nonetheless leave the basic fabric of the social structure unchanged.

In attempting to avoid the least hint of a revolutionary social agenda, however, the practicability of Wakefield's proposal for extending women's employment is called into question. *The Victim of Prejudice* and *The Wanderer*, while written by novelists who are often taken to represent the opposite poles of radicalism and respectability, both focus on the predicament of an unprotected, destitute woman and her efforts to support herself independently. For example Mary, in Hays's novel, follows up Wakefield's suggestion that 'women whose refinement of manners unfit them for any occupation of a sordid menial kind' (p. 97) should support themselves through the use of such feminine arts as painting, colouring of prints, and so on. She gains employment drawing and painting flowers, a skill acquired during her youthful study of botany, only to find herself the object of her employer's sexual advances when her (undeserved) reputation as a fallen woman reaches him.[60] Juliet, in *The Wanderer*, similarly discovers that her employment in Miss Matson's milliner's shop leaves her a prey to the unwelcome attentions of Sir Lyell Sycamore and reflects anxiously on 'the improprieties to which her defenceless state made her liable'.[61] Both heroines attempt a variety of jobs in their search for 'the dignity of INDEPENDENCE'[62] and in the hope of attaining 'that sort of independence, that belongs, physically, to sustaining life by her own means';[63] but, although Burney's novel manages a conventional happy ending, neither can see anything to hope for but harsh treatment and sexual harassment for the unattached middle-class woman who wishes to work for herself, at least as society was then constituted. In reaching this conclusion, both novels implicitly criticise Wakefield's attempt to divorce her appeal for women's employment from a commitment to social change.

The conservative reaction of which Wakefield's views were a part, however, also dictated that *The Victim of Prejudice* and *The Wanderer*, despite their critique, could not find the optimism of earlier years in their treatment of women and work; while the experiences of their protagonists suggest the necessity of social reorganisation, neither novel sees any prospect of such an eventuality, or indeed any ways in which women might make the current order work in their favour. Hays's novel ends with a desperate and far from hopeful appeal for a radical change in male attitudes towards sexuality and chastity, while Burney's (in a movement perhaps reflected in the novel's general preference for the term 'self-dependence' rather than 'independence') finally submits to a rhetoric of internalised independence which can contain its earlier criticism and is appropriate for the closing union between Juliet and Harleigh: 'Yet even DIFFICULTIES such as these are not insurmountable, where mental courage, operating through patience, prudence, and principle, supply physical force, combat disappointment, and keep the untamed spirits superior to failure, and ever alive to hope.'[64]

Conclusion

In the introduction to his *Treatise on Political Economy* (1803), Jean-Baptiste Say asserts that the ancients 'knew, what has always been known wherever the right of property has been sanctioned by laws, that riches are increased by economy and diminished by extravagance'.[1] Although other contemporary economists (notably Malthus and Sismondi) disagreed with him and retained a Mandevillian emphasis on the importance of prodigality in the production of wealth, Say's view at once confirmed the rectitude of Adam Smith's attack on Mandeville and represented what was to become the orthodoxy in the theory of political economy during the following century.[2] The triumph of frugality over prodigality in economic theory finds its analogue in the triumph of self-control over sensibility in novelistic discourse. Self-control, an appropriate quality to possess in cultivation of frugal habits, is also suited to the ideal of femininity required by the developing capitalist society.

The contradictions within such a society are manifest. As Terry Lovell has pointed out, capitalism is 'Janus-faced', requiring frugality from its producers and prodigality from its consumers – two groups which inevitably overlap to a greater or lesser degree.[3] Furthermore, the triumph of self-control over sensibility in the novel during the years after 1800 is by no means complete. From the height of its popularity in the 1770s, sentimentalism as a fashionable literary movement might have had its day by the first decade of the nineteenth century. It is important to recognise, however, that many of its conventions, values and approaches were still powerfully influential in the very novels that sought to challenge it.

Mary Brunton's *Self-Control* (1811), for example, announces its ideological allegiance in its title and imagines, as Nicola Watson puts it, destructive passion 'as being generated by, and in terms of, the fictions of sensibility'.[4] Laura's own sensibility, like that of so many heroines of the 1790s, is something she has 'been taught to consider as a weakness to be subdued, not as an ornament to be gloried in ...'[5] Yet it is still a vital component in her status as heroine; while she is vexed at the 'ill-timed sensibility' which causes her to faint on meeting Hargrave, it is that quality which guarantees her worth. As in earlier novels, sensibility can be divided into the false and the true. Laura's selfish mother, for example, finds on meeting her future husband that his 'fine person' aroused 'the only sort of sensibility' she possessed (I, 4), while with Lady Pelham, Laura speculates on 'the nature of that sensibility which could thus enlarge to a stranger on the defects of an only child' (II, 26). Yet 'the religious character' requires 'a mind of sensibility and reflection' (I, 10), and the final sentence of the novel reinforces the importance of feeling in its characteristically sentimental appeal to those like-minded individuals who will understand: 'The joys that spring from chastened affection, tempered desires, useful employment, and devout meditation, must be felt – they cannot be described' (II, 468).

Laura has much in common with Austen's Fanny Price, as Nicola Watson has noticed: both heroines exhibit, she argues, 'a self-sufficiency of virtue that at times culminates in social iconoclasm'.[6] In addition, Fanny, as much as Laura, combines that self-sufficiency with a sensibility that crucially differentiates her from her insensitive cousins and Mary Crawford. Her feelings are 'very acute', she possesses 'delicacy of taste, of mind, of feeling', and the affectionate relationship between herself and her brother William provides Henry Crawford with a picture which he 'had moral taste enough to value. Fanny's attractions increased – increased twofold – for the sensibility which beautified her complexion and illumined her countenance, was an attraction in itself.'[7] The link between sensibility and fine moral discrimination is, if anything, stronger in Fanny than in Laura. Her heart and mind work in unison, as Edmund's plea to his father in her favour indicates: 'Fanny is the only one who has judged rightly throughout, who has been consistent. Her feelings have been steadily against it from first to last' (p. 168).

Tied firmly as it is to a discourse of self-control – or the importance of 'hardship and discipline', as *Mansfield Park* has it (p. 432) – sensibility in these later novels is clearly working within a different discursive field than that represented by, for example, *Lady Julia Mandeville* or *The History of Lady Barton*. When we come to such later novels as those by Hays, Wollstonecraft and West, however, the similarities between these works and those of Austen and Brunton are at least as striking as the differences.

If even a cursory consideration of the novel of the early nineteenth century emphasises that 1800 did not mark the end of 'eighteenth-century' sensibility in the novel, it also suggests a continuing preoccupation with dependence and independence, and with the relation between women and economic activity. Again, *Self-Control* provides a useful example. Laura, like Mary in *The Victim of Prejudice* before her, endeavours to earn money through her artistic skill. Although a single woman, this attempt is not primarily to support herself, but to look after her sick father. The sanction of working for the sake of the family, as Mrs Bilson and Caroline Traverse did and as Amelia offered to do, differentiates Laura's labours from those of Anna, until, on the death of her father, she is left as destitute as Bennett's heroine. Her reflections at this juncture are significant:

> But her personal charms were such as no degree of humility could screen from the knowledge of their possessor, and she was sensible how much this dangerous distinction increased the disqualifications of her sex and age for the character of an artist. As an artist, she must be exposed to the intrusion of strangers, to public observation if successful; to unpitied neglect if she failed in her attempt. Besides, it was impossible to think of living alone and unprotected, in the human chaos that surrounded her. (II, 8)

Unlike the women in *Lady Barton*, 'she fears not to labour for her subsistence' and sees independence, theoretically at least, as a perfectly reasonable end at which to aim. But unlike Mary in *The Victim of Prejudice* she also anticipates the inevitable result of setting up as a female artist and rejects the possibility accordingly, considering 'the tuition of youth ... as the most eligible means of procuring necessary subsistence, and protection, more necessary still' (II, 10). The emphasis on protection over subsistence throws into greater relief Laura's position as a woman, for whom virtue is more crucial than sustenance. Her earlier willingness to half starve herself in order to feed her father adequately assures the reader that she is capable of 'death before dishonour'. However, her visit to Lady Pelham results first in that lady taking her on (in effect) as an unpaid companion and subsequently in the payment of the arrears of an annuity due to her: 'independence' is internalised much as it had been for West's heroine.

The continuing relevance of sensibility, and of issues related to women and economic activity, in novels of the early 1800s is a subject too far beyond the scope of this book to do more than indicate its presence. It might have been expected, however, that issues of such earnest debate at the end of the eighteenth century would not simply disappear. What this study has demonstrated, I hope, is the inescapable link between eighteenth-century sensibility and the economic – a link that ensured that the sentimental novel recognised and dealt with a whole range of discourses, especially economic but also political, not usually associated with the genre. With a wide variety of strategies, from ironic commentary (in, for example, *David Simple* and *Lady Julia Mandeville*) to the use of analogy (especially *Anna* and *Barham Downs*), from evasion (in *The History of Lady Barton*) to appropriation (in, amongst others, *A Gossip's Story*), the sentimental novel was able to take part in contemporary debates on economic policy, forms of government, revolutionary politics and, infusing all these, definitions of femininity. Far from being a politically irrelevant or narrow genre, the sentimental novel was a versatile vehicle for comment.

Notes

CHAPTER 1

1. Henry Mackenzie, *The Man of Feeling* (1771; Oxford: Oxford University Press, 1987), pp. 34–5.
2. Mary Collyer, *Letters from Felicia to Charlotte* (1744–9; rpt 2 vols, London: R. Baldwin, 1755), vol. I, pp. 5–6.
3. Samuuel Richardson, *The History of Sir Charles Grandison* (1753; Oxford: Oxford University Press, 1986), vol. IV, Letter ix, p. 311.
4. As James Thompson points out in *Models of Value: Eighteenth-Century Political Economy and the Novel* (Durham and London: Duke University Press, 1996), p. 4. Examples of earlier treatment of economic aspects of eighteenth-century literature include the now classic work of Maximillian E. Novak, *Economics and the Fiction of Daniel Defoe* (Berkeley: University of California Press, 1962) and more recent studies such as Mona Scheuermann, *Her Bread to Earn: Women, Money and Society from Defoe to Austen* (Lexington, KY: Kentucky University Press, 1993), Colin Nicholson, *Writing and the Rise of Finance: Capital Satires of the Early Eighteenth Century* (Cambridge: Cambridge University Press, 1994) and Edward Copeland, *Women Writing about Money: Women's Fiction in England 1790–1820* (Cambridge: Cambridge University Press, 1995).
5. Thompson, p. 3. Thompson's central argument is that, 'as separate as these two stories might seem, they go hand in hand' (p. 3): 'Holding together as contiguous but polar opposites – on the one side coinage, banking and credit, on the other side love, marriage, and the home – political economy and the novel work together in the eighteenth century to describe a partitioned but symmetrical social whole' (pp. 13–14). The difference in the construction of value in these two areas is part of 'the changing conception of public and private across this period ... . Inverses of one another, political economy and the novel map, respectively, a zone of finance and zone of affect, or money and feeling' (pp. 22–3). But these zones are not hermetically sealed against one another, and because they are 'by definition ideological and therefore largely invisible, they can be traced only through moments or places of transgression – the presence of subjectivity in the discourse of civil society and financial exchange which constitutes political economy, or, conversely, the presence of financial exchange in the discourse of domesticity which constitutes the novel' (p. 24).
6. As Mary Poovey has commented, in the course of the eighteenth century, 'sentimental virtues were increasingly identified as feminine virtues' ('Ideology and *The Mysteries of Udolpho*', *Criticism*, 21 [1979], pp. 308–9), while in *The Proper Lady and the Woman Writer* (Chicago and London: University of Chicago Press, 1984) she points out that 'even critics of excessive sentimentalism ... agreed that women were

"naturally" suited to this species of composition' (p. 38) In *Feminist Literary History: A Defence* (Oxford: Polity Press, 1988), Janet Todd underlines the crucial connections between eighteenth-century women writers and male writers such as Richardson, commenting that the 'gender polarities of that century cut across sex lines to label his prose "feminine"' (p. 42). See also Jane Spencer, *The Rise of the Woman Novelist: From Aphra Behn to Jane Austen* (Oxford and New York: Blackwell, 1986; rpt 1987), pp. 77–8.

7. See Nancy Armstrong, 'The Rise of the Domestic Woman', in N. Armstrong and L. Tennenhouse (eds), *The Ideology of Conduct* (London: Methuen, 1987) and Spencer, pp. xi and 77–8.

8. The political dimensions of sentimental fiction have, of course, been more widely recognised and discussed with regard to the 1790s than the earlier decades of the eighteenth century, particularly in the last few years. See especially Chris Jones's *Radical Sensibility: Literature and Ideas in the 1790s* (London: Routledge, 1993).

9. Compare Armstrong, *Desire and Domestic Fiction: A Political History of the Novel* (New York and Oxford: Oxford University Press, 1987) pp. 9–10, where she argues that 'We are taught to divide the political world in two and detach the practices that belong to a female domain from those that govern the marketplace. In this way, we compulsively replicate the symbolic behavior that constituted a private domain of the individual outside and apart from social history ... political events cannot be understood apart from women's history, from the history of women's literature, or from changing representations of the household.' Her stance, of course, is part of the longstanding questioning of the public/private divide in feminist (particularly socialist feminist) criticism.

10. John Mullan, *Sentiment and Sociability: the Language of Feeling in the Eighteenth Century* (Oxford: Clarendon Press, 1988), p. 198.

11. Robert Markley, 'Sentimentality as Performance: Sterne, Shaftesbury and the Theatrics of Virtue' in Felicity Nussbaum and Laura Brown (eds), *The New Eighteenth Century: Theory, Politics, English Literature* (New York and London: Methuen, 1987), p. 211.

12. Mullan, p. 126.

13. What follows first appeared, in largely the same form, as part of my article '"The Price of a Tear": Economic Sense and Sensibility in Sarah Fielding's *David Simple*', in *Literature and History*, 3rd Series, 1 (Spring, 1992). James Thompson undertakes a similar and helpful discussion of 'economy' in *Models of Value*, pp. 41–3.

14. Erik Erämetsä, 'A Study of the Word "Sentimental" and of Other Characteristics of Eighteenth-Century Sentimentalism in England', *Annales Academiae Scientarum Fennicae*, B, 74 (Helsinki, 1951), p. 8.

15. Samuel Johnson, *A Dictionary of the English Language: in which the Words are Deduced from their Originals, and Illustrated in their Different Significations by Examples from the Best Writers* (2 vols, London: J. and P. Knapton *et al.*, 1755).

16. George Berkeley, *An Essay towards preventing the Ruin of Great Britain* (1721), in Stephen Copley (ed.), *Literature and the Social Order in*

Eighteenth-Century England (London, Sydney and Dover, New Hampshire: Croom Helm, 1984), pp. 90–1.

17. Oliver Goldsmith, 'Of the Pride and Luxury of the Middling Class of People', *The Bee* (1759), in *Collected Works of Oliver Goldsmith*, ed. Arthur Friedman (5 vols, Oxford: Clarendon Press, 1966), vol. I, pp. 486–7 (my emphasis). Also compare Adam Smith's view that 'In all the middling and inferior professions, real and solid professional abilities, joined to prudent, just, firm, and temperate conduct, can very seldom fail of success' in *The Theory of Moral Sentiments* (1759; 11th edn, Edinburgh: Bell and Bradfoute *et al.*, 1808).

18. *The Economy of Human Life* (Manchester: G. Nicholson, 1797), p. 11. This edition proclaims itself to be 'by Robert Dodsley'. The work first appeared anonymously in 1750, but is sometimes attributed to Philip Dormer Stanhope, fourth Earl of Chesterfield.

19. Wetenhall Wilkes, *A Letter of Genteel and Moral Advice to a Young Lady* (1740; 8th edn, London: L. Hawes *et al.*, 1766), p. 201.

20. Ibid., p. 220.

21. Samuel Richardson, *Clarissa, or the History of a Young Lady* (1747–8; London: Penguin Books, 1985), pp. 1468, 1471.

22. Sarah Fielding, *The Adventures of David Simple* (1744 and 1753; Oxford: Oxford University Press, 1987), Book II, Chapter x, p. 139.

23. *David Simple*, II, x, 145.

24. For discussion of the roots of civic humanism and the values it espouses, see J. G. A. Pocock, *The Machiavellian Moment: Florentine Political Thought and the Atlantic Republican Tradition* (Princeton and London: Princeton University Press, 1975), especially Chapters 3 and 14, and Stephen Copley's Introduction to *Literature and the Social Order*.

25. *David Simple*, IV, iii, p. 351.

26. Bernard Mandeville, 'Remark L', *The Fable of the Bees: or, Private Vices, Publick Benefits*, ed. F. B. Kaye (1714–28; 2 vols, Oxford: Clarendon Press, 1924), vol. I, p. 107.

27. Mandeville, 'The Grumbling Hive: Or, Knaves turn'd Honest', *Bees*, I, 37.

28. John Barrell, *English Literature in History 1730–1780: An Equal Wide Survey* (London: Hutchinson, 1983), p. 24.

29. *The Poems of Alexander Pope*, ed. John Butt (1963; London: Methuen, 1965), p. 510, ll. 165–70.

30. Mandeville, 'Remark Y' and 'An Essay on Charity and Charity-Schools', *Bees*, I, 249 and 267.

31. Richard Steele, *The Guardian*, no. 105, 11 July 1713 in Copley, p. 136.

32. Mandeville, 'An Essay on Charity and Charity-Schools', *Bees*, I, 267.

33. See, for example, Copley, pp. 19–20, where he comments that literary texts generally in the eighteenth century 'seem to lack or exclude an appropriate vocabulary to describe and celebrate the workings of contemporary commercial culture ... the moral vocabulary of humanism is adopted very widely in literary texts, while the new vocabularies of economic analysis find virtually no place in them.'

34. J. G. A. Pocock, *Virtue, Commerce and History: Essays on Political Thought and History, Chiefly in the Eighteenth Century* (Cambridge, New York and Melbourne: Cambridge University Press, 1985), p. 9.

35. Michel Foucault, *The History of Sexuality, Volume I: An Introduction*, trans. Robert Hurley (1976; Harmondsworth: Peregrine Books, 1984), p. 100.
36. See, for example, Albert O. Hirschman, *The Passions and the Interests: Political Arguments for Capitalism before its Triumph* (Princeton, NJ: Princeton University Press, 1977).
37. John Brown, *An Estimate of the Manners and Principles of the Times* (London: L. Davis and C. Reymers, 1757), p. 29.
38. Harriet Guest, 'A Double Lustre: Femininity and Sociable Commerce, 1730–60', *Eighteenth-Century Studies*, 23 (Summer, 1990), pp. 479–501.
39. *David Simple*, V, i, 314.
40. For contemporary response to Mandeville's work, see Gertrude Himmelfarb, *The Idea of Poverty: England in the Early Industrial Age* (London and Boston: Faber & Faber, 1984; New York: Alfred A. Knopf, Inc., 1984; Toronto: Random House, 1984), pp. 30–1 and Elizabeth Bellamy, *Private Virtues, Public Vices: Commercial Morality and the Novel, 1740–1800* (unpublished PhD thesis; Cambridge, 1988), Chapters 1 and 2.
41. In *Private Virtues, Public Vices* Elizabeth Bellamy writes, 'Many of the arguments put forward in *The Wealth of Nations* had been truisms of the economic tradition since before Smith was even born, and his writing represents the culmination of an old tradition as much as the start of a new one' (p. 19). She further comments that Smith's departure from earlier writing was based partly on 'his reinvestment of economic discourse with some code of personal behaviour' and continues, 'It was in part for this reason that the economic writings of Hume and Smith were regarded as more socially acceptable than those of their predecessors. Unlike the primitive writers they made some attempt to engage with the moral attacks on both their discourse and the commercial society which it described' (p. 122).
42. Adam Smith, *The Wealth of Nations* (1776; 2 vols, Oxford: Clarendon Press, 1976), vol. I, p. 25, and see Hirschman, p. 107.
43. Since beginning this project nine years ago, valuable and innovative work has been produced on the sentimental novel in the eighteenth century, much of which I have profited by and I hope fully acknowledged. I am sorry that Markman Ellis's *The Politics of Sensibility: Race, Gender and Commerce in the Sentimental Novel* (Cambridge: Cambridge University Press, 1996) came to my attention too late to enable me to include it in my discussions, but I am also delighted that the very title of his study confirms my conviction that the broader significances of the sentimental novel deserve much greater attention.

CHAPTER 2

1. For an assessment of Henry Fielding which sees him as having rather more in common with Richardson, and thus with sentimentalism, than is often allowed, see April London, 'Controlling the Text: Women in *Tom Jones*', *Studies in the Novel*, 19 (Fall, 1987), pp. 323–3.

See also Ann Jessie Van Sant, *Eighteenth-Century Sensibility and the Novel: the Senses in Social Context* (Cambridge: Cambridge University Press, 1993), pp. 6–7, where links (and differences) between sentimentalism in Fielding and Sterne are discussed.

2. Henry Fielding, *Tom Jones* (1749; Oxford: Clarendon Press, 1974), Book IV, Chapter xiv, p. 208. Subsequent page references in the text are to this edition.

3. Sarah Fielding, *The Adventures of David Simple* (1744; Oxford: Oxford University Press, 1987), Book VII, Chapter v, p. 412. Subsequent page references in the text are to this edition.

4. Jina Politi, *The Novel and its Presuppositions: Changes in the Conceptual Structure of Novels in the Eighteenth and Nineteenth Centuries* (Amsterdam: Adolf M. Hakkert N.V., 1976), p. 63.

5. John Mullan, *Sentiment and Sociability: the Language of Feeling in the Eighteenth Century* (Oxford: Clarendon Press, 1988), p. 80.

6. Politi, p. 160.

7. *The Poems of Alexander Pope*, ed. John Butt (1963; London: Methuen, 1965), p. 567, l. 216. This association of excess with the aristocracy is of course in keeping with the anti-aristocratic views discussed in Chapter 1, p. 5–6.

8. Janet Todd, *Sensibility: an Introduction* (London and New York: Methuen 1986), p. 97.

9. In *Models of Virtue: Eighteenth-Century Political Economy and the Novel* (Durham and London: Duke University Press, 1996), James Thompson considers the use of money in *Tom Jones* in much more detail, and sees the novel's 'monetary subplots' as bespeaking 'a conservative drive to stabilize cash and paper credit, to represent and contain currency within traditional patterns of property and possession, a desire which is determined by a specific stage in the development of money' (p. 133). He concludes that 'the true protagonist of *Tom Jones* is Paradise Hall. Tom's becoming a worthy steward to this estate is but part of a larger history, the possessive and genealogical continuity represented by the dynastic estate itself' (p. 155).

10. Politi, p. 87.

11. See Chapter 1, p. 6.

12. Henry Fielding, 'Of too frequent and expensive Diversions among the Lower Kind of People', *An Enquiry into the Causes of the Late Increase in Robbers* (1751), in *An Enquiry into the Causes of the Late Increase in Robbers and Related Writings*, ed. Malvin R. Zirker (Oxford: Oxford University Press, 1988), p. 80.

13. Ibid., p. 77.

14. Ibid., pp. 77, 78–9, 83–4.

15. Ibid., p. 71.

16. Michel Foucault, *The History of Sexuality, Volume I: An Introduction*, trans. Robert Hurley (1976; Harmondsworth: Peregrine Books, 1984), p. 92. Of course, Henry Fielding's work also offers a famous example of such an unpicking of the class system in *Joseph Andrews* (1742; Oxford: Clarendon Press, 1967) in which, having described 'the picture of dependence like a kind of ladder', the narrator suggests that

'to a philosopher the question might only seem whether you would chuse to be a great man at six in the morning, or at two in the afternoon' (II, xiii, pp. 157–8). Such radical scepticism, however, is never allowed to infect the novel's final conclusion, and it is the willingness of *Volume the Last* to do just this in the case of *David Simple*, I would argue, that makes Sarah's use of the trope the more biting.

17. Miguel de Cervantes Saavedra, *The Adventures of Don Quixote*, trans. J. M. Cohen (Harmondsworth: Penguin Books, 1950; rpt 1968), p. 33.
18. *Poems*, p. 195, ll. 15–16.
19. Ibid., l. 14.
20. See John Barrell, *English Literature in History 1730–80: An Equal, Wide Survey* (London: Hutchinson, 1983), pp. 32–6, 52.
21. Ruth Perry, *Women, Letters, and the Novel* (New York: AMS Press, Inc., 1980), p. 137. On the decline of women's employment, see also Bridget Hill, *Eighteenth-Century Women: An Anthology* (London: Allen & Unwin, 1984; rpt 1987), pp. 197–201 and my Chapter 3, pp. 38–9.
22. Samuel Johnson, *A Dictionary of the English Language: in which the Words are deduced from their Originals, and Illustrated in their Different Significations by Examples from the best Writers* (2 vols, London: J. and P. Knapton *et al.*, 1755).
23. Todd, p. 94.
24. Malcolm Kelsall, Introduction to *David Simple* (Oxford: Oxford University Press, 1987), p. xv.
25. Bernard Mandeville, 'Remark Y', *The Fable of the Bees* (1714–28; 2 vols, Oxford: Clarendon Press, 1924), vol. I, p. 249.
26. Mary Collyer, *Letters from Felicia to Charlotte* (1744–9; rpt 2 vols, London: R. Baldwin, 1755), vol. II, p. 21.
27. Todd, p. 89.
28. Sarah Fielding, *The History of the Countess of Dellwyn* (2 vols, London: A. Millar, 1759), vol. I, p. 36. Subsequent references in the text are to this edition.
29. Wetenhall Wilkes, *A Letter of Genteel and Moral Advice to a Young Lady* (1740; 8th edn, London: L. Hawes *et al.*, 1766), p. 202.
30. Ibid., p. 177.
31. Ibid., p. 195.
32. Todd, p. 97.
33. Priscilla Wakefield, *Reflections on the Present Condition of the Female Sex: with Suggestions for its Improvement* (1798; 2nd edn, London: Darton, Harvey, and Darton, 1817), pp. 78–9.
34. Sarah Scott, *Millenium Hall* (London: J. Newbery, 1762), p. 203.
35. Adam Smith, *The Theory of Moral Sentiments* (1759; 11th edn, 2 vols, Edinburgh: Bell and Bradfoute, *et al.*, 1808), vol. I, p. 253.
36. Mullan, p. 45.
37. Smith, I, 8.
38. Many charities were founded during the eighteenth century – the SPCK in 1699, the Royal Maternity Charity in 1757, the Magdalen Hospital in 1758, the Royal Humane Society in 1774, and the Royal Literary Fund in 1790, to name a few. See David Owen, *English Philanthropy 1660–1960* (Cambridge, Mass. and London: Harvard University Press and Oxford University Press, 1965).

39. Smith, I, 355.
40. 'Philogamus', *The Present State of Matrimony: Or, The Real Causes of Conjugal Infidelity and Unhappy Marriages* (London: John Hawkins, 1739).
41. Collyer, I, 5.
42. Mullan, p. 56.

CHAPTER 3

1. Charlotte Charke, *A Narrative of the Life of Mrs Charlotte Charke* (1755; rpt London: Constable, 1929), p. 30.
2. James Fordyce, *Sermons to Young Women* (3rd edn, 2 vols, London: A. Millar *et al.*, 1766), vol. I, p. 108.
3. James Thompson cites Kristina Straub's *Sexual Suspects: Eighteenth-Century Players and Sexual Ideology* (Princeton, NJ: Princeton University Press, 1992) to further confirm this connection: 'As Kristina Straub notes in her discussion of the representation of eighteenth-century actors' sexuality, almost by definition any location of a woman – any stance that is not retired, not private, and not domestic – is inevitably associated with sale and prostitution' (*Models of Value: Eighteenth-Century Political Economy and the Novel* [Durham and London: Duke University Press, 1996], p. 175).
4. Wetenhall Wilkes, *A Letter of Genteel and Moral Advice to a Young Lady* (1740; 8th edn, London: L. Hawes *et al.*, 1766), p. 194.
5. Chris Middleton, 'Women's Labour and the Transition to Pre-Industrial Capitalism', in Lindsey Charles and Lorna Duffin (eds), *Women and Work in Pre-Industrial England* (London, Sydney and Dover, New Hampshire: Croom Helm, 1985), p. 200.
6. Bridget Hill, *Women, Work and Sexual Politics in Eighteenth-Century England* (Oxford: Blackwell, 1989), p. 263.
7. Ivy Pinchbeck, *Women Workers and the Industrial Revolution* (1930; rpt London: Virago, 1985), p. 3.
8. Betsy Rodgers, *Cloak of Charity: Studies in Eighteenth-Century Philanthropy* (London: Methuen, 1949), p. 49.
9. Mary Wollstonecraft, *A Vindication of the Rights of Woman* (1792), in Janet Todd and Marilyn Butler (eds), *The Works of Mary Wollstonecraft* (7 vols, London: William Pickering, 1989), vol. 5, p. 218.
10. Henry Fielding, *Amelia* (1751; Oxford: Clarendon Press, 1983), Book XI, Chapter iii, p. 466. Subsequent references in the text are to this edition.
11. Sarah Fielding, *David Simple* (1744; Oxford: Oxford University Press, 1987), Book III, Chapter ii, pp. 165–6.
12. Jane Jack, Introduction to Daniel Defoe, *Roxana* (1724; Oxford: Oxford University Press, 1964; rpt 1986), p. viii.
13. *Roxana*, pp. 25, 28, 29, 2.
14. 'Roxana's narrative traverses a zone of financial growth and a zone of affective degeneration, as the skilled capitalist is transformed into the guilty mother … in *Roxana* the dogged persistence of Susan colors the whole last third of the novel, and all of Roxana's material success is unable to help her evade her daughter's quest for a mother'

(James Thompson, *Models of Value: Eighteenth-Century Political Economy and the Novel* [Durham and London: Duke University Press, 1996], p. 121).

15. John Cleland, *Memoirs of a Woman of Pleasure* (1748/9; Oxford: Oxford University Press, 1985; rpt 1986), p. 176.
16. Ibid., p. 187.
17. Adam Smith, *The Theory of Moral Sentiments* (1759; 11th edn, 2 vols, Edinburgh: Bell and Bradfoute *et al.*, 1808), vol. I, p. 396.
18. Philip E. Simmons, 'John Cleland's *Memoirs of a Woman of Pleasure*: Literary Voyeurism and the Techniques of Novelistic Transgression', *Eighteenth-Century Fiction*, 3 (October 1990), p. 44.
19. See Peter Sabor's Introduction to the cited edition, in which he gives Brigid Brophy, Erica Jong and Marghanita Laski as examples of critics who have held the latter view; and Janet Todd, Nancy Miller and Anne Taylor as examples of those who incline to the former.
20. Simmons, p. 46.
21. Sarah Fielding, *The History of Ophelia* (2 vols, London: R. Baldwin, 1760), vol. I, p. 55. Subsequent page references in the text are to this edition.
22. Terry Castle, *Masquerade and Civilisation: the Carnivalesque in Eighteenth-Century English Culture and Fiction* (London: Methuen, 1986), pp. 216, 219.
23. Although Mrs Atkinson is free from vice, she is not free from imprudence, as events throughout the novel demonstrate; she lives uneconomically with her first husband, and on at least one occasion has a drop too much to drink during her second marriage. Her economic judgement is exercised, it seems, only in extra-domestic ways; the qualities embodied in Amelia or Mrs Bilson which would make her the perfect housewife are always directed beyond the 'domestic inclosure', rather than within it.
24. Jean Hagstrum, *Sex and Sensibility: Ideal and Erotic Love from Milton to Mozart* (Chicago: University of Chicago Press, 1980), p. 10.
25. Fordyce, I, 93; compare also Wilkes, pp. 114–15: 'Chastity is a kind of quick and delicate feeling in the soul, which makes her shrink, and withdraw herself, from every thing that is wanton, or has danger in it' and Addison's comment that modesty is 'such an exquisite Sensibility, as warns a woman to shun the first Appearance of every thing which is hurtful' (quoted in Chris Jones, *Radical Sensibility: Literature and Ideas in the 1790s* [London and New York: Routledge, 1993], p. 5).
26. It is interesting to compare this all-female Eden with Hagstrum's comment (p. 14) that there is an 'insistent and recurring suggestion all through the Age of Sensibility … that men and women, finding themselves in love … identified themselves with Milton's primal pair.' Here it is the advent of a man which destroys Edenic harmony.
27. Adam Smith, *The Wealth of Nations* (1776; 2 vols, Oxford: Clarendon Press, 1976), vol. I, pp. 82, 25.
28. Ibid., I, 37–46.
29. Castle, p. 85.

30. One of Ophelia's companions at the masquerade, Lady Rochester, looks upon it as 'the English Saturnalia' (I, 220); Terry Castle discusses the masquerade's links with 'the ancient and powerful world of carnival', p. 11.

31. Sheridan Baker, 'Fielding's *Amelia* and the Materials of Romance', *Philological Quarterly*, 41 (1962), p. 449.

32. Carolyn Williams, 'Fielding and Half-learned Ladies', *Essays in Criticism*, 38 (1988), p. 28.

33. Sheridan Baker recognises the strong sentimentalism in *Amelia* – if in less than complimentary terms: 'with the comic controls removed entirely, the realism turns Fielding's habitual romance techniques sentimental, and lures him into the further temptations and pious self-deceptions of sentimentalism' (p. 449).

34. In Jean-Jacques Rousseau's *La Nouvelle Héloïse*, for example, St Preux laments: 'Had it not been for thee, thou fatal beauty, I could never have experienced the insupportable contrast between the greatness of my soul, and the low estate of my fortune' (1761; first translated into English 1762; rpt of 1803 translation, Oxford: Woodstock Books, 1989), p. 140.

35. As James Thompson notes, *Amelia* 'images a world almost totally ruled by money' (*Models of Value: Eighteenth-Century Political Economy and the Novel* [Durham and London: Duke University Press, 1996], p. 144).

36. Adam Smith, *Moral Sentiments*, I, 74. In *Models of Value*, James Thompson comments that 'In Fielding's attack on the decadent aristocracy in *Amelia*, social obligation has become explicitly financial, transformed into a kind of social capital deployed to oppress the lower orders' (p. 145).

37. Charke, p. 67.

38. Henry Fielding, *A Proposal for Making an Effectual Provision for the Poor* (London: A. Millar, 1753), p. 6.

39. Ibid., pp. 3–4.

40. Smith, *Moral Sentiments*, I, 333–4. Hume also felt that 'A certain degree of poverty produces contempt' but went on, 'a degree beyond causes compassion and good-will. We may under-value a peasant or a servant; but when the misery of a beggar appears very great, or is painted in very lively colours, we sympathize with him in his afflictions, and feel in our heart evident touches of pity and benevolence' (*A Treatise of Human Nature* [1739–40; Oxford: Clarendon Press, 1978], p. 387; quoted in Jones, *Radical Sensibility*, p. 29). Sympathy with beggars did not prevent Hume from sharing Smith's inclination to see the different classes as in entirely different categories from one another, however: see Chapter 5, n. 14.

41. David Blewett, Introduction to *Amelia* (Harmondsworth: Penguin, 1987), p. x; George Sherburn, 'Fielding's *Amelia*: An Interpretation', in Ronald Paulson (ed.), *Fielding: A Collection of Critical Essays* (Englewood Cliffs, NJ: Prentice-Hall, Inc., 1962), p. 147; Baker, p. 445; Castle, pp. 186–7.

42. Castle, p. 241.

CHAPTER 4

1. Sir James Steuart, *An Inquiry into the Principles of Political Œconomy: Being an Essay on the Science of Domestic Policy in Free Nations*, (2 vols, London: Millar and Cadell, 1767), vol. I, p. 1. Subsequent page references in the text are to this edition.

2. Louis Dumont, *From Mandeville to Marx: The Genesis and Triumph of Economic Ideology* (Chicago and London: The University of Chicago Press, 1977), p. 35.

3. Frances Brooke, *The History of Lady Julia Mandeville* (1763), in Mrs Barbauld (ed.), *The British Novelists*, vol. 27 (London: F. C. and J. Rivington *et al.*, 1820), p. 8. Subsequent page references in the text are to this edition.

4. Oliver Goldsmith, *The Vicar of Wakefield* (1766) in Arthur Friedman (ed.), *Collected Works of Oliver Goldsmith* (5 vols, Oxford: Clarendon Press, 1966), vol. 4, p. 167. Subsequent page references in the text are to this edition.

5. H. T. Dickinson, *Liberty and Property: Political Ideology in Eighteenth-Century Britain* (New York: Holmes and Meier, 1977), p. 21. It is also perhaps useful at this point to stress that, while Steuart uses a patriarchal model to describe his theory of political economy, he was politically opposed to the kind of absolute patriarchy favoured by Filmer, believing rather that the power of the ruler should be limited and that the development of a commercial society would be directly favourable to such limitation. Albert O. Hirschman writes that there is a distinction 'implicit in Steuart, between "arbitrary" abuses of power that stem from the riches and passions of the rulers ... on the one hand, and the "fine tuning" carried out by a hypothetical statesman exclusively motivated by the common good, on the other. According to Steuart, modern economic expansion puts an end to the former type of intervention, but creates a special need for the latter if the economy is to move along a reasonably smooth trajectory.' See Hirschman, *The Passions and the Interests: Political Arguments for Capitalism before its Triumph* (Princeton, NJ: Princeton University Press, 1977), p. 86. I develop such ideas further in Chapter 6.

6. John Bender, 'Prison Reform and the Sentence of Narration in *The Vicar of Wakefield*', in Felicity Nussbaum and Laura Brown (eds), *The New Eighteenth Century: Theory, Politics, English Literature* (New York and London: Methuen, 1987), p. 182.

7. Sheridan Baker, 'Fielding's *Amelia* and the Materials of Romance', *Philological Quarterly*, 41 (1962), p. 445.

8. *The Poems of Alexander Pope*, ed. John Butt (1963; London: Routledge, 1989), p. 510, ll. 169–70.

9. Lorraine McMullen, *An Odd Attempt in a Woman: the Literary Life of Frances Brooke* (Vancouver: University of British Columbia Press, 1983), pp. 57–60.

10. Wetenhall Wilkes, *A Letter of Genteel and Moral Advice to a Young Lady* (1740; 8th edn, London: L. Hawes, 1766), p. 220.

11. McMullen, p. 61.

12. Elizabeth Bellamy also makes this point in *Private Virtues, Public Vices: Commercial Morality and the Novel 1740–1800* (unpublished PhD thesis; Cambridge, 1988), p. 271.

13. Bender, p. 115.

14. Dumont, p. 35. The phrase 'the mercantilist period' is generally used to signify, rather loosely, the seventeenth century and the eighteenth century up to the last decades.

15. Sarah Fielding, *David Simple* (1744; Oxford: Oxford University Press, 1987), Book III, Chapter vi, pp. 189–90.

16. Similar kinds of redefinition of 'luxury' had been earlier attempted by Hume and Hutcheson. See Bellamy, pp. 93ff.

17. Compare John Dyer, for whom Chinese tea and vases are 'Things elegant, ill-titled luxuries,/In temp'rance us'd delectable and good' (*The Fleece: A Poem* [London: R. and J. Dodsley, 1757], Book IV, ll. 379–80).

18. Adam Smith, *The Theory of Moral Sentiments* (1759; 11th ed., 2 vols, Edinburgh: Bell and Bradfoute *et al.*, 1808), vol. II, p. 290.

19. Gertrude Himmelfarb, *The Idea of Poverty: England in the Early Industrial Age* (London and Boston: Faber & Faber 1984), pp. 30–1.

20. David Hume, *A Treatise of Human Nature* (1739–40), edited by L. A. Selby-Bigge (Oxford: Oxford University Press, 1888; 2nd edition 1978; rpt 1987), p. 537.

21. Hume, p. 534.

22. John Barrell, *English Literature in History 1730–80: An Equal, Wide Survey* (London: Hutchinson, 1983), p. 33.

23. Barrell, p. 40.

24. Bellamy, p. 268.

25. Adam Smith, *The Wealth of Nations* (1776; 2 vols, Oxford: Clarendon Press, 1976), vol. I, p. 82.

26. For the fullest discussion of the conservative politics of *Humphry Clinker*, see John Sekora, *Luxury: the Concept in Western Thought, Eden to Smollett* (Baltimore and London: The Johns Hopkins University Press, 1977), especially Part Three. See also John P. Zomchick, 'Social Class, Character, and Narrative Strategy in *Humphry Clinker*', *Eighteenth-Century Life*, 10 (1986), pp. 172–85.

27. Tobias Smollett, *The Expedition of Humphry Clinker* (The Everyman Library; London: J. M. Dent & Vermont: Charles E. Tuttle, 1993), p. 321. (Subsequent references in the text are to this edition.) It is typical of Bramble's position in the text that there are two drowning episodes – the first, comical, incident in which Humphry Clinker mistakenly believes him to be drowning while sea-bathing at Scarborough (pp. 187–8) and the second, in which Clinker actually saves his life (p. 321).

28. Zomchick, p. 173.

29. Sekora, p. 265.

30. It is of course noteworthy that Liddy's love turns out not to be imprudent at all, since the strolling-player is in reality an eminently eligible young gentleman temporarily estranged from his worthy family. In his recent full-length study of Smollett, John Skinner finds this the one aspect of *Humphry Clinker* that could be seen as challenging Smollett's

pervasive misogyny, since although 'the male correspondents, Bramble and his nephew Jery, insistently undermine the conventions of romance, invested above all in the ingenuous Lydia … yet Lydia's romantic intuition about the true identity of Denny/Wilson proves entirely justified. Her reading is the correct one.' See John Skinner, *Constructions of Smollett: A Study of Genre and Gender* (Newark: University of Delaware Press & London: Associated University Presses, 1996), p. 237.

31. For Jery's progress in this regard, see p. 10, where he declares, 'My uncle is an odd kind of humorist, always on the fret, and so unpleasant in his manner, that rather than be obliged to keep him company, I'd resign all claim to the inheritance of his estate. – Indeed his being tortured by the gout may have soured his temper, and, perhaps, I may like him better on further acquaintance: certain it is, all his servants, and neighbours in the country, are fond of him, even to a degree of enthusiasm, the reason of which I cannot as yet comprehend.' Understanding the 'enthusiasm' others feel for Bramble, and appreciating the soundness of both his reasoning and his feelings, is the process of education Jery must undergo in order to become a worthy successor. See Sekora, *Luxury*, pp. 252–4, for an account of Jery's transformation.

  John Skinner sees the relationship between Bramble's and Jery's narratives somewhat differently, suggesting that 'it is precisely the promiscuity and miscegenation detested by Bramble and apparently celebrated by Jery, that provide the mainspring of comedy in *Humphry Clinker*.' However, that 'apparently' is of the utmost importance for, as Skinner points out, 'Jery finds social miscegenation more attractive when he is a detached spectator, and he expresses horror at the thought of his own sister marrying an actor' (p. 196). Despite the contrast in tone, then, the views of uncle and nephew are likely to coincide in essentials.

32. The most important instance is, of course, the scene of sentimental reunion already discussed, but there are other examples, such as the case of the blacksmith's widow (p. 190) and Lismahago's plight (p. 193).

33. Thomas R. Preston, 'Smollett and the Benevolent Misanthrope Type', *PMLA*, 79 (1964), p. 52. Without reference to Preston, Ann Jessie Van Sant also refers to Bramble in these terms, noting that 'Smollett brings together the man of feeling and the man of humor, defining excess by acuteness of sensation rather than humoral imbalance. Bramble is, in other words, a traditional physiological character type with a new physiology' (*Eighteenth-Century Sensibility and the Novel: The Senses in Social Context* [Cambridge: Cambridge University Press, 1993], p. 103.)

34. See Zomchick, p. 177, for his analysis of this scene.

35. Acts 9. 36.

36. There is an irony here in that it is the mob, for whom Bramble professes so much fear and hatred, which acts as an apparently natural curb on the social aspirations he so equally disapproves of.

37. Zomchick, p. 183.

38. Ibid., p. 184.

39. Bramble continues, a little further on: 'I believe it will be found upon inquiry, that nineteen out of twenty, who are ruined by extravagance, fall a sacrifice to the ridiculous pride and vanity of silly women, whose parts are held in contempt by the very men whom they pillage and enslave' (p. 301). Later, Dennison underlines the point once more: '"the pride, envy, and ambition of ... wives and daughters. – These are the rocks upon which all the small estates in the country are wrecked"' (p. 335).

CHAPTER 5

1. Elizabeth Griffith, *Essays Addressed to Young Married Women* (London, 1782), pp. 109–10. For similar advice, see for example, Lady Pennington, *An Unfortunate Mother's Advice to her Absent Daughters, in a Letter to Miss Pennington* (1761), p. 63, and John Gregory, *A Father's Legacy to his Daughters* (London: Strahan, Cadell, Balfour & Creech, 1774), pp. 52–3.
2. Griffith, *Essays*, p. 108.
3. Janet Todd, *Sensibility: An Introduction* (London: Methuen, 1986), p. 3.
4. John Mullan, *Sentiment and Sociability: The Language of Feeling in the Eighteenth Century* (Oxford: Clarendon Press, 1988), pp. 118–19.
5. Sir James Steuart, *An Inquiry into the Principles of Political Œconomy* (2 vols, London: Millar and Cadell, 1767), vol. I, p. 1.
6. Robert Markley, 'Sentimentality as Performance: Shaftesbury, Sterne and the Theatrics of Virtue', in Felicity Nussbaum and Laura Brown (eds), *The New Eighteenth Century: Theory, Politics, English Literature* (London and New York: Methuen, 1987), p. 210.
7. Elizabeth Griffith, *The History of Lady Barton, A Novel in Letters* (1771; 2nd edn, 3 vols, London: T. Davies & T. Cadell, 1773), vol. I, p. 68. Subsequent references in the text will be to this edition.
8. Griffith, *A Series of Genuine Letters Between Henry and Frances* (1757; 3rd edn, 2 vols, London: W. Johnston, 1767), vol. I, p. xxiv.
9. *Genuine Letters*, I, 44.
10. Tony Tanner, *Adultery in the Novel: Contract and Transgression* (Baltimore and London: The Johns Hopkins University Press, 1979), p. 12.
11. *Genuine Letters*, I, 57. In this Frances agrees with David Hume, who wrote in *A Treatise of Human Nature* (1739–40; Oxford: Clarendon Press, 1987, p. 573) that 'Courage, which is the point of honour among men, derives its merit, in a great measure, from artifice, as well as the chastity of women'.
12. Anonymous, *The Economy of Human Life* (1750; 'by Robert Dodsley', Manchester, 1797), p. 12.
13. Henry Mackenzie, *The Man of Feeling* (Oxford: Oxford University Press, 1987), p. 24 (subsequent references in the text will be to this edition); Mullan, p. 61.
14. David Hume, *A Treatise of Human Nature* (1739–40; Oxford: Clarendon Press, 1978), p. 402: 'The skin, pores, muscles, and nerves of a

day-labourer are different from those of a man of quality: So are his sentiments, actions and manners. The different stations of life influence the whole fabric, external and internal ...'; Adam Smith, *The Theory of Moral Sentiments* (1759; 11th edn, Edinburgh, 1808), 2 vols, vol. I, p. 444; *The Economy of Human Life*, p. 33. In *Radical Sensibility*, Chris Jones notes how Hutcheson too 'had counselled his benevolent readers against thinking of lower-class characters as having the same sensibility of their hardships as the sympathizing middle-class onlooker. Their minds and bodies are "soon fitted to their state" and this should "support a compassionate Heart, too deeply touched with apprehended Miseries, of which the *Sufferers* are themselves insensible"' (London and New York: Routledge, 1993, p. 68).

15. John Millar, *The Origin of the Distinction of Ranks* (1771; 3rd edn, 1779), reprinted in William C. Lehmann, *John Millar of Glasgow 1735–1801: His Life and Thought and his Contributions to Sociological Analysis* (Cambridge: Cambridge University Press, 1960), p. 176. In *Models of Value: Eighteenth-Century Political Economy and the Novel* (Durham and London: Duke University Press, 1996), James Thompson underlines this point when he refers to the way in which Adam Smith 'assumes that the subject is defined by his income, by his property, what C. B. Macpherson terms "possessive individualism." This interrelation has considerable significance for understanding the ways in which individual subjects are represented in eighteenth-century literature, particularly the novel which proceeds by defining subjects according to their possessions – what they own, and how they own, and why they own' (pp. 84–5).

16. Fanny's economic independence, it should be noted, is owing to the way in which Sir George is a significantly absent authority for much of the novel. When he does appear, it is to be more under the direction of Fanny than vice versa.

17. Harriet Guest, 'A Double Lustre: Femininity and Sociable Commerce, 1730–60', *Eighteenth-Century Studies*, 23 (Summer, 1990), p. 490.

18. Elizabeth Bellamy, *Private Virtues, Public Vices: Commercial Morality and the Novel, 1740–1800*, unpublished PhD thesis (Cambridge, 1988), p. 313.

19. Mackenzie, *The Man of the World* (1773), in *Works* (8 vols, Edinburgh: Archibald Constable & Co., 1808), vol. I, p. 318.

20. See, for example, *The Mirror* (1779–80), nos. 12 and 25 and *The Lounger* (1785–87), nos. 17 and 98, in Rev. Robert Lynam (ed.), *The British Essayists* (30 vols, London: J. F. Dove, 1827), vols 24 and 25.

21. Bellamy, p. 313.

22. Nancy Armstrong, *Desire and Domestic Fiction: a Political History of the Novel* (New York and Oxford: Oxford University Press, 1987), p. 30.

23. Todd, p. 119.

24. Jane Spencer, *The Rise of Woman Novelist: From Aphra Behn to Jane Austen* (Oxford: Blackwell, 1986), p. 124.

25. Todd, p. 117.

26. Compare, for example, Peter in *The Man of Feeling* (pp. 18–19), or Le Blanc in Mackenzie's *Julia de Roubigné*.

27. Mary Astell, *A Serious Proposal to the Ladies, for the Advancement of their True and Greatest Interest* (1694; 2nd edn, London: R. Wilkin, 1695), especially pp. 48–9; Sarah Scott, *Millenium Hall* (London: J. Newbury, 1762).

28. Scott, pp. 1, 69.
29. See, for example, Millar, p. 220.
30. Guest, p. 483.
31. Raymond Williams, *The Country and the City*, quoted in Mullan, p. 126.
32. Mullan, p. 126.
33. Ibid., p. 125.
34. *Genuine Letters*, I, 57–8.
35. Adam Smith, *The Theory of Moral Sentiments* (1759; 11th edn, 2 vols, Edinburgh: Bell and Bradfoute *et al.*, 1808), vol. I, pp. 287–8.
36. Spencer, p. 126.
37. Laurence Sterne, *A Sentimental Journey* (1768; Oxford: Oxford University Press, 1984; rpt 1987), p. 21. Subsequent references in the text are to this edition.
38. John Mullan usefully discusses the 'innocence' of *A Sentimental Journey* in *Sentiment and Sociability*, commenting:

> It is as if the *Sentimental Journey*, most graphically in the act of omission with which it concludes, dares its readers to find anything except innocence in its thrills and encounters. As Sterne declared to an admiring, aristocratic reader, 'If it is not thought a chaste book, mercy on them that read it, for they must have warm imaginations indeed!' Attuned to contemporary ideas of reading as a moral (or immoral) activity, Sterne produces a narrative which 'is all quite innocent provided one takes it so'. (p. 196)

39. See Arthur Hill Cash, *Sterne's Comedy of Moral Sentiments: The Ethical Dimension of the Journey* (Pittsburgh, PA: Duquesne University Press, 1966).
40. Mullan, pp. 191–2.
41. Mullan, p. 193.
42. Markley, p. 211.
43. In *Eighteenth-Century Sensibility and the Novel* (Cambridge: Cambridge University Press, 1993), Ann Jessie Van Sant also discusses this episode as 'a scene of substituted sexual pleasure' (p. 109) but, in concentrating on its physiological and interiorising aspects, does not mention the financial transaction to which it ultimately leads.

CHAPTER 6

1. Adam Smith, *Lectures on Justice, Police, Revenue and Arms*, ed. Edwin Cannan (Oxford: Clarendon Press, 1896), p. 259; quoted in Albert O. Hirschman, *The Passions and the Interests: Political Arguments for Capitalism before its Triumph* (Princeton, NJ: Princeton University Press, 1977), p. 61.
2. Elizabeth and Richard Griffith, *A Series of Genuine Letters Between Henry and Frances* (1757; 3rd edn, 2 vols, London: W. Johnston, 1767), vol. I, p. xxiv.

3.   Sylvana Tomaselli, 'The Enlightenment Debate on Women', *History Workshop Journal*, 19 (1985), p. 121. Tomaselli discusses, among others, Montesquieu's *De l'esprit des lois* (1748), Diderot's 'Sur les femmes' (1772), John Millar's *Origin of the Distinction of Ranks* (1771) and William Alexander's *History of Women* (1782). In his *Distinction of Ranks*, John Millar wrote that the condition of women 'is naturally improved by every circumstance which tends to create more attention to the pleasures of sex, and increase the value of those occupations that are suited to the female character; by the cultivation of the arts of life; by the advancement of opulence, and by the gradual refinement of taste and manners' (3rd edn, 1779; reprinted in William C. Lehmann, *John Millar of Glasgow* [Cambridge: Cambridge University Press, 1960], p. 203).

4.   John Gregory, *A Father's Legacy to His Daughters* (London: Strahan, Cadell, Balfour & Creech, 1774), p. 7.

5.   Hannah More, *Essays on Various Subjects, principally designed for the young ladies* (4th edn, London: T. Cadell, 1785), p. 13.

6.   More, *Sensibility: an Epistle to the Honourable Mrs. Boscawen* (1782); reprinted in *Poems* (London: T. Cadell & W. Davies, 1816), p. 186.

7.   William Robertson, *A View of the Progress of Society in Europe* (1769); reprinted in *Works* (12 vols, London: William Baynes, 1824), vol. XII, p. 82; quoted in Hirschman, p. 61.

8.   See Hirschman, pp. 60–1.

9.   Henry Brooke, *The Fool of Quality* (1765–70; London: Routledge, 1906), pp. 25–6. Subsequent page references in the text are to this edition.

10. John Mullan, *Sentiment and Sociability: the Language of Feeling in the Eighteenth Century* (Oxford: Clarendon Press, 1988), p. 134. For other discussions of *The Fool of Quality* see for example Elizabeth Bellamy, *Private Virtues, Public Vices: Commercial Morality and the Novel 1740–1800* (unpublished PhD thesis; Cambridge, 1988), pp. 264–5, and Janet Todd, *Sensibility: an Introduction* (London and New York: Methuen, 1987), pp. 95–6.

11. Robert Markley, 'Sentimentality as Performance: Shaftesbury, Sterne and the Theatrics of Virtue' in Nussbaum and Brown (eds), *The New Eighteenth Century*, p. 230.

12. Tomaselli, p. 114.

13. Hirschman, p. 129.

14. See my Chapter 5, p. 92.

15. Robert Bage, *Barham Downs* (2 vols, London: G. Wilkie, 1784), vol. I, p. 2. Subsequent page references in the text are to this edition.

16. Peter Faulkner, in his *Robert Bage* (Boston: Twayne Publishers, 1979), quotes this pertinent passage from *The History of Birmingham* (1782) written by Bage's life-long friend and business partner, William Hutton: 'Civility and humanity are ever the companions of trade; the man of business is the man of liberal sentiment; a barbarous and a commercial people is a contradiction; if he is not the philosopher of nature, he is the friend of his country', and comments that 'Bage's novels embody a similar mercantile confidence' (p. 18).

17. An interesting comparison is provided by the argument Henry Mackenzie puts forward in favour of a 'liberal education' for men of

business. 'Letters', he says, 'give room for the exercise of that discernment, that comparison of objects, that distinction of causes, which is to increase the skill of the physician, to guide the speculation of the merchant, and to prompt the arguments of the lawyer ...' (*The Lounger*, no. 100 [30 December 1786], in Rev. Robert Lynam (ed.), *The British Essayists*, [30 vols; London: J. F. Dove, 1827], vol. 25, p. 505).

18. This recalls Adam Smith's view that 'The mere want of fortune, mere poverty, excites little compassion ... . The fall from riches to poverty, as it commonly occasions the most real distress to the sufferer, so it seldom fails to excite the most sincere commiseration in the spectator' (see my Chapter 3, p. 52), and further confirms his assurance that the sufferer 'is almost always so much pitied, that he is scarce ever allowed to fall into the lowest state of poverty' and is indulged in his 'imprudence' by the lenity of his creditors (*The Theory of Moral Sentiments*, [1759; 11th edn, 2 vols, Edinburgh: Bell & Bradfoute *et al.*, 1808], vol. I, pp. 333–4).

19. Agnes Maria Bennett, *Anna; or Memoirs of a Welch Heiress: Interspersed with Anecdotes of a Nabob* (1785; 2nd edn, 4 vols, London: William Lane, 1786), vol. III, p. 240. Subsequent page references in the text are to this edition. Although Agnes Maria Bennett is hardly known today, it is worth bearing in mind Dorothy Blakey's comment about Bennett in her history of the Minerva Press: 'when Mrs Bennett died in 1808 the whole body of her work ranked her, in the eyes of contemporaries at least, with Fielding and Richardson' (*The Minerva Press, 1790–1820* [London: Printed for the Bibliographical Society at the University Press, Oxford, 1939], p. 57).

20. Compare the words of 'Barbara Heartless' in no. 90 of *The Lounger* (21 October 1786): 'from my rank in life, being a tradesman's daughter, left an orphan at six years old, I had little title to know any thing about sensibility or feeling' (Lynam (ed.), p. 444).

21. Louis Dumont, *From Mandeville to Marx: the Genesis and Triumph of Economic Ideology* (Chicago and London: The University of Chicago Press, 1977), p. 35. See also my Chapter 4, pp. 72–3 and 86–7.

22. See Henry Mackenzie, *The Man of Feeling* (1771; Oxford: Oxford University Press, 1987), p. 66, and my Chapter 5, p. 98.

23. See, for example, the passage where O'Donnel's fellow officer Parry reflects that '"a push of the sword, or a pull of the trigger, may make wretched widows and orphan children, or childless and disconsolate parents; destroy the promising prospects of families and consign them to beggary and ruin"' (*Barham Downs*, II, 336).

24. See Chapter 5, pp. 102–3.

25. Hirschman, p. 63.

26. This applies equally to the character of Arabella, the milliner who marries Clement in *The Fool of Quality*. Her exemplary conduct as a wife links her with Amelia, Mrs Bilson and Caroline Traverse; in the same way as the latter, an illness deprives her of the use of her hands and thus of the ability to earn money (p. 112).

27. Janet Todd, *The Sign of Angellica: Women, Writing and Fiction, 1660–1800* (London: Virago, 1989), p. 205.

28. See Hirschman, pp. 82–93, for discussion of ideas in Montesquieu, Sir James Steuart and John Millar on the potential of commerce for

restricting the exercise of arbitrary and authoritarian power. Millar comments that the regulations in modern European nations 'which have made the greatest improvements in commerce and manufactures', 'tend to moderate the excessive and arbitrary power assumed by the head of a family, [and] are supported by every consideration of justice and utility. The opinion of Sir Robert Filmer, who founds the doctrine of passive obedience to a monarch, upon the unlimited submission which children owe to their father, seems, at this day, unworthy of the serious refutation which it has met with …' (*Distinction of Ranks*, p. 243).

29. See Elizabeth Griffith, *The History of Lady Barton* (1771; 2nd edn, 3 vols, London: T. Davies & T. Cadell, 1773), vol. III, p. 214, and my Chapter 5, p. 105.

30. Richard Price, *Observations on the Nature of Civil Liberty, the Principles of Government, and the Justice and Policy of the War with America* (2nd edn, London: T. Cadell, 1776), p. 11.

31. Mary Wollstonecraft, *Thoughts on the Education of Daughters* (1787); Todd and Butler (eds), *The Works of Mary Wollstonecraft* (7 vols; London: William Pickering, 1989), vol. 4, p. 25.

32. See my Chapter 2, p. 35.

33. Smith, *Lectures on Justice*, p. 258.

34. See for example III, 106: 'They were sitting on white sattin [*sic*] Ottomans, a superb breakfast equipage before them; the room breathed perfumes; it was decorated with the choicest and most beautiful flowers in the finest china vases; the toilette magnificently set out with silver fillagree boxes; and the assemblage of every elegance luxury could invent, or money purchase, were here in the height of profusion.'

35. As exemplified in her 'domestic establishment' in which 'happiness and decorum were more consulted than shew or grandeur, although there appeared no deficiency in the latter' (IV, 55).

36. Chris Jones, *Radical Sensibility: Literature and Ideas in the 1790s* (London and New York: Routledge, 1993), p. 82.

37. *The Monthly Review*, September 1784, vol. 71 (London: R. Griffiths, 1785), p. 224.

38. Gary Kelly, *The English Jacobin Novel 1780–1805* (Oxford: Clarendon Press, 1976), pp. 30–1.

39. Montesquieu, *Oeuvres Complètes* (Daniel Oster (ed.), Paris: 1964), vol. XIX, p. 644; quoted in Tomaselli, p. 113.

40. See my Chapter 3, pp. 43–4.

41. Kelly, p. 41.

42. Price, *Observations on Reversionary Payments* (1773; 4th edn, London: T. Cadell, 1783), p. 206.

43. Todd, *The Sign of Angellica*, p. 103.

44. Kelly, p. 8.

45. Chris Jones, *Radical Sensibility*, p. 83.

46. Faulkner, *Robert Bage*, p. 72.

47. Adam Smith, *An Inquiry into the Nature and Causes of the Wealth of Nations* (1776; 2 vols, Oxford: Clarendon Press, 1976), vol. I, p. 283.

48. See *Wealth of Nations*, I, 541 and especially Book V, chapter iii, 'Of publick Debts'.

49. See *Wealth of Nations*, II, 924, in which Smith roundly criticises such a view put forward in J. F. Melon's *Essai politique sur le Commerce* (1734; trans. D. Bindon 1738). See also Terence Hutchison, *Before Adam Smith: The Emergence of Political Economy 1662-1776* (Oxford: Blackwell, 1988), p. 400, n. 10 which explains how Isaac de Pinto's *Traité de la circulation et du crédit* (1773, English translation 1774) 'maintained that the public debt supported "circulation" and that England's economic advance had been promoted by her public debt and public credit.'

50. Hirschman, p. 76.

51. Price, *Civil Liberty*, p. 109.

52. Elizabeth Bellamy, writing of Bage's later novel *Man As He Is* in her unpublished PhD thesis *Private Virtues, Public Vices: Commercial Morality and the Novel 1740–1800* (Cambridge, 1988), p. 291.

53. Peter Faulkner, Introduction to *Hermsprong* (Oxford: Oxford University Press, 1985), p. vii.

54. For a discussion of the extent of the radical debt to country ideology, see H. T. Dickinson, *Liberty and Property: Political Ideology in Eighteenth-Century Britain* (New York: Holmes & Meier, 1977), Chapter 6, 'The Development of a Radical Ideology'.

55. Jane Austen, *Mansfield Park* (1814; London, New York, Toronto: Oxford University Press, 1970), p. 432.

56. See Marilyn Butler, *Jane Austen and the War of Ideas* (Oxford: Clarendon Press, 1975; reissued with a new Introduction, 1987), pp. 242–5.

57. Austen, *Mansfield Park*, p. 52; Tony Tanner, Introduction to the Penguin edition of *Mansfield Park* (London, 1966; rpt. 1985), p. 11. While there is not space to explore it here, the exact social position of the Crawfords is admittedly a complicated one in that they possess an estate; their values, however, do seem to me to indicate the rejection of commercial attitudes, as Tanner suggests.

58. See Harriet Guest, 'A Double Lustre: Femininity and Sociable Commerce, 1730–60', *Eighteenth-Century Studies*, 23 (Summer, 1990), pp. 479–501, and my Chapter 5, pp. 107–8.

59. It also looks forward, interestingly, to Mary Wollstonecraft's opinion in the *Vindication* that 'It is vain to expect virtue from women till they are, in some degree, independent of men' (*Works*, vol. 5, p. 211).

60. Guest, p. 482.

61. Griffith, *The History of Lady Barton*, I, 70.

62. See my Chapter 5, p. 108.

63. Todd, *The Sign of Angellica*, p. 202.

CHAPTER 7

1. Helen Maria Williams, *Julia* (2 vols, Dublin: Chamberlaine and Rice *et al.*, 1790), vol. II, p. 192. Subsequent page references in the text are to this edition. Mary Wollstonecraft, *A Vindication of the Rights of Woman* (1792); Janet Todd and Marilyn Butler (eds), *The Works of Mary Wollstonecraft* (7 vols, London: William Pickering, 1989), vol. 5, p. 155.

2. For a discussion of this moment in the novel see Vivien Jones, 'Women Writing Revolution: Narratives of History and Sexuality in Wollstonecraft and Williams', in Stephen Copley and John Whale (eds), *Beyond Romanticism* (London: Routledge, 1992).

3. Most notable examples of this are probably Laetitia Matilda Hawkins, who in her *Letters on the Female Mind, its Powers and Pursuits* (2 vols, London: Hookham & Carpenter, 1793) wished to convince Helen Maria Williams 'that there is but one side a female can take in politics', and described politics as 'the climax of unfitness' as a study for women (I, 5; 21); and Hannah More, whose *Strictures on the Modern System of Female Education* (2 vols, London: T. Cadell & W. Davies, 1799) contained the following assurance: 'I am not sounding an alarm to female warriors, or exciting female politicians: I hardly know which of the two is the most disgusting and unnatural character' (I, 6).

4. Examples include Gertrude and D'Oyley in Charles Lloyd's *Edmund Oliver* (1798), and Geraldine and Fitzosborne in Jane West's *A Tale of the Times* (1799) as well as, from a different political standpoint, Anna and Coke Clifton in Thomas Holcroft's *Anna St. Ives* (1792). See also Janet Todd, *The Sign of Angellica: Women, Writing and Fiction, 1660–1800* (London: Virago, 1989), in which she remarks how in novels of the 1790s 'The particular feminine trajectory stood in for the trajectory of the nation' (p. 233). As Chris Jones writes in *Radical Sensibility*, 'The debates of the 1790s were characterized by a politicizing of issues raised within the school of sensibility to the extent that one's stand on matters such as the conduct of the private affections, charity, education, [etc.] became political statements, aligned with conservative or radical ideologies. Under the suppression of direct political expression, these issues became a code in which conservative and progressive thinkers proclaimed their allegiances and worked out terms of accommodation' (London: Routledge, 1993, p. 13).

5. Edmund Burke, *Reflections on the Revolution in France* (1790); L. G. Mitchell (ed.), *The Writings and Speeches of Edmund Burke* (Oxford: Clarendon Press, 1989), vol. 8, p. 84.

6. More, *Strictures* (II, 173–4). And compare for example Fanny Burney, *Camilla* (1796; Oxford: Oxford University Press, 1983; rpt 1986), in which Mr Tyrold tells his wife that he holds 'it as much a moral duty not to refuse receiving good offices, as not to avoid administering them. That species of independence, which proudly flies all ties of gratitude, is inimical to the social compact of civilized life, which subsists but by reciprocity of services' (p. 232); also Jane West, *A Gossip's Story* (1796; 4th edn, 2 vols, London: T. N. Longman & O. Rees, 1799), where the narrator, Mrs Prudentia Homespun, informs the reader that Christianity, 'Upon the basis of mutual wants, general imperfection, and universal kindred ... builds the fair structure of candour and benevolence' (I, 49).

7. William Godwin, *Enquiry concerning Political Justice* (1793; London: Penguin, 1976; rpt 1985), 'Summary of Principles', p. 76. See also Wollstonecraft, *A Vindication of the Rights of Woman*, especially p. 110 where the naturalisation of dependence is described as acting against

the 'wise designs of nature', which lead towards independence. See also Nicola Watson, *Purloined Letters: Revolution, Reaction, and the Form of the Novel, 1790–1825* (Unpublished DPhil thesis; Oxford: 1990), in which she describes conservative upholders of 'the Burkean ideal of the patriarchal familial network of affections and obligations as the microcosm, and the foundation, of a stable society' as 'horrified' by Godwin's suggestion that 'universal benevolence could only exist when individuals were freed of obligations and unfettered by inequality of property, or relationships (filial or marital) based on property' (p. 101).

8. See, for example, Susan E. Brown, 'Rational Creatures and Free Citizens: The Language of Politics in the Eighteenth-Century Debate on Women', *Historical Papers/Communications Historiques*, Canadian Historical Association, 1988, p. 47. Also Marilyn Butler's *Jane Austen and the War of Ideas* (Oxford: Clarendon Press, 1975; reissued with a new introduction, 1987; rpt 1990), in which she writes 'In sexual matters the jacobins thought and as a group behaved (whatever their opponents claimed) like forerunners of the Evangelicals. Their advocacy of reason and restraint often makes them read like their opponents, the conservative moralists ...' (p. 45), and Janet Todd, *The Sign of Angellica: Women, Writing and Fiction, 1660–1800* (London: Virago, 1989), p. 234, where she identifies strategies and conclusions common to women writers of the 1790s across the political spectrum.

9. Jones, *Radical Sensibility*, p. 15. The point is further reinforced in the following passage: 'The varieties of sensibility are all linked, and considerable force is needed to compress them into one type or typical narrative trajectory. Neither radical nor conservative sensibility denied the pleasures of taste, sympathy, and enthusiasm. Radical sensibility could offer just as much in the way of discipline and social usefulness as the conservative alternative, and aim at that extensive benefit to society which was derided as illusory by conservative writers' (p. 17).

10. Brown, p. 47, quotes Richard Polwhele's *The Unsex'd Females* (1798) as finding the ideals and principles of conservatives such as Hannah More 'diametrically opposite to [those of] Miss Wollstonecraft'.

11. See, for example, Jane West, *The Advantages of Education, or, the History of Maria Williams* (2 vols, London: Minerva, 1793), in which the narrator (Mrs Prudentia Homespun) protests that 'real evils in abundance exist, to stem the torrent of refined whimseys, and sentimental extravagance' (I, 34). Of course sentimental vocabulary was also under attack from radical writers, most famously in Wollstonecraft's *Vindication of the Rights of Men*, in which she termed Burke's rhetoric 'sentimental jargon' (*Works*, vol. 5, p. 30). I discuss this further below.

12. Sarah Fielding, *The History of the Countess of Dellwyn* (2 vols, London: A. Millar, 1759), vol. I, p. 202.

13. Janet Todd, *Sensibility: An Introduction* (London and New York: Methuen, 1986), p. 130.

14. Watson, p. 44. See also John Whale's essay, 'Preparations for Happiness: Mary Wollstonecraft and Imagination', in Robin Jarvis

and Philip Martin (eds), *Reviewing Romanticism* (London: Macmillan, 1992), in which he suggests that Wollstonecraft 'rails against the chaos of strong feelings not simply as a rationalist who wishes to dismiss them altogether, but as a moralist who wishes to appropriate their affective power for her own concerns' (p. 178).

15. In *Jane Austen and the War of Ideas*, Marilyn Butler agrees with Erämetsä, who recorded 'how the word "sensibility" became a pejorative term before the turn of the century, and the process could be illustrated in Mary Wollstonecraft's strictures on Burke' (p. 39). Butler goes on to quote Wollstonecraft's 'Sensibility is the *manie* of the day ...', from the *Vindication of the Rights of Men* (*Works*, vol. 5, p. 8). There seems to me, however, to be a marked contrast between Wollstonecraft's criticism of sensibility in both her *Vindications* and her use of sensibility in her novels, *Mary* (1788) and *The Wrongs of Woman*, as my discussion below shows. Further, the view that '"sensibility" had become a pejorative term before the turn of the century' fails to take account of the fact that, even as discussion of the word heightened many authors' awareness of its undesirable aspects (and even at the same time as they warned against its dangers), it is still one of the key terms used to describe the distinctive quality of virtuous characters in novels by writers of both sexes and across the political spectrum throughout the 1790s. Examples include Fanny Burney's use of the word in *Camilla* (see, for instance, pp. 298, 373, 404, 539, 547, 650, 878); Jane West's usage in both *A Gossip's Story* (1796) (see discussion below) and *A Tale of the Times* (1799) and Helen Maria Williams, *Julia* (see especially I, 104). Finally, it is worth bearing in mind Hannah More's detailed critique of sensibility in her *Strictures* (1799), in which 'sensibility' is described as 'this amiable quality' (I, 74) and in which More makes it quite clear that it is 'ungoverned' or 'ill-directed' sensibility which is to be avoided, while 'very exquisite sensibility' although not designed to contribute to happiness, 'may yet be made to contribute so much to usefulness, that it may, perhaps, be considered as bestowed for an exercise to the possessor's own virtue, and as a keen instrument with which he may better work for the good of others' (II, 103). Thus, while sensibility must, in More's work, be checked and restrained, it continues to confer particular status on its possessor, who has a greater potential for good and virtuous deeds than less favoured mortals.

16. Thomas Paine, *The Rights of Man* (1790–2; London and New York: Dent and Dutton [Everyman's Library], 1915; rpt. 1966), p. 157 and compare for example Jean-Baptiste Say, *A Treatise on Political Economy; or the Production, Distribution, and Consumption of Wealth* (1803; trans. from the 4th edn of the French; 5th American edn, Philadelphia: Grigg & Elliott, 1832): 'the sense of mutual interest begets international kindness, extends the sphere of useful intercourse, and leads to a prosperity, permanent, because it is natural' (p. 47).

17. Paine, p. 159. See also pp. 214ff.

18. See, for example, *Political Justice*, p. 728, and the essay 'Of Trades and Professions' in *The Enquirer: Reflections on Education, Manners and*

Literature (1797; New York: Augustus M. Kelley, 1965) in which Godwin asserts that the trader's 'whole mind is buried in the sordid care of adding another guinea to his income' (p. 217). Elsewhere, however, Godwin did appear to acknowledge a certain importance for commerce in the progress of mankind, seeing it for example as one of the influences responsible for the downfall of feudalism (*Political Justice*, p. 791).

19. See Mary Wollstonecraft, *Mary* and *The Wrongs of Woman* (1788 and 1798; Oxford: Oxford University Press, 1980), p. 95, n. 4.

20. Mary Wollstonecraft, *A Vindication of the Rights of Men* (1790), *Works*, vol. 5, p. 52. Here, of course, there is an important coincidence of argument between Wollstonecraft and Godwin. In *Political Justice*, as Chris Jones points out, Godwin 'notoriously ... attacks gratitude, the slavish dependence, bred of unequal institutions, which makes men the objects of demeaning and ostentatious charity rather than fellow-beings who may claim a just right to the means of life' (*Radical Sensibility: Literature and Ideas in the 1790s* [London: Routledge, 1993], p. 92).

21. Paine asserts the reciprocal operation of rights and duties in his *Rights of Man*: 'A Declaration of Rights is, by reciprocity, a declaration of duties also. Whatever is my right as a man is also the right of another; and it becomes my duty to guarantee as well as to possess' (p. 98).

22. Wollstonecraft, *Rights of Men*, p. 11.

23. Ibid., p. 11.

24. Burke, *Reflections*, p. 88.

25. Thomas Holcroft, *Anna St. Ives* (1792; Oxford: Oxford University Press, 1970), p. 175. Subsequent page references in the text are to this edition.

26. See Butler, p. 31 and note.

27. Elizabeth Inchbald, *Nature and Art* (1796) in Mrs Barbauld (ed.), *The British Novelists* (50 vols, London: F. C. and J. Rivington *et al.*, 1820), vol. 27, p. 242. Subsequent page references in the text are to this edition.

28. Thomas Robert Malthus, *An Essay on the Principle of Population* (1798), E. A. Wrigley and David Souden (eds), *The Works of Malthus* (8 vols, London: William Pickering, 1986), vol. 1, p. 35.

29. Ibid., pp. 29 and 33. See also Guy Routh, *The Origin of Economic Ideas* (1975; 2nd edn, Basingstoke: Macmillan, 1989), in which he discusses the ways in which Malthus justifies the sufferings of the poor, which develop from seeing them as 'the helpless victims of natural law' to, in the expanded 1803 edition of the *Essay*, explaining to them 'patiently ... that their sufferings are all their own fault' (pp. 112–13).

30. See Gary Kelly, *The English Jacobin Novel 1780–1805* (Oxford: Clarendon Press, 1975): 'The events of 1794, the Treason Trials and the nationwide conservative reaction, made English Jacobin novels and English Jacobin ideas of general reform not only dangerous, but peripheral, and Pantisocracy was only one way out, a retrograde step seen in several English Jacobin novels of the time, a literary return to the ideal of rustic independence and sympathetic mutual help which had scarcely ever existed outside the world of fiction' (p. 111).

31. Butler, p. 96.

32. Ibid., p. 101.

33. Ibid., p. 101.
34. Jane West, *A Gossip's Story, and a Legendary Tale* (1796; 4th edn, 2 vols, London: Longman and Rees, 1799), vol. I, p. iii. Subsequent page references in the text are to this edition.
35. In *Sense and Sensibility* (1811; London, New York, Toronto: Oxford University Press, 1970), see, for example, Elinor's reaction to Colonel Brandon's narrative and his own difficulty in relating it: 'He could say no more, and rising hastily walked for a few minutes about the room. Elinor, affected by his relation, and still more by his distress, could not speak. He saw her concern, and coming to her, took her hand, pressed it, and kissed it with grateful respect. A few minutes more of silent exertion enabled him to proceed with composure' (p. 179). The paralysis induced by overwhelming feeling and the expressive gestures are both hallmarks of the sentimental tableau.
36. Godwin, *Political Justice*, p. 728.
37. Hawkins, *Letters on the Female Mind*, I, 54.
38. Mary Hays, *Memoirs of Emma Courtney* (1796; Oxford: Oxford University Press, 1996), p. 10. Subsequent page references in the text are to this edition.
39. Janet Todd, *Sensibility: an Introduction* (London and New York: Methuen, 1986), p. 138.
40. See, for example, the way in which Emma tells of her damaging propensity to foster 'the sickly sensibility of my soul' (p. 61), while Mrs Harley urges Augustus, '"It would be a comfort to my declining years to see you the husband of a woman of virtue and sensibility ..."' (p. 72).
41. Hannah More, of course, had the answer to this question: 'The profession of ladies, to which the bent of their instruction should be turned, is that of daughters, wives, mothers, and mistresses of families ...' (*Strictures*, I, 107).
42. For example, *Emma Courtney*: 'Active, industrious, willing to employ my faculties in any way, by which I might procure an honest independence, I beheld no path open to me, but that to which I could not submit – the degradation of servitude' (p. 163).
43. Charles Lloyd, *Edmund Oliver* (2 vols, Bristol: Joseph Cottle, 1798), vol. I, pp. 36, 40. Subsequent page references in the text are to this edition.
44. Butler, p. 109. Although compare p. 43 where Lloyd is one of the 'Writers of revolutionary tendencies'.
45. Mary Wollstonecraft, *The Wrongs of Woman* (1798); *Works*, vol. 1, p. 101. Subsequent references in the text are to this edition.
46. See n. 19 above.
47. See, for example, Darnford's comment on the American women ('"I could only keep myself awake in their company by making downright love to them"' [102]) and his confession that, on his return to London, '"the women of the town (again I must beg pardon for my habitual frankness) appeared to me like angels"' (102). I can only agree that Darnford is 'a hopelessly compromised revolutionary' (Watson, p. 72).
48. Todd, *Sign of Angellica*, p. 202.

49. Wollstonecraft, *Vindication of the Rights of Woman*, p. 211.
50. Ibid., p. 219.
51. Ibid., pp. 129–31.
52. See especially Mary's 'rhapsody on sensibility', *Works*, vol. 1, p. 59.
53. *Rights of Woman*, p. 133.
54. Watson, p. 44.
55. See Wollstonecraft, *Thoughts on the Education of Daughters* (1787); *Works*, vol. 4, p. 26; and *Rights of Woman*, p. 218.
56. Taken from West's *A Tale of the Times*, I, 107.
57. See Todd, *Sensibility*, pp. 130–1 and *Sign of Angellica*, pp. 224–7; also Butler, ch. 4.
58. Despite its late date, *The Wanderer* was conceived and begun in the 1790s and is very much a work of that decade. See Margaret Doody's Introduction to the World's Classics edition (Oxford: Oxford University Press, 1991), pp. viii, xii–xiii.
59. Priscilla Wakefield, *Reflections on the Present Condition of the Female Sex* (1798; 2nd edn, London: Darton, Harvey, and Darton, 1817), pp. 61–2. Subsequent references in the text are to this edition.
60. Mary Hays, *The Victim of Prejudice* (1799; Peterborough, Ontario: Broadview Press, 1994), pp. 139-40.
61. Fanny Burney, *The Wanderer; or, Female Difficulties* (1814; Oxford: Oxford University Press, 1991), p. 448.
62. *Victim*, p. 138.
63. *Wanderer*, p. 146.
64. Ibid., p. 873.

CONCLUSION

1. Jean-Baptiste Say, *A Treatise on Political Economy; or the Production, Distribution, and Consumption of Wealth* (1803; trans. from the 4th edn of the French; 5th American edn, Philadelphia: Grigg & Elliott, 1832), vol. I, p. xxx.
2. See Guy Routh, *The Origin of Economic Ideas* (1975; 2nd edn, Basingstoke: Macmillan, 1989), p. 140; also my Chapter 4, where I discuss the disjunction between overt opposition to Mandeville's views and covert appropriation of them.
3. Terry Lovell, *Consuming Fiction* (London: Verso, 1987), p. 31.
4. Nicola Watson, *Purloined Letters: Revolution, Reaction and the Form of the Novel, 1790–1825* (unpublished DPhil thesis; Oxford, 1990), p. 166.
5. Mary Brunton, *Self-Control* (2 vols, Edinburgh: Manners and Miller, 1811), vol. II, p. 26. Subsequent page references in the text are to this edition.
6. Watson, pp. 185–6.
7. Jane Austen, *Mansfield Park* (1814; London, New York, Toronto: Oxford University Press, 1970), pp. 11, 73, 212. Subsequent page references in the text are to this edition.

Bibliography

PRIMARY TEXTS

Astell, Mary. *A Serious Proposal to the Ladies, for the Advancement of their True and Greatest Interest. By a Lover of her Sex.* 1694; 2nd edn, London: R. Wilkin, 1695.

Austen, Jane. *Sense and Sensibility*, ed. Claire Lamont (Oxford English Novels, Gen. Ed. James Kinsley). 1811; London, New York, Toronto: Oxford University Press, 1970.

—— *Mansfield Park*, ed. John Lucas (Oxford English Novels). 1814; London, New York, Toronto: Oxford University Press, 1970.

Bage, Robert. *Barham Downs*. 2 vols. London: G. Wilkie, 1784.

—— *Hermsprong; or, Man As He Is Not*, ed. Peter Faulkner (World's Classics). 1796; Oxford: Oxford University Press, 1987.

Bennett, Agnes Maria. *Anna: or Memoirs of a Welch Heiress: Interspersed with Anecdotes of a Nabob*. 4 vols. 1785; London: William Lane, 1786.

Brooke, Frances. *The History of Lady Julia Mandeville*. 1763; in *The British Novelists*, ed. Mrs Barbauld. 50 vols. London: F. C. and J. Rivington *et al.*, 1820. Vol. 27.

Brooke, Henry. *The Fool of Quality*. 1765–70; London and New York: Routledge and Dutton, 1906.

Brown, John. *An Estimate of the Manners and Principles of the Times*. London: L. Davis and C. Reymers, 1757.

Brunton, Mary. *Self-Control: A Novel*. 2 vols. Edinburgh: Manners and Miller, 1811.

Burke, Edmund. *Reflections on the Revolution in France* (1790), in *The Writings and Speeches of Edmund Burke*, ed. L. G. Mitchell. Vol. 8. Oxford: Clarendon Press, 1989.

Burney, Fanny. *Camilla; or, A Picture of Youth*, ed. Edward A. and Lillian D. Bloom (World's Classics). 1796; Oxford: Oxford University Press, 1983; rpt 1986.

—— *The Wanderer; or, Female Difficulties*, ed. Margaret Anne Doody, Robert L. Mack and Peter Sabor (World's Classics). 1814; Oxford and New York: Oxford University Press, 1990.

Cervantes Saavedra, Miguel de. *The Adventures of Don Quixote*, trans. J. M. Cohen. Harmondsworth: Penguin, 1950; rpt 1968.

Charke, Charlotte. *A Narrative of the Life of Mrs Charlotte Charke*. 1755; London: Constable, 1929.

Cleland, John. *Memoirs of a Woman of Pleasure*, ed. Peter Sabor (World's Classics). 1748–9; Oxford: Oxford University Press, 1985; rpt 1986.

Collyer, Mary. *Letters from Felicia to Charlotte: containing A Series of the most interesting Events, interspersed with Moral Reflections, chiefly tending to prove, the Seeds of VIRTUE are implanted in the Mind of EVERY Reasonable Being*. 1744–9; 3rd edn, London: R. Baldwin, 1755.

Defoe, Daniel. *Roxana; or, the Fortunate Mistress*, ed. Jane Jack (World's Classics). 1724; Oxford: Oxford University Press, 1981.

Dyer, John. *The Fleece: A Poem*. London: R. and J. Dodsley, 1757.

Economy of Human Life, The. 1750; Manchester: G. Nicholson, 1797.

Fielding, Henry. *Joseph Andrews* and *Shamela*, ed. Martin C. Battestin (the Wesleyan Edition of the Works of Henry Fielding). 1742 and 1741; Oxford: Clarendon Press, 1967.

────── *The History of Tom Jones, A Foundling*, ed. Martin C. Battestin and Fredson Bowers (Wesleyan Edition). 2 vols. 1749; Oxford: Clarendon Press, 1974.

────── *Amelia*, ed. Martin C. Battestin (Wesleyan Edition). 1751; Oxford: Clarendon Press, 1983.

────── *An Enquiry into the Causes of the Late Increase of Robbers and Related Writings*, ed. Malvin R. Zirker (Wesleyan Edition). Oxford: Clarendon Press, 1988.

────── *A Proposal for Making an Effectual Provision for the Poor*. London: A. Millar, 1753.

Fielding, Sarah. *The Adventures of David Simple*, ed. Malcolm Kelsall (World's Classics). 1744 and 1753; Oxford: Oxford University Press, 1987.

──────*The History of the Countess of Dellwyn*. 2 vols. London: A. Millar, 1759.

────── *The History of Ophelia*. 2 vols. London: R. Baldwin, 1760.

Fordyce, James. *Sermons to Young Women*. 2 vols. 1766; 3rd edn, London: A. Millar & T. Cadell, J. Dodsley & J. Payne, 1766.

Godwin, William. *Enquiry Concerning Political Justice and its Influence on Modern Morals and Happiness*. 1793; London: Penguin, 1985.

────── 'Of Trades and Professions', in *The Enquirer: Reflections on Education, Manners and Literature*. 1797; New York: Augustus M. Kelley, 1965.

Goldsmith, Oliver. *The Vicar of Wakefield: A Tale Supposed to be Written by Himself* (1766), in *The Collected Works of Oliver Goldsmith*, ed. Arthur Friedman. 5 vols. Oxford: Clarendon Press, 1966. Vol. 4.

────── 'Of the Pride and Luxury of the Middling Class of People', *The Bee* (1759), in *Works*, Vol. 1.

Gregory, John. *A Father's Legacy to His Daughters*. London: Strahan, Cadell, Balfour & Creech, 1774.

Griffith, Elizabeth. *The History of Lady Barton, A Novel in Letters*. 1771; 2nd edn, London: T. Davies and T. Cadell, 1773.

────── *Essays Addressed to Young Married Women*. London: T. Cadell & J. Robson, 1782.

Griffith, Elizabeth and Richard. *A Series of Genuine Letters Between Henry and Frances*. 1757; 3rd edn, London: W. Johnston, 1767.

Hawkins, Laetitia Matilda. *Letters on the Female Mind, its Powers and Pursuits*. 2 vols. London: Hookham & Carpenter, 1793.

Hays, Mary. *Memoirs of Emma Courtney*, ed. Eleanor Ty (World's Classics). 1796; Oxford: Oxford University Press, 1996.

────── *The Victim of Prejudice*, ed. Eleanor Ty (Broadview Literary Texts). 1799; Peterborough, Ont: Broadview Press, 1994.

Holcroft, Thomas. *Anna St Ives*, ed. Peter Faulkner (Oxford English Novels). 1792; London, New York and Toronto: Oxford University Press, 1970.

Hume, David. *A Treatise of Human Nature*, ed. L. A. Selby-Brigge. 2nd edn revised, P. H. Nidditch. 1739–40; Oxford: Clarendon Press, 1978.

Inchbald, Elizabeth. *Nature and Art* (1796) in *The British Novelists*, ed. Mrs Barbauld. 50 vols. London: F. C. and J. Rivington *et al.*, 1820. Vol. 27.

Johnson, Samuel. *A Dictionary of the English Language: in which the Words are deduced from their Originals, and Illustrated in their Different Significations by Examples from the best Writers*. 2 vols. London: J. and P. Knapton, 1755.

Lloyd, Charles. *Edmund Oliver*. 2 vols. Bristol: Joseph Cottle, 1798.

Lounger, The in *The British Essayists*, ed. Rev. Robert Lynam *et al.* 30 vols. London: J. F. Dove, 1827.

Mackenzie, Henry. *The Man of Feeling*, ed. Brian Vickers (World's Classics). 1771; Oxford: Oxford University Press, 1987.

——— *The Man of the World* (1773) in *The Works of Henry Mackenzie, Esq.* 8 vols. Edinburgh: Archibald Constable and Co., 1808. Vols 1 and 2.

——— *Julia de Roubigné* (1777) in *The British Novelists*, ed. Mrs Barbauld. 50 vols. London: F. C. and J. Rivington *et al.*, 1820. Vol. 29.

Malthus, Thomas Robert. *An Essay on the Principle of Population* (1798), in *The Works of Malthus*, ed. E. A. Wrigley and David Souden. 8 vols. London: William Pickering, 1986. Vol. 1.

Mandeville, Bernard. *The Fable of the Bees: or, Private Vices, Publick Benefits*, ed. F. B. Kaye. 1714–28; Oxford: Clarendon Press, 1924.

Millar, John. *The Origin of the Distinction of Ranks* (1771; 3rd edn, 1779), in William C. Lehmann, *John Millar of Glasgow 1735–1801: His Life and Thought and his Contributions to Sociological Analysis*. Cambridge: Cambridge University Press, 1960.

Mirror, The in *The British Essayists*, ed. Rev. Robert Lynam *et al.* 30 vols. London: J. F. Dove, 1827.

Monthly Review, The. Vols 71 (September 1784) and 72 (August 1785). London: R. Griffiths, 1785 and 1786.

More, Hannah. *Essays on Various Subjects, principally designed for the young ladies.* 1777; 4th edn, London: T. Cadell, 1785.

———*Sensibility: An Epistle to the Honourable Mrs. Boscawen* (1782), in *Poems*. London: T. Cadell & W. Davies, 1816.

———*Strictures on the Modern System of Female Education*. 2 vols. 1799; 2nd edn, London: T. Cadell Jun. & W. Davies, 1799.

Paine, Thomas. *The Rights of Man*, introduction by Arthur Seldon (Everyman's Library). 1791–2; London and New York: Dent and Dutton, 1915; rpt 1966.

Pennington, Sarah. *An Unfortunate Mother's Advice to her Absent Daughters, in a Letter to Miss Pennington.* 1761; 5th edn, London: J. Walter, 1770.

'Philogamus'. *The Present State of Matrimony: Or, The Real Causes of Conjugal Infidelity and Unhappy Marriages*. London: John Hawkins, 1739.

Pope, Alexander. *Poems*, ed. John Butt. 1963; London: Methuen, 1965.

Price, Richard. *Observations on Reversionary Payments*. 1771; 4th edn, London: T. Cadell, 1783.

———— *Observations on the Nature of Civil Liberty, the Principles of Government, and the Justice and Policy of the War with America.* 1776; 2nd edn, London: T. Cadell, 1776.

Richardson, Samuel. *Clarissa, or the History of a Young Lady.* 1747–8; Harmondsworth: Penguin, 1985.

———— *The History of Sir Charles Grandison*, ed. Jocelyn Harris (World's Classics). 1753; Oxford: Oxford University Press, 1986.

Robertson, William. *A View of the Progress of Society in Europe* (1769) in *Works.* 12 vols. London: William Baynes, 1824.

Rousseau, Jean-Jacques. *La Nouvelle Héloïse.* 1761; Oxford: Woodstock Books, 1989.

Say, Jean-Baptiste. *A Treatise on Political Economy; or, the Production, Distribution, and Consumption of Wealth.* 1803; trans. from the 4th edn of the French; 5th American edn, Philadelphia: Grigg & Elliott, 1832.

Scott, Sarah. *A Description of Millenium Hall.* London: J. Newbery, 1762.

Smith, Adam. *The Theory of Moral Sentiments.* 1759; 11th edn, 2 vols, Edinburgh: Bell and Bradfoute, *et al.* and London: Lackington, Allen and Co. *et al.*, 1808.

———— *Lectures on Justice, Police, Revenue and Arms*, ed. Edwin Cannan. *c.* 1763; Oxford: Clarendon Press, 1896.

———— *An Inquiry into the Nature and Causes of the Wealth of Nations*, ed. R. H. Campbell, A. S. Skinner and W. B. Todd (the Glasgow Edition of the Works and Correspondence of Adam Smith). 2 vols. 1776; Oxford: Clarendon Press, 1976.

Smollett, Tobias. *The Expedition of Humphry Clinker*, ed. Peter Miles (Everyman Library). 1771; J. M. Dent: London & Charles E. Tuttle: Vermont, 1993.

Sterne, Laurence. *A Sentimental Journey*, ed. Ian Jack (World's Classics). 1768; Oxford: Oxford University Press, 1984; rpt 1987.

Steuart, Sir James. *An Inquiry into the Principles of Political Œconomy.* London: Millar and Cadell, 1767.

Wakefield, Priscilla. *Reflections on the Present Condition of the Female Sex; with Suggestions for its Improvement.* 1798; 2nd edn, London: Darton, Harvey, and Darton, 1817.

West, Jane. *The Advantages of Education, or, the History of Maria Williams.* 2 vols. London: Minerva, 1793.

———— *A Gossip's Story, and a Legendary Tale.* 2 vols. 1796; 4th edn, London: T. N. Longman and O. Rees, 1799.

———— *A Tale of the Times.* 1799; 2nd edn, 3 vols. London: T. N. Longman and O. Rees, 1799.

Wilkes. Rev. Wetenhall. *A Letter of Genteel and Moral Advice to a Young Lady.* 1740; 8th edn, London: L. Hawes, C. Clarke and R. Collins, 1766.

Williams, Helen Maria. *Julia, a Novel; Interspersed with some Poetical Pieces.* 2 vols. Dublin: Chamberlaine and Rice *et al.*, 1790.

Wollstonecraft, Mary. *Thoughts on the Education of Daughters* (1787) in *The Works of Mary Wollstonecraft*, ed. Janet Todd and Marilyn Butler. 7 vols. London: William Pickering, 1989. Vol. 4.

———— *A Vindication of the Rights of Men* (1790) in *Works*, Vol. 5.

———— *A Vindication of the Rights of Woman* (1792) in *Works*, Vol. 5.

———— *Mary, a Fiction* and *The Wrongs of Woman* (1788, 1798) in *Works*, Vol. 1.

SECONDARY TEXTS

Armstrong, Nancy. *Desire and Domestic Fiction: A Political History of the Novel*. New York and Oxford: Oxford University Press, 1987.
—— 'The Rise of the Domestic Woman', in *The Ideology of Conduct*, ed. N. Armstrong and L. Tennenhouse. London: Methuen, 1987.
Baker, Sheridan. 'Fielding's *Amelia* and the Materials of Romance', *Philological Quarterly* 41 (1962) 437–49.
Barrell, John. *English Literature in History 1730–1780: An Equal Wide Survey*. London: Hutchinson, 1983.
Bellamy, Elizabeth. *Private Virtues, Public Vices: Commercial Morality and the Novel 1740–1800*. Unpublished PhD thesis. Cambridge, 1988.
Bender, John. 'Prison Reform and the Sentence of Narration in *The Vicar of Wakefield*', in *The New Eighteenth Century: Theory, Politics, English Literature*, ed. Felicity Nussbaum and Laura Brown. New York and London: Methuen, 1987.
Blakey, Dorothy. *The Minerva Press, 1790–1820*. London: Printed for the Bibliographical Society at the University Press, Oxford, 1939.
Blewett, David. Introduction to Henry Fielding's *Amelia*. Harmondsworth: Penguin, 1987.
Brown, Susan E. 'Rational Creatures and Free Citizens: the Language of Politics in the Eighteenth-Century Debate on Women', *Historical Papers/Communications Historiques*, Canadian Historical Association, 1988.
Butler, Marilyn. *Jane Austen and the War of Ideas*. Oxford: Clarendon Press, 1975; reissued with new introduction, 1987.
Cash, Arthur Hill. *Sterne's Comedy of Moral Sentiments: The Ethical Dimension of the 'Journey'*. Pittsburgh, Pa: Duquesne University Press, 1966.
Castle, Terry. *Masquerade and Civilization: The Carnivalesque in Eighteenth-Century English Culture and Fiction*. London: Methuen, 1986.
Copeland, Edward, *Women Writing About Money: Women's Fiction in England 1790–1820*. Cambridge: Cambridge University Press, 1995.
Copley, Stephen, ed. *Literature and the Social Order in Eighteenth Century England*. London, Sydney and Dover, New Hampshire: Croom Helm, 1984.
Dickinson, H. T. *Liberty and Property: Political Ideology in Eighteenth-Century Britain*. New York: Holmes and Meier, 1977.
Dumont, Louis. *From Mandeville to Marx: The Genesis and Triumph of Economic Ideology*. Chicago and London: The University of Chicago Press, 1977.
Erämetsä, Erik. 'A Study of the Word "Sentimental" and of Other Linguistic Characteristics of Eighteenth-Century Sentimentalism in England', *Annales Academiae Scientarum Fennicae* B 74 (Helsinki, 1951).
Faulkner, Peter. *Robert Bage*. Boston: Twayne Publishers, 1979.
—— Introduction to Bage's *Hermsprong* (World's Classics). Oxford: Oxford University Press, 1987.
Foucault, Michel. *The History of Sexuality: An Introduction*. 1976; Harmondsworth: Penguin, 1981; rpt 1987.
Guest, Harriet. 'A Double Lustre: Femininity and Sociable Commerce, 1730–60', *Eighteenth-Century Studies* 23 (Summer, 1990) 479–501.

Hagstrum, Jean H. *Sex and Sensibility: Ideal and Erotic Love from Milton to Mozart.* Chicago: University of Chicago Press, 1980.

Hill, Bridget. *Eighteenth-Century Women: An Anthology.* 1984; London: Allen & Unwin, 1987.

——— *Women, Work and Sexual Politics in Eighteenth-Century England.* Oxford: Blackwell, 1989.

Himmelfarb, Gertrude. *The Idea of Poverty: England in the Early Industrial Age.* London and Boston: Faber & Faber, 1984.

Hirschman, Albert O. *The Passions and the Interests: Political Arguments for Capitalism Before its Triumph.* Princeton, NJ: Princeton University Press, 1977.

Hutchison, Terence. *Before Adam Smith: The Emergence of Political Economy 1662–1776.* Oxford: Blackwell, 1988.

Jack, Jane. Introduction to Defoe's *Roxana* (World's Classics). Oxford: Oxford University Press, 1981.

Jones, Chris. *Radical Sensibility: Literature and Ideas in the 1790s.* London: Routledge, 1993.

Jones, Vivien. 'Women Writing Revolution: Narratives of History and Sexuality in Wollstonecraft and Williams', in *Beyond Romanticism*, ed. Stephen Copley and John Whale. London: Routledge, 1992.

Kelly, Gary. *The English Jacobin Novel 1780–1805.* Oxford: Clarendon Press, 1976.

——— Notes to Mary Wollstonecraft's *Mary* and *The Wrongs of Woman* (World's Classics). Oxford: Oxford University Press, 1980.

Kelsall, Malcolm. Introduction to Sarah Fielding's *David Simple* (World's Classics). Oxford: Oxford University Press, 1987.

London, April. 'Controlling the Text: Women in Tom Jones', *Studies in the Novel* 19 (Fall, 1987) 323–33.

Lovell, Terry. *Consuming Fiction.* London: Verso, 1987.

Markley, Robert. 'Sentimentality as Performance: Sterne, Shaftesbury and the Theatrics of Virtue' in *The New Eighteenth Century: Theory, Politics, English Literature*, ed. Felicity Nussbaum and Laura Brown. New York and London: Methuen, 1987.

McMullen, Lorraine. *An Odd Attempt in a Woman: The Literary Life of Frances Brooke.* Vancouver: University of British Columbia Press, 1983.

Middleton, Chris. 'Woman's Labour and the Transition to Pre-Industrial Capitalism', in *Women and Work in Pre-Industrial England*, ed. Lindsey Charles and Lorna Duffin. London, Sydney and Dover, New Hampshire: Croom Helm, 1985.

Mullan, John. *Sentiment and Sociability: the Language of Feeling in the Eighteenth Century.* Oxford: Clarendon Press, 1988.

Nicholson, Colin, *Writing and the Rise of Finance: Capital Satires of the Early Eighteenth Century.* Cambridge: Cambridge University Press, 1994.

Novak, Maximillian E. *Economics and the Fiction of Daniel Defoe.* Berkeley: University of California Press, 1962.

Owen, David. *English Philanthropy 1660–1900.* Cambridge, Mass. and London: Harvard University Press and Oxford University Press, 1965.

Perry, Ruth. *Women, Letters and the Novel.* New York: AMS Press, Inc., 1980.

Pinchbeck, Ivy. *Women Workers and the Industrial Revolution 1750–1850.* 1930; London: Virago, 1981; rpt 1985.

Pocock, J. G. A. *The Machiavellian Moment: Florentine Political Thought and the Atlantic Republican Tradition.* Princeton and London: Princeton University Press, 1975.

———— *Virtue, Commerce and History: Essays on Political Thought and History, Chiefly in the Eighteenth Century.* Cambridge, New York and Melbourne: Cambridge University Press, 1985.

Politi, Jina. *The Novel and its Presuppositions: Changes in the Conceptual Structure of Novels in the Eighteenth and Nineteenth Centuries.* Amsterdam: Adolf M. Hakkert N.V., 1976.

Poovey, Mary. 'Ideology and The Mysteries of Udolpho', *Criticism* 21 (1979) 307–30.

———— *The Proper Lady and the Woman Writer.* Chicago and London: University of Chicago Press, 1984.

Preston, Thomas R. 'Smollett and the Benevolent Misanthrope Type', *PMLA* 79 (1964) 51–7.

Rodgers, Betsy. *Cloak of Charity: Studies in Eighteenth-Century Philanthropy.* London: Methuen, 1949.

Routh, Guy. *The Origin of Economic Ideas.* 1975; 2nd edn. Basingstoke and London: Macmillan, 1989.

Sabor, Peter. Introduction to Cleland's *Memoirs of a Woman of Pleasure* (World's Classics). Oxford: Oxford University Press, 1985; rpt 1986.

Scheuermann, Mona. *Her Bread to Earn: Women, Money, and Society from Defoe to Austen.* Lexington, KY: Kentucky University Press, 1993.

Sekora, John. *Luxury: The Concept in Western Thought, Eden to Smollett.* Baltimore and London: The Johns Hopkins University Press, 1977.

Sherburn, George, 'Fielding's *Amelia*: an Interpretation', in *Fielding: A Collection of Critical Essays*, ed. Ronald Paulson. Englewood Cliffs, NJ: Prentice-Hall, 1962.

Simmons, Philip E. 'John Cleland's *Memoirs of a Woman of Pleasure*: Literary Voyeurism and the Techniques of Novelistic Transgression', *Eighteenth-Century Fiction* 3 (October 1990) 43–63.

Skinner, Gillian. '"The Price of a Tear": Economic Sense and Sensibility in Sarah Fielding's *David Simple*', *Literature and History*, 3rd Series, 1 (Spring 1992).

Skinner, John. *Constructions of Smollett: A Study of Genre and Gender.* Newark: University of Delaware Press & London: Associated University Presses, 1996.

Spencer, Jane. *The Rise of the Woman Novelist: From Aphra Behn to Jane Austen.* Oxford: Blackwell, 1986.

Tanner, Tony. *Adultery in the Novel: Contract and Transgression.* Baltimore and London: The Johns Hopkins University Press, 1979.

———— Introduction to *Mansfield Park.* London: Penguin, 1966 (Penguin English Library); rpt London: Penguin, 1985 (Penguin Classics).

Thompson, James. *Models of Value: Eighteenth-Century Political Economy and the Novel.* Durham and London: Duke University Press, 1996.

Todd, Janet. *Sensibility: An Introduction.* London: Methuen, 1986.

———— *Feminist Literary History: A Defence.* Oxford: Polity Press, 1988.

———— *The Sign of Angellica: Women, Writing, and Fiction, 1660–1800*. London: Virago, 1989.

Tomaselli, Sylvana. 'The Enlightenment Debate on Women', *History Workshop Journal* 19 (1985) 101–24.

Van Sant, Ann Jessie. *Eighteenth-Century Sensibility and the Novel: The Senses in Social Context*. Cambridge: Cambridge University Press, 1993.

Watson, Nicola. *Purloined Letters: Revolution, Reaction and the Form of the Novel, 1790–1825*. Unpublished DPhil thesis. Oxford, 1990.

Whale, John. 'Preparations for Happiness: Mary Wollstonecraft and Imagination', in *Reviewing Romanticism*, ed. Robin Jarvis and Philip Martin. Basingstoke and London: Macmillan, 1992.

Williams, Carolyn D. 'Fielding and Half-learned Ladies', *Essays in Criticism* 38 (1988) 22–34.

Zomchick, John P. 'Social Class, Character, and Narrative Strategy in *Humphry Clinker*', *Eighteenth-Century Life* 10 (1986), pp. 172–85.

Index

Addison, Joseph 198 *n*
Alexander, William
    History of Women 206 *n*
aristocracy
    in *The Countess of Dellwyn* (Sarah
        Fielding) 31, 36
    and degeneracy 126, 179
    and excess 5–6, 18
    linked with trade 102 (*The Man
        of Feeling*), 123–8 (*Barham
        Downs* and *Anna*)
    and luxury 20
    and tyranny 133
    see also bourgeois values, class,
        middle classes
Armstrong, Nancy 103–4, 192 *n*
Astell, Mary 107
Austen, Jane
    Mansfield Park 148, 188, 209 *n*
    Sense and Sensibility 164, 165, 214 *n*

Bage, Robert
    Barham Downs 4, 117–53 *passim*
    Hermsprong 141, 146
Baker, Sheridan 48, 54, 55, 199 *n*
Barrell, John 8, 75, 76, 196 *n*
Bellamy, Elizabeth 78 *n* 24, 102 *n*
    18, 103 *n* 21, 194 *n*, 201 *n*,
    206 *n*
Bender, John 63, 72
benefactor 26–7, 33, 40, 50–1, 61,
    71, 80
    married woman as 101–2
    see also benevolence, community,
        obligation
benevolence 50–1
    and class 100–1
    and commercial considerations
        (*Humphry Clinker*) 86
    contradictory nature of 53
    and self-interest 52
    in *The Rights of Men*
        (Wollstonecraft) 160
    undermined 50, 54, 56

    in *The Vicar of Wakefield*
        (Goldsmith) and *Lady Julia
        Mandeville* (Frances Brooke)
        66
    see also benefactor, charity
Bennett, Agnes Maria
    *Anna: or Memoirs of a Welch
        Heiress* 4, 117–53 *passim*
    contemporary admiration for the
        work of 207 *n*
Blakey, Dorothy 207 *n*
Blewett, David 54
bourgeois values
    and property 101–2
    set against aristocratic vice 31
    see also class, middle classes
British Merchant 125, 166
    and commerce 13
    unites competing class interests
        11
Brooke, Frances
    Lady Julia Mandeville 4, 61–81
        passim, 134
Brooke, Henry
    The Fool of Quality 119–21, 207 *n*
Brophy, Brigid, 198 *n*
Brown, John
    *An Estimate of the Manners and
        Principles of the Times* 11–12
Brown, Susan E. 211 *n*
Brunton, Mary
    Self-Control 187–8, 189
Burke, Edmund 155
    equality unattainable 160
Burney, Fanny
    Camilla 210 *n*, 212 *n*
    *The Wanderer; or, Female
        Difficulties* 184, 185–6,
        215 *n*
Butler, Marilyn 209 *n*, 211 *n*
    on *Edmund Oliver* (Charles
        Lloyd) 175
    on *A Gossip's Story* (Jane West)
        164–5

Cash, Arthur 113
Castle, Terry 42, 46–7, 54, 55
charity
    as important component of a
        woman's moral economy
        (*Lady Barton*) 95, 99, 102
    opposing views of humanists
        and Mandevillians 9
    in *The Countess of Dellwyn* (Sarah
        Fielding) 33–5
    in *The Fool of Quality* (Henry
        Brooke) 120
    in *The History of Ophelia* (Sarah
        Fielding) 53
    Wollstonecraft's views (*Rights of
        Men*) 160
    see also benefactor, benevolence,
        obligation
Charke, Charlotte 51
    *A Narrative of the Life of Mrs
        Charlotte Charke* 37–8
chastity
    in women morally analogous to
        courage in men 98
    see also virtue
civic humanism 7–10, 20, 49, 193 *n*
    use of its discourse by a woman
        26
    opposed to Mandevillian views
        on the utility of vice 66
class
    in *Amelia* (Henry Fielding) 49
    in *Anna* (Agnes Maria Bennett)
        124, 132
    in *David Simple* (Sarah Fielding)
        21–2
    in debates over luxury 5–6, 8
    and discourses of femininity 11,
        100–5 (*Man of Feeling* and
        Lady Barton)
    and gender 103–11 *passim*
    in Henry Fielding's work 19–21
    in *The History of Ophelia* (Sarah
        Fielding) 46
    in *Humphry Clinker* (Smollett)
        89
    and trade 11, 28
    union of competing interests
        via figure of British
        Merchant 11

    see also aristocracy, bourgeois
        values, middle classes
Cleland, John
    *Memoirs of a Woman of Pleasure
        (Fanny Hill)* 40–1
Collyer, Mary 1
    Letters from Felicia to Charlotte 30,
        35
commerce 11
    as antidote to the progress of
        tyranny 133–40 *passim*
    as civilising influence 117–53
        passim
    in *Emma Courtney* (Mary Hays)
        170, 173
    and figure of British Merchant 13
    in *Humphry Clinker* (Smollett)
        86–7
    importance for the radical
        woman writer 184
    linked with sentimental values
        30, 32, 71–2, 117–53 *passim*
    and masculine vocabulary of
        nobility and heroism 126–9
    opposition to produces
        essentially conservative
        novels 177
    and *Reflections on the Present
        Condition of the Female Sex*
        (Priscilla Wakefield) 184–5
    related to dependence and
        independence 158–9
    and sentimental protagonist 94
    in *The Wrongs of Woman*
        (Wollstonecraft) 178–9
    see also trade
community
    female 107–8
    sentimental 12, 16: affinities with
        discourse of political
        economy 60; and early
        modern
    commercial world 30; and
        patriarchal organisation
        60–1; role of benefactor
        within 26–7
conduct literature 31, 35, 140
    and requirement for controlled
        sensibility 67, 69
    vocabulary of in *Fanny Hill* 40

conservative
  as political label in the 1790s 156
Copeland, Edward 191 *n*
Copley, Stephen 7, 210 *n*
country ideology
  opposed to court interest 147
  radical debt to 209 *n*

dependence 154–86 *passim*
  associated with conservative
    ideal 155
  and commerce 158–9
  as ideal of the sentimental
    community 157
  related to sensibility 180
  revealed as humiliating
    submission by sentimental
    novelists 157
Defoe, Daniel
  Roxana 39–40
de Pinto, Isaac 145
Dickinson, H. T. 62, 209 *n*
Diderot, Denis
  'Sur les femmes' 206 *n*
disinterest
  see patriarch
Doody, Margaret
  introduction to *The Wanderer*
    (Burney) 215 *n*
Don Quixote 24
Dumont, Louis 60, 72, 86, 125
Dyer, John
  The Fleece 201 *n*

economic activity
  accounts of women's involvement
    in through history 38
  and Anne Wilmot in *Lady Julia
    Mandeville* (Frances Brooke)
    69–70
  in *Emma Courtney* (Mary Hays)
    171–3
  as enabling avoidance of male
    tyranny 135–7
  heroine's analysis of in *The
    History of Ophelia* (Sarah
    Fielding) 45, 47
  as inherently immoral for women
    37–8, 41–2

and Louisa in *A Gossip's Story*
  (Jane West) 167, 168
and Tabitha Bramble in *Humphry
  Clinker* 87–90
and the virtuous woman 57–8
in *The Wrongs of Woman*
  (Wollstonecraft) 182–4
see also prostitution, working
  woman
economic discourse
  affinities with workings of the
    sentimental community 60,
    158
  use of by women 23–4, 26
economy 91–116 *passim*
  defined by Sir James Steuart 59
  in *Lady Julia Mandeville* (Frances
    Brooke) 66, 67
  meanings of 4–10, 91
  radical appropriation of in
    Barham Downs (Robert Bage)
    144–6
  related to women 6–7, 41
  see also frugality, prudence
Economy of Human Life, The 6, 98,
  100
Edenic communities 44–5, 78–9,
  198 *n*
  in *Edmund Oliver* (Charles Lloyd)
    175, 177
  patriarch's attempts to reconcile
    with the commercial world
    79
effeminacy 126, 127, 134
Ellis, Markman 194 *n*

Fanny Hill
  see Cleland, John
Faulkner, Peter 144, 146, 206 *n*
femininity 37–58 *passim*, 95–9, 102
  and class 11–12
  and discourses of sensibility 10
  and economic ability 10–12
  necessary display of virtuous
    107–8, 148–52
  as refining influence 116–17
feminisation
  of commerce 11, 117–53 *passim*
  of novel 2–3

of sentimental hero 11–12, 71,
98–9, 103, 112, 172–3
Fielding, Henry
Amelia 37–58 *passim*
Covent-Garden Journal 39
Joseph Andrews 21, 195–6 *n*
*A Proposal for Making an Effectual
Provision for the Poor* 51–2
Tom Jones 15–31 *passim*, 36, 44
Fielding, Sarah
The Countess of Dellwyn 31–6, 37,
114, 157
David Simple 2, 4, 7, 12, 15–31
passim, 39, 60, 73: compared
with *A Sentimental Journey*,
115
David Simple, Volume the Last 8,
26–31 *passim*, 53, 55, 71, 72
The History of Ophelia 37–58
passim
Filmer, Robert 208 *n*
Patriarcha 62
Fordyce, James 38, 43 *n* 25, 48
Foucault, Michel 9, 22
French Revolution 154, 155, 156,
159, 162
friendship between women 106–8
frugality
as antidote to luxury 5–6
as panacea for England's political
and economic ills 5–6
triumph of in economic theory
187
see also economy, prudence

gender
interaction with class 103–11
passim
Godwin, William 165
*Enquiry Concerning Political
Justice* 156
views on trade 159, 212–13 *n*
Goldsmith, Oliver 6, 19
Man in Black 85
The Vicar of Wakefield 4, 61–81
passim, 116
Gregory, John
A Father's Legacy to his Daughters
118, 203 *n*

Griffith, Elizabeth
*A Series of Genuine Letters between
Henry and Frances* 95, 98,
110, 117
*Essays Addressed to Young Married
Women* 91
The History of Lady Barton 92–111
passim
Guest, Harriet 12, 102, 107, 149,
209 *n*

Hagstrum, Jean 43, 198 *n*
Hawkins, Laetitia Matilda 168–9,
210 *n*
Hays, Mary
Memoirs of Emma Courtney 169–77
The Victim of Prejudice 184, 185–6
Hill, Bridget 38
Himmelfarb, Gertrude 74, 194 *n*
Hirschmann, Albert O. 118, 129,
145, 194 *n*, 200 *n*, 205 *n*, 207–8 *n*
Holcroft, Thomas
Anna St. Ives 161–2, 210 *n*
Hume, David 100, 199 *n*, 203 *n*
role of governors in society 75
sympathy 34
Hutcheson, Frances 204 *n*
Hutchison, Terence 209 *n*
Hutton, William
The History of Birmingham 206 *n*

Inchbald, Elizabeth
Nature and Art 162–4
independence 131–3, 149, 154–86
passim
able to accommodate women's
sensibility 181–4
appropriated by Malthus 163–4
and commerce 158–9
as crucial to Godwinian ideal of
social organisation 155–6
internalised as self-control in
women (*A Gossip's Story*)
166–9
masculine version in *Edmund
Oliver* (Charles Lloyd) 175–6
as threatening women's
sensibility 180
in *Nature and Art* (Inchbald) 163

individualism
  and women 101–2
internalisation
  as precondition of social
    amelioration 163–4
  as producing a feminised version
    of independence (*A Gossip's
    Story*) 166–9

Jack, Jane 39
Johnson, Samuel
  Dictionary 5, 28 *n* 22
Jones, Chris 138
  Radical Sensibility 143–4, 156,
    192 *n*, 198 *n*, 199 *n*, 204 *n*,
    210 *n*, 213 *n*
Jones, Vivien 210 *n*
Jong, Erica 198 *n*

Kelly, Gary 139, 141, 159, 178
  The English Jacobin Novel 143
  events of 1794 213 *n*
Kelsall, Malcolm 29

land
  ownership as a guarantee of
    disinterest 75–8
Laski, Marghanita 198 *n*
Lehmann, William C. 204 *n*
liberty
  women as inheritors of ideal of
    British 140–3
Lloyd, Charles
  Edmund Oliver 169, 174–7, 210 *n*
Lock Hospital 39
London, April 194 *n*
Lovell, Terry 187
luxury 31, 32
  in *Anna* (Agnes Maria Bennett)
    134
  in *The Countess of Dellwyn* (Sarah
    Fielding) 32
  in *David Simple* (Sarah Fielding)
    23–4
  and 'economy' in debates
    surrounding 5–6
  in Henry Fielding's work 19–21
  in *The History of Ophelia* (Sarah
    Fielding) 45

in *Humphry Clinker* (Smollett) 87,
    89
  Mandeville's definition of 8
  redefinition in Steuart's *Political
    Œconomy* 74

Mackenzie, Henry
  The Lounger 102, 206–7 *n*
  The Man of Feeling 1, 92–116
    passim
  The Man of the World 102
  The Mirror 102
Malthus, Thomas Robert 187
  *An Essay on the Principle of
    Population* 163–4
Mandeville, Bernard 20–1, 30, 34,
    45, 49, 53, 74, 187
  The Fable of the Bees 8, 12, 74
Markley, Robert 3, 94, 114, 120
masquerade
  in *The History of Ophelia* (Sarah
    Fielding) 46–7, 199 *n*
McMullen, Lorraine 67, 68
Melon, J. F. 145
Memoirs of a Woman of Pleasure
  see Cleland, John
mercantilism 72 *n* 14
middle classes
  conflation of sensibility and
    commercial instinct in
    defence of 36
  financial hardship of more
    moving than that of working
    classes 52
  as initiators of sentimentalism 34
  in *Lady Barton* (Elizabeth Griffith)
    104–5
  see also aristocracy, bourgeois
    values, class
Middleton, Chris 38
Millar, John
  Origin of the Distinction of Ranks
    101, 206 *n*, 207–8 *n*
Miller, Nancy 198 *n*
moderation
  see patriarch
money
  in *The Countess of Dellwyn* (Sarah
    Fielding) 33

in *David Simple* (Sarah Fielding) 19
in *The History of Ophelia* (Sarah Fielding) 45
in *Humphry Clinker* (Smollett) 86
in *Lady Barton* (Elizabeth Griffith) and *The Man of Feeling* (Mackenzie) 94
in *Lady Julia Mandeville* (Frances Brooke) 72
in *A Sentimental Journey* (Sterne) 114–16
in *Tom Jones* (Henry Fielding) 19, 21, 195 *n*
see also wealth
Montesquieu
De l'esprit des lois 118, 121, 140, 207 *n*
Monthly Review, The 138 *n* 37
moral choice
as a criterion for a critical text 109–10
More, Hannah
Essays on Various Subjects 118
Sensibility (poem) 118
Strictures on the Modern System of Female Education 155, 210 *n*, 212 *n*, 214 *n*
Mullan, John 3, 4, 17 n. 5, 92, 94, 98, 108, 109, 110, 113, 119, 205 *n*
on Adam Smith's 'sympathy' 34

Nicholson, Colin 191 *n*

obligation 60, 61, 155–86 *passim*
in *Amelia* (Henry Fielding) 50–1
in *Anna* (Agnes Maria Bennett) 130–2
in *Anna St. Ives* (Holcroft) 161–2
associated with conservative ideal 155
in *The Countess of Dellwyn* (Sarah Fielding) 33
in *David Simple* (Sarah Fielding) 26, 30–1
in *The History of Ophelia* (Sarah Fielding) 51
in *Lady Julia Mandeville* (Frances Brooke) 68
in *Nature and Art* (Inchbald) 162–4

Wollstonecraft's views (*Rights of Men*) 160
see also benefactor, benevolence, community
Owen, David 196 *n*

Paine, Thomas
Rights of Man 159, 213 *n*
views on commerce 158–9
patriarch 59–90 *passim*
disinterest as defining feature of 65, 75
Hume's 'governors' 75
and moderation 71, 74
union of sentimental and prudential views within patriarchal figures 66
patriarchal government 59–90 *passim*
and the sentimental community 60–1
Pennington, Lady
An Unfortunate Mother's Advice to her Absent Daughters ... 203 *n*
Perry, Ruth 28
'Philogamus' 35 *n* 40
Pinchbeck, Ivy 38, 39
Pocock, J. G. A. 9, 193 *n*
Politi, Jina 16–17
political economy
see economic discourse; Steuart, Sir James
Polwhele, Richard 211 *n*
Poor Laws
Malthus' views on 163–4
Poovey, Mary 191 *n*
Pope, Alexander
Essay on Man 8, 25–6, 66
'ev'ry Woman is at heart a rake' 18
Windsor Forest 25–6
Preston, Thomas R.
Matthew Bramble as 'benevolent misanthrope' type 85
Price, Richard 141, 145
Observations on the Nature of Civil Liberty 133, 146
Observations on Reversionary Payments 141 *n* 42

property
   as giving distinction to the
      bourgeois individual 101–2
   women viewed as 136, 138
prostitution 39–40
   see also economic activity,
      working woman
prudence
   in *Fanny Hill* (Cleland) 40–1
   in *The History of Ophelia* (Sarah
      Fielding) 42, 57
   in *Humphry Clinker* (Smollett)
      88
   in *Lady Julia Mandeville* (Frances
      Brooke) and *The Vicar of
      Wakefield* (Goldsmith) 65–71
   in *The Man of Feeling* (Mackenzie)
      98–9, 109
   in *Tom Jones* (Henry Fielding)
      17–18, 21
public/private
   divide 2–3, 191 *n*, 192 *n*
   analogies between spheres
      141–2, 155

radical
   as political label in the 1790s
      156
Richardson, Samuel
   Clarissa 6, 17, 60, 102
   Sir Charles Grandison 1–2, 26, 34
rights, theories of 159–61
Robertson, William
   *View of the Progress of Society in
      Europe* 118, 129
Rodgers, Betsy 39 *n* 8
romance structure (*Amelia* and
      Ophelia) 54–8
Rousseau, Jean-Jacques
   La Nouvelle Héloïse 199 *n*
Routh, Guy 213 *n*

Sabor, Peter 198 *n*
Say, Jean-Baptiste
   Treatise on Political Economy 187,
      212 *n*
Scheuermann, Mona 191 *n*
Scott, Sarah
   Millenium Hall 34, 107

self-control
   as internalised form of
      independence for
      conservative women writers
      166–9
   tension between sensibility and,
      resolved, 181
   as urged by radical writers 173
   triumph over sensibility in
      novelistic discourse 187
   see also prudence
self-interest
   associated with prudence 71, 88
   as barely disguised basis for
      benevolent community 52
   differentiating between public
      interest and 75, 77
Sekora, John 82, 201 *n*, 202 *n*
sensibility
   as civilising influence 117–53
      passim
   as depriving its possessor of the
      power to act 71, 180
   as seen by conservatives and
      radicals in 1790s 157–8
   commercial values and 30, 71–2
   compatible with economic values
      32, 36, 115–16, 117–53 *passim*
   discourses of femininity and 10
   economic ability and 10–11, 35,
      44
   in *Emma Courtney* (Mary Hays)
      171, 214 *n*
   excessive 66, 67, 71, 166–7 (*A
      Gossip's Story*), 171 (*Emma
      Courtney*)
   'masculinisation' 127–32
   politicisation of 3, 192 *n*
   prudence and 65
   radical potential within 173,
      181–4
   reason and 181
   'right sensibility' 122
   satire and 85
   sexuality and 35, 43
   still valued during 1790s 212 *n*
   suffering and 29
   varieties of 211 *n*
   in women 35, 43

in *The Wrongs of Woman*, 180–4
see also sentimentalism
sentimentalism
 conflict between patriarchal and
  sentimental values 65–71
 importance of linking its virtues
  with economic activity 34
 sentimental novel as a feminine
  form 3, 191–2 *n*
 sentimental virtues compatible
  with economic values 32,
  117–53 *passim*
 substituting emotional for
  material methods of
  evaluation 49–50
 under attack 92, 121, 157–8, 211 *n*
 undermined by theories of rights
  159–60
 see also community
Sherburn, George 54
Simmons, Philip 41
simplicity
 always already compromised in
  women 44
 in *David Simple* (Sarah Fielding)
  28–31
 in relation to Ophelia and Amelia
  43–4
Skinner, John 201 *n*, 202 *n*
Smith, Adam 12–13, 45, 51, 52, 111,
 117, 134, 187
 limits of sympathy 52
 The Theory of Moral Sentiments 12,
  13, 34, 35, 40–1, 74, 100, 193 *n*,
  207 *n*
 The Wealth of Nations 13, 45, 145
 see also sympathy
Smith, Charlotte
 Emmeline 138
Smollett, Tobias
 Humphry Clinker 81–90
Spencer, Jane 105, 111, 192 *n*
Steele, Richard 9, 34
Sterne, Laurence
 A Sentimental Journey 3, 93, 112–16
 Sermons 113
Steuart, Sir James
 Principles of Political Œconomy 5,
  59–60, 74, 93, 200 *n*, 207 *n*

Straub, Kristina 197 *n*
sympathy
 difference of definition between
  Adam Smith and David
  Hume 34
 limits of for Smith 52

Tanner, Tony 96, 148
Taylor, Anne 198 *n*
Thompson, James 2, 40, 191 *n*, 192 *n*,
 195 *n*, 197 *n*, 199 *n*, 204 *n*
Todd, Janet 18, 28–9, 30 *n* 27, 32,
 92, 103–4, 106, 132–3, 143, 152,
 157–8, 171, 179, 192 *n*, 198 *n*,
 206 *n*, 210 *n*, 211 *n*
Tomaselli, Sylvana 117, 121, 140
trade 11, 19, 22
 absence of in *Lady Barton*
  (Elizabeth Griffith)
 associated with self-interest 76,
  77
 disparagement of, and
  progressive change of
  attitude 72–3, 86
 linked with the aristocracy 102
  (*The Man of Feeling*) 123–8
  (*Barham Downs* and *Anna*)
 vice as a means to profit in 23, 40
 women ousted from 28
 women reappropriating 32
 see also commerce
tyranny 133, 135–43
 women as natural opposers of
  140

Van Sant, Ann Jessie 195 *n*, 202 *n*,
 205 *n*
virtue
 and femininity (*Lady Barton*)
  95–8
 and sexual innocence in women
  43–4
 see also chastity

Wakefield, Priscilla 32
 *Reflections on the Present Condition
  of the Female Sex* 184–5
Watson, Nicola 158, 187, 188, 211 *n*,
 214 *n*

wealth
  source of as issue in sentimental
    fiction 3–4
  source of patriarch's wealth in
    Lady Julia Mandeville
    (Frances Brooke) and *The
    Vicar of Wakefield*
    (Goldsmith) 64–5
  see also money
West, Jane
  The Advantages of Education
    211 *n*
  *A Gossip's Story, and a Legendary
    Tale* 164–9, 210 *n*, 217 *n*
  A Tale of the Times 183 *n* 56, 210 *n*,
    212 *n*
Whale, John 210 *n*, 211–12 *n*
Wilkes, Wetenhall 31, 67–8
  *Letter of Genteel and Moral Advice
    to Young Lady* 6, 38 *n* 4, 198 *n*
Williams, Carolyn 48
Williams, Helen Maria
  Julia 154, 212 *n*
Williams, Raymond 108 *n* 31
Wollstonecraft, Mary 39, 138, 154
  *Thoughts on the Education of
    Daughters* 133, 182
  A Vindication of the Rights of Men
    159–60, 211 *n*

  *A Vindication of the Rights of
    Woman* 152, 179–80, 181,
    182–3, 209 *n*, 210–11 *n*
  The Wrongs of Woman 159, 177–84
working woman 10–12, 28
  in *Amelia* (Henry Fielding) 48–9
  in *Anna* (Agnes Maria Bennett)
    129–36
  combination of sensibility and
    commercial instinct within
    36
  in *The Countess of Dellwyn* (Sarah
    Fielding) 32
  in *The History of Ophelia* (Sarah
    Fielding) 48, 51, 57
  inherently immoral 37–8
  see also economic activity,
    prostitution
women
  as monitors of social and moral
    health 117–53 *passim*
  as reforming influence 95–7

xenophobia
  in *Anna* (Agnes Maria Bennett)
    143

Zomchick, John P. 81 *n* 28, 89, 201 *n*,
  202 *n*